A HISTORY OF THE
CLASSICAL
WORLD

A HISTORY OF THE CLASSICAL WORLD

THE STORY OF ANCIENT GREECE AND ROME

ELIZABETH WYSE

This edition published in 2022 by Arcturus Publishing Limited
26/27 Bickels Yard, 151–153 Bermondsey Street,
London SE1 3HA

AD008797UK

Printed in the UK

CONTENTS

PART III
TRANSITIONS   109

PART IV
REPUBLIC   133

PART V
IMPERIUM   181

INTRODUCTION

The long and chequered history of Greece and Rome permeates our culture, our language and our philosophy. We can still see the physical remnants of these great civilizations, marvel at the scale and grandiosity of their ambition, and feel a connection with our extraordinary forebears. Tracing the development of their societies takes us on a fascinating journey of discovery.

FROM THE 3RD MILLENNIUM BCE the island of Crete, and eventually the Greek mainland as well, was peppered with palace-based societies, where a ruling elite and ordinary people coalesced around small, economically self-sufficient palaces and their hinterland. In the rugged terrain of Greece these polities were defensible, while access to the trade routes of the Mediterranean Sea enabled economies to thrive and cultures to flourish. These energetic and inventive Greek societies had disappeared by 1100 BCE, either because of internal dissolution or invasion, but the collapse of the feudal and hereditary ruling elites paved the way for the emergence of the new power structures of the Greek polis that began to emerge in the 8th century BCE. Throughout Greece independent, self-governing city-states evolved, their development powered by dynamic experiments in government and social structures, which led to rule by aristocrats, oligarchies, tyrannies and famously, in 6th-century Athens, to democracy, or rule by the people.

The institutions and beliefs of the Greek world – from temples, theatres, stadia and gymnasia to a pantheon of deities, with their accompanying oracles and shrines – gradually became recognizable and defined. From the 8th century BCE Greek settlers carried this strong sense of identity to distant colonies, most notably in Sicily, southern Italy, and the shores of the Black Sea, leaving their imprint all over the eastern Mediterranean world. Inevitably, there was conflict, both with the mighty Persian

Empire to the east and between individual city-states or allied leagues. However, the inventions, innovations and insights of the Greek world continued to multiply, diversify and disseminate at an astonishing rate, and included: the Greek alphabet; philosophy; poetry; mathematics; astronomy; medicine; theatre; the Olympic Games; architectural styles and sculpture.

Eventually, internal conflicts intensified, and Macedonia in northern Greece emerged as the dominant power. In 336 BCE the Macedonian ruler Alexander the Great erupted on the Mediterranean stage. In the space of just over a decade (334–323 BCE) he led his Greek army on an epic journey through Egypt, Asia Minor, Persia and ultimately to the Himalayas, conquering new territories, founding cities, transplanting Greek ideas and institutions, absorbing Oriental ideas, encouraging his men to inter-marry with subject peoples, and leaving a compelling legacy: Hellenistic Greece. His successors ruled from Egypt to Bactria in modern-day Afghanistan, where they created flourishing and diverse civilizations, which absorbed existing cultures and blended them with Greek ideals.

Meanwhile, in central Italy, a very different civilization was emerging. Rome had begun its story in the 8th century BCE as a small village scattered over the Palatine Hill, one of the seven hills that rose above the River Tiber in central Italy. It rapidly grew in size, prosperity and sophistication, and eventually, in 509 BCE, its aristocratic families overthrew the Etruscan kings who ruled there and set about creating a Roman republic, a government in which citizens elected representatives to vote on their behalf, presided over by the Senate.

Rome was inspired by Greek civilization and influenced by Greek ideas, art, architecture and institutions, but it developed very differently. From the outset, Roman society was ambitious, martial and disciplined, able to withstand invasion, for example by the Gallic invaders from the north, and to gradually conquer the other tribal groups that ruled the Italian peninsula. The three Punic Wars, which took place between 264 BCE and 146 BCE, which brought Rome into conflict with the Carthaginian civilization of North Africa, helped to forge Rome's identity and self-belief. Its victory, and subsequent expansion, was the first stage in its imperial expansion.

Civil wars and conflicts between dominant leading Romans, such as Julius Caesar, Pompey the Great, and Mark Antony, eventually led to the transition from republic to empire. Augustus the Great was given extraordinary powers by the Roman Senate in 27 BCE, and became the first in a long, and diverse, line of Roman emperors, who ranged from dangerous megalomaniacs, such as Nero and Caligula, to expansionist conquerors, such as Trajan, and intelligent realists, such as Hadrian and Marcus Aurelius.

Throughout its long imperial history, Rome relentlessly expanded, absorbing huge tracts of territory, from Britain in the north-west to Armenia in the east, and acquiring an ever-growing population. Conquered peoples provided manpower, notably for the huge standing army that was required to police the empire and its frontiers, and tax revenues. The money that flowed into the imperial coffers financed ambitious public works programmes – aqueducts and sewers, grandiose monuments, a sophisticated road network and defensive walls.

For centuries the Roman Empire was able to absorb, tolerate and profit from its multi-racial diversity of subjects, but eventually it unravelled under the external pressure of 'barbarians', Germanic peoples from beyond the empire, who began to cross the borders in ever-increasing numbers. Eventually, following the sack of Rome by a huge Goth army in 410 CE, the empire collapsed. However, its legacy was woven into the fabric of successor civilizations and still underpins many of our beliefs, social structures and customs to this day. The world's largest religion, Christianity, was espoused by the Roman Empire in 313 CE; we write using the Latin alphabet; our legal systems owe much to Roman models; our calendar was inspired by the Romans; we build using concrete, a Roman invention; our roads follow Roman routes. Many Europeans live in cities that were originally founded by the Romans, or – like our Roman forebears – aspire to own weekend retreats in the countryside.

The story of the classical civilizations of Greece and Rome is a chronicle of achievement, dynamism and inspired creativity, as well as a catalogue of conflict, corruption and cruelty. The triumphs and failures of classical civilization together form a rich and palpable heritage which, some 2,000 years later, can still provide inspiration and lessons for the modern world.

PART 1
Beginnings

The gold funerary 'Mask of Agamemnon' was unearthed in 1876 during excavations at Mycenae by the German archaeologist Heinrich Schliemann, who believed it to belong to the Homeric hero of the Trojan War. However, it has been dated to 1580–1550 BCE – 300 years before Agamemnon, if he did exist, would have lived. Nevertheless, the mask was found still on its corpse, and the richness of the goods located with the body indicates that it covered somebody of great importance.

MINOAN CRETE

Described by the poet Homer as a 'rich and lovely land' in the 'wine-dark sea', the southern Mediterranean island of Crete is the home of one of Europe's oldest civilizations, and the palace-based societies that developed there in the 2nd millennium BCE would spread their influence throughout the eastern Mediterranean.

THE EARLIEST EVIDENCE OF HUMAN SETTLEMENT on Crete dates to the 7th millennium BCE. By the 4th millennium BCE, the Cretans were coalescing into communities of farmers and craftsmen, and it is likely that a ruling elite was beginning to emerge. By 2000 BCE, these small beginnings had evolved into the great palaces of Crete, at Knossos, Phaistos, Mallia and Khania. The British archaeologist Sir Arthur Evans, who excavated the palace of Knossos from 1900–05, named the entire civilization 'Minoan', after the mythical Cretan King Minos.

These palaces did not appear to be pompous projections of royal hegemony. Rather, they acted as local administrative and trading centres, controlling a hinterland of small towns, villages and farms, acting as religious and judicial centres, as well as storehouses for wine, oil, ceramics and precious metals. The largest, Knossos, is about the size of a small medieval monastery. The palaces were elaborate stone-built, multi-storey structures, which featured colonnades, porticoes, stairways, processional ramps, courtyards, ceilings supported by wooden columns, and a drainage system. There is little evidence of fortifications, indicating that the various Minoan communities coexisted relatively peacefully, although finds of weapons and armour suggest that peace was not invariably maintained.

The palaces were also religious centres, and remains of Minoan wall paintings, art and architecture conjure up a world where a voluptuous mother-goddess, who brandishes a snake in each hand, is worshipped, as well as a young, spear-carrying male god. Religious rituals include libations, processions, feasts and sporting events, such as acrobatic bull vaulting, which is depicted on frescoes on the palace walls.

Minoan frescoes are full of dynamic life and movement and depict rituals or scenes from nature, such as leaping dolphins, in vivid colours using pigments that include saffron, iron ore and indigo. Pottery is decorated with naturalistic flowers, plants, flying fish and sinuous octopuses with writhing tentacles. The Minoans made great strides in metalworking, in particular gold and bronze, ivory carving, exquisite filigree jewellery and pottery.

The Minoans developed their own script, Linear A, which dates from about 2500–1400 BCE, but this remains undeciphered. The palace of Knossos, uniquely, also used Linear B script, which appeared in the later Mycenaean palaces on the mainland and encodes the earliest form of Greek. The Knossos tablets demonstrate that the script was employed primarily as an economic and administrative tool, recording the palace's economic assets, which included sheep and wool, and orchards in which figs, olives and grapes were cultivated. Much of this produce was stored within the palace compound, and it is possible that it was redistributed to the hinterland.

In addition, the Minoans were traders who transported their surplus goods, such as oil, wine and pottery, far afield to Egypt, Syria, Anatolia, Mesopotamia, Cyprus and mainland Greece, in exchange for precious commodities, such as copper from Cyprus, ivory from Egypt and tin from Asia Minor. This extensive trade network supported a great florescence of luxury goods on Crete: gemstones, fine bronzes, terracotta and beautifully worked gold, silver and faience.

Minoan culture declined because of the rise of the more dominant Mycenaean culture on the Greek mainland, which eventually reached Crete. It is also speculated that civilization on Crete was devastated by natural events, such as earthquakes or a volcanic eruption on the neighbouring island of Thera (Santorini) in the 16th century BCE, and the consequent tsunami. It is likely that it was a combination of natural disasters and invasion from the mainland that dealt Cretan civilization its final deathblow: most Minoan sites were effectively abandoned by the 12th century BCE.

The Legend of King Minos

The son of the god Zeus and the Phoenician princess Europa, King Minos built a mighty kingdom on the island of Crete.

Here, he created a powerful navy and conquered Athens, demanding that 14 young Athenians were sent annually to Crete to be sacrificed to the fearsome minotaur, half-man, half-bull, who lived in a labyrinth on the island. Cretan sculptors, artists and metalworkers have left an extensive legacy of artefacts that depict the sacred bull and 'bull-sports', indicating that bulls may have played an important role in Cretan culture, symbolizing strength, potency and fertility.

Bull-leaping fresco from the palace of Knossos, Crete, c.1400 BCE. This reconstructed image is a composite of at least seven panels, each about 78 cm (31 in) high. It depicts an acrobatic figure vaulting over a bull's back, while another figure grabs the bull's horns and prepares to leap, and a third figure appears to have just 'dismounted'. The main leaper is painted brown, which follows Egyptian convention and indicates that he is male. It is possible that the bull-leaping scene depicted with such fluidity and dynamism was a rite-of-passage ceremony.

MYCENAEN GREECE

Mycenaean civilization flourished in mainland Greece in the late Bronze Age (c.1600–1100 BCE) and extended its influence throughout the Peloponnese and across the Aegean Sea to Crete and the Cycladic islands. More militaristic and austere than Minoan Crete, Mycenaean culture made a lasting impression on later Greeks, especially in their myths of the Trojan Wars and Bronze Age heroes such as Achilles and Odysseus.

THE INDIGENOUS GREEKS OF THE PELOPONNESE had come into trading contact with the Minoans, which may have had a major cultural impact. They began to develop their own centres, such as Mycenae, Tiryns, Pylos, Sparta and Athens, and by the end of the 15th century BCE had become the dominant culture in the Aegean. Their societies were strictly feudal, headed by a king (*wanax*), who was supported by a warrior elite.

The Mycenaeans were fierce warriors and great engineers who built sturdy bridges and elaborate drainage and irrigation systems. Like the Minoans, they evolved a palace-based culture, where the palace acted as an administrative and economic centre. However, the Mycenaeans were militaristic, and their palaces were invariably fortified citadels, surrounded by impressive walls of large, unworked stone blocks called Cyclopean masonry (an indication that only the mythical giant could have lifted them). These walls boasted monumental doorways, capped by impressive lintels. The Mycenaean writing system, Linear B, comprises about 200 syllabic signs and logograms, and about 6,000 tablets have been found. It was used exclusively to catalogue produce and commodities and support the palace bureaucracy.

Mycenaean palace complexes shared many features. They were built around a large central hall, called the 'megaron', which was the heart of the palace, as well as the throne room. Private apartments and storerooms were set around the megaron. Richly decorated with wall paintings, the palaces were stone-built, with wooden columns and ceilings. Monumental stone 'tholos' tombs were dome-shaped burial chambers with a corbelled roof made from overlapping stone blocks to create arches, often earth-covered and approached by a stone passageway. These were arranged in prominent gravesites, and the dead were buried with a rich array of grave goods, including jewellery, gold masks, swords and daggers.

Little is known about Mycenaean religion, though there is some evidence of the beginnings of the Greek pantheon. Texts refer to Poseidon (at the time probably associated with earthquakes), the Lady of the Labyrinth, Ares, Hermes, Artemis and Dionysos. Very few shrines or temples have been found and it is thought that sacrifices and libations took place on open ground or in remote sanctuaries.

Contact with Minoan Crete played an important role in shaping Mycenaean art. While still inspired by natural forms, Mycenaean art was much more stylized than Minoan art, and geometric designs, often featuring spiral devices, were popular. Decorations were symmetrical and disciplined, while Mycenaean frescoes, like their Minoan counterparts, depicted plants and bull-leaping scenes, but also introduced a new range of subject matter: lions, griffins, battles, warriors, chariots and boar hunts.

Local workshops produced textiles, pottery, bronze weapons, carved gems, jewellery and glass ornaments. The Mycenaeans were enterprising traders, travelling as far afield as Spain and the Levant, exporting ceramic vessels, wine and oil and importing precious

Ivory head of a warrior wearing a boar's tusk helmet, from a Mycenaean chamber tomb, 14th–13th centuries BCE. Helmets were made using slivers of boars' tusks, attached to a leather base padded with felt. Boar hunting was a popular activity in Mycenaean Greece, and tusks would have been widely available.

19

gems and metals, including ivory from Syria and even lapis lazuli from distant Afghanistan.

Mycenaean civilization may have declined because of population movement or conflict. It is believed that migrations would have been precipitated by an attack from outside Greece, possibly from the so-called Sea Peoples, who are thought to have originated in the Levant. Internal conflict may have arisen within Mycenaean society, with the impoverished classes rising against the ruling elite. The end of Mycenaean civilization, around 1100 BCE, led to the complete destruction of several of the palaces and heralded the start of the Greek Dark Ages.

HOMERIC GREECE

Mythical heroes, and their epic journeys and battles, throng Homer's Iliad *and* Odyssey – *the first long texts in Greek, probably composed in the 8th century BCE, that survive. Although they depict a legendary past, they also present a poetic vision of Greece in the 'Dark' Ages, c.1100–800 BCE, when literacy was lost and only oral accounts of a heroic past persisted.*

THE *ILIAD* IS HOMER'S GREAT EPIC of the Trojan War, and the names of the heroic warriors still resound down the centuries: Achilles, Patroclus, Priam, Ajax and Hector. The action occurs over 51 days in the tenth year of the Trojan War and takes its title from Ilium, the Greek name for Troy. The poem is geographically accurate, referring to real places on the island of Crete, within the Mycenaean world, and Troy itself, on the coast of modern-day Turkey. A long and detailed 'catalogue' of ships lists the towns, many of them traceable through archaeology, which were said to have sent troops to Troy. The events depicted in the *Iliad* – from the death of Patroclus to the reconciliation between the warrior hero Achilles and Priam, the last king of Troy, all take place against a background of the interventions of the gods, in particular Athena and Apollo, who in many ways seem less heroic than their mortal counterparts.

Scholars are still debating whether the Trojan War actually took place, and it seems likely that the poem is depicting customs and narratives that were an amalgam of several centuries of Greek history. The heroes of the Trojan War wear bronze armour, not the iron armour of Homer's own age, and they are cremated, an Iron Age practice, rather than being buried, a Bronze Age practice. A helmet is described as being made of boars' tusks, a Mycenaean practice that had disappeared in Homeric Greece.

Roman bust of Homer from the 2nd century CE, based on a Hellenistic original. The question of Homer continues to be debated: while some scholars believe that most of the Iliad *and some of the* Odyssey *was composed by an individual poet named Homer, other scholars believe that the poems were composed, and reworked, by many individual poets, and that 'Homer' denotes an entire tradition.*

The *Odyssey* is a poem set in the aftermath of the Trojan War, and is about a hero's journey and a return, much disrupted by godly interventions, to his wife, whom he must reclaim by slaying her suitors. It tells of Odysseus' journey on a capricious sea to the furthest outpost of the known and fabled world, even taking him to the underworld, the realm of the dead. He must weather storms and shipwrecks and encounter remote islands peopled by fabulous or monstrous inhabitants, such as the Sirens or the Cyclops. Ultimately, his loyalty and perseverance is rewarded.

Above all, in both these texts Homer evoked and propagated an understanding of common values that would continue to define and shape Greek culture. His poems codify notions of heroism and nobility, which became an aspirational model for all Greeks. He dismisses lives of safe mediocrity, glorifying in heroic deeds, which bring their own immortality.

> *'A man who has been through bitter experiences and travelled far enjoys even his sufferings after a time.'*
>
> HOMER, *ODYSSEY*

Homer

Very little is known about Homer. He is thought to have been born in Ionia, since the poems are in the Ionic dialect, in the late 9th century or early 8th century BCE. It is even doubtful whether the *Iliad* and *Odyssey* were composed by the same man, since they embody very different styles: the *Iliad* is heroic and martial, whereas the *Odyssey* is picaresque and fantastical. He emerged from an oral tradition, where poetry was passed down by word of mouth. Indeed, Homer himself refers to the poet as a 'singer', one who builds up a repertoire of poetic songs that recount heroic exploits from a distant past. Homer's innovation appears to have been the sheer length of his epic poems (the *Iliad* comprises 16,000 verses), which would have taken at least four or five evenings to recite. Greece acquired an alphabetic system in the 9th or early 8th century BCE, and it is conceivable that Homer used writing to aid him in his compositions. However, it is beyond dispute that Homer's medium was primarily oral, and that the poems were probably not written down until the 7th century BCE, when they were disseminated by professional reciters.

Red-figure kylix, or drinking cup, c.500 BCE, depicting Achilles tending Patroclus, who has been wounded in the arm by an arrow and is sitting on his shield, with his head turned away. The cup, which was made by the 'Sosias painter' in the Etruscan city of Vulci, demonstrates the universality of Homer's tales of Trojan heroes. Achilles and Patroclus were close comrades in the Trojan War, and were frequently depicted as lovers.

THE GREEK DARK AGES

The period between the collapse of Mycenaean civilization (c.1100 BCE) and the Archaic period (c.800 BCE) is commonly referred to as the Greek Dark Ages, a time of warfare and instability, when the great palace-based centres were abandoned and the early polysyllabic writing system, Linear B, was lost.

ONCE THE GREAT MYCENAEAN PALACES had been destroyed or had fallen into disuse, there were limited attempts to rebuild and reoccupy, and in general people retreated to smaller, more scattered settlements in locations that were easily defensible. It seems likely that the population shrank and some areas of Greece, for example the southern Argolid, were more or less abandoned. The tendency seems to have been for populations to retreat into isolation, and for contact between them to disappear. This is reflected in burial practices, which began to show considerable regional variation: in Attica, cremation, with incinerated remains placed in an urn, became the norm; in Euboea, cremation and inhumation coexisted; in Thessaly, small Mycenaean-style tholos tombs were retained; in Crete, communal burial in chamber tombs persisted.

This lack of unity is further evidenced in pottery styles, which began to show marked regional variations, in contrast to the stylistic cohesion of the Mycenaean world. Decorative styles were predominantly geometric and abstract; figurative art more or less disappeared during the Greek Dark Ages. These simple, diagrammatic styles seemed to emerge from a less sophisticated society, and the marked regional variation in artistic approaches indicate that there was very little contact between different groups, or indeed much input from outside Greece.

For ordinary people, life would remain relatively unchanged: farming, weaving, metalworking and pottery making were still the dominant activities. The only real innovation in the era was the use of iron. Iron smelting was learned from Cyprus and the Levant, and hitherto unexploited deposits of iron ore within Greece were soon being used to make weapons and armour.

The loss of the Mycenaean palace system meant that there was no longer a redistributive economy, which had ensured that the palace hinterlands were self-sustaining. As a result, populations began to shrink as the old world of organized armies, kings and bureaucracies disappeared. While undoubtedly people gathered together in settlements where higher-status individuals, or chiefs, emerged, their standard of living was not significantly higher than their lower-status counterparts. This collapse of the old hereditary, feudal class structure that had prevailed in the Mycenaean world paved the way for the innovative sociopolitical institutions that would ultimately lead to the rise of democracy in the 5th century BCE.

There are numerous signs that Greece was coming out of the Greek Dark Ages in the 8th century BCE. These included: the emergence of the Greek alphabet and literacy; a much more varied material culture; increased contacts with areas beyond Greece; and the development of an early form of city-state. All these phenomena are indicative of a period of population growth, stabilization and recovery; the age of the polis was about to begin.

The Temple of Artemis was built on Corfu between 600 and 580 BCE and is the oldest known true Doric temple. The west pediment shows the gorgon Medusa, with living snakes instead of hair, fleeing Perseus, the founder of Mycenae and a heroic slayer of monsters. On either side, figures of panthers represent the protectors of the temple. These stocky felines were frequent motifs in Egyptian art, which is clearly a strong influence on this Archaic sculpture.

PART II
Polis

The imposing remains of the Doric temple at Corinth, which is now considered to be the Temple of Apollo. Thought to have been constructed in c.560 BCE, it stands on the rocky outcrop known as Temple Hill. It became emblematic of the city of Corinth, which was a flourishing and prosperous city-state.

EVOLUTION OF THE CITY-STATE 750–600 BCE

The mountainous terrain of Greece, with its isolated valleys, deep inlets and myriad scattered islands, provided ideal territory for the evolution of the polis, or city-state. These ruggedly independent political units comprised an urban centre, its surrounding territory, and its citizens and inhabitants. Eventually, there were more than 1,000 city-states in classical Greece.

THE ORIGINS OF THE POLIS are unclear. It may have evolved from the remnants of Mycenaean palace-based settlements, emerged as part of a Greece-wide recovery in population levels in the 9th century BCE, or developed separately when the Greeks began to establish colonies abroad in the 8th century BCE. Among the most important city-states to emerge in this period were Athens, Sparta, Rhodes, Corinth, Thebes and Aegina.

The polis can be defined as a small self-governing community of citizens who, along with wives, children and slaves, live together in a settlement and its hinterland, which may include many villages. The urban centre within the polis was often fortified, built on a natural acropolis (high ground) or harbour. Over the centuries, the rights of a 'citizen' evolved. The defining force that drew citizens together was loyalty; primarily, they were warriors who were willing to fight for, and defend, their territory. Each polis was involved in international affairs, engaging in conflict, trade and diplomacy with other poleis or non-Greek states.

The poleis of Greece evolved in isolation and developed many unique characteristics, but certain features were universal. The urban area, the home to most of the population, always encompassed a sacred space, with one or more temples. Gradually, more impressive buildings were added, for example gymnasia, theatres and an agora (an outdoor space where the citizens could meet). Fortifications were the norm from the 7th century BCE, although Sparta was an exception.

In theory, each citizen of a polis had equal rights based on ownership of property. But as city-states were founded, from as early as the 9th century BCE, magistrates and ruling councils began to emerge. These were made up of men from a small ruling class, the aristocrats (from *aristoi,* 'the best'), who became ruling dynasties of families, each dominating their region. These families may well have been able to trace their antecedents back to Mycenaean Greece.

Aristocrats were responsible for the conduct of war between city-states, and were skilled fighters and horsemen. They were also shipowners, who used their vessels to raid other territories; by the 8th century BCE, warships, powered by two tiers of oarsmen, were beginning to appear. When they were not fighting, aristocrats were responsible for the smooth running of their city societies, serving as magistrates and arbitrating disputes and delivering justice. They also presided over the city's deities and were responsible for rites and offerings, which were administered by the priesthood. Their wives and daughters frequently served as priestesses.

Noblemen had to communicate with their citizenry and the art of rhetoric was beginning to be admired. They were also expected to be physically fit, capable of riding without stirrups, wielding a sword or spear, leading a hunt or participating in athletic contests. These virile pursuits were complemented by more courtly activities: dancing, singing, music making, conversation and companionship. Over time, especially after the introduction of coinage, members of the aristocracy were able to grow wealthy by lending money or engaging – through merchant intermediaries – in commerce, and the gap between rich and poor widened.

The success of the polis depended on the loyal support of its inhabitants, and the poleis developed many ways of unifying and bonding them. Some were spiritual, including specific gods and cults, unique festivals and feast days, and patron deities. On a more practical level, city-minted coinage and unique law codes helped to define and codify the city-state. Symbols were used to denote the city-state, such as the owl on Athenian coins representing the goddess Athena, reinforcing a feeling of identity. A sense of history and reverence for the polis' past and its heroic founders and defenders was nurtured through statues of gods and prominent individuals. Most importantly of all, from the 8th century BCE onwards, individual poleis began to project their unique identities into a wider world, founding their own colonies all over the Mediterranean, and thereby exporting their values.

The François vase is a large Attic krater dating to 570–560 BCE. It was used for wine and water, and was made for a symposium given by an Athenian aristocratic family. The black-figure friezes that decorate the vase depict scenes from Greek mythology.

TYRANTS

By the mid-7th century BCE, the political power of the aristocratic families was beginning to be broken. Starting in Corinth, the ruling cliques began to be replaced by a single ruler, called a turannos, or 'tyrant', and for more than a century tyrannies flourished in many city-states. The Greek word turannos simply means a 'sole ruler'; it only gained its negative connotations during the transition to democracy in Athens in the 5th century BCE.

THE COLLAPSE OF THE ARISTOCRATIC MONOPOLY may be connected to the rise of the hoplite in the early 7th century BCE. Armed with a large shield, which protected him from chin to knee, the hoplite infantryman could wield a short sword or thrusting spear in close combat, while the overlapping shields provided protection for an entire phalanx. Faced with this impenetrable wall, the cavalry of the aristocrats was powerless, and gradually horses became peripheral to Greek warfare.

Hoplites were ordinary citizens, armed and ready to fight for their territory without the flair and leadership of aristocratic champions. They broke the long-established dominance of the noble warriors, creating circumstances in which tyrants could flourish. In addition, the aristocrats were giving in to factional disputes and conflicts; their increasingly luxurious lifestyles gave them the leisure to socialize together, but harmonious gatherings could easily turn into violent brawls, where insults were revenged, and loyal clan members fuelled the fire.

As nobles became wealthier and spent freely, a chain reaction began to develop, and the merchants and craftsmen on whom the aristocracy depended for their luxuries began to accrue wealth of their own while some even began to rival the aristocrats. It was scarcely surprising that these newly emerging prosperous classes began to question the morality and justice of their 'superiors', especially when personal feuds and resentments coloured their judgement.

Tyrants were individual rulers who emerged from this social melee with a simple agenda. They claimed that they would stop factionalism and in-fighting, and that they would open up the high offices to men who were competent and qualified, rather than merely of good family. They took control of the political election of magistracies, and expelled or eliminated rivals. Once they were established as rulers, they concentrated their power on maintaining their position at home; rivalries with other tyrants were risky endeavours that could jeopardize their position.

Once the tyrants had seized power, usually through a violent coup, which was supported by the emerging middle class and the peasants, they regarded the position as hereditary. Often, it was with the second and third generation of tyrants, who were frequently less able and disciplined than their fathers, that trouble began, and firm rule turned into oppression.

During the 6th century BCE, the heyday of the Archaic tyrannies, numerous popular revolts overturned aristocracies throughout the Greek world, and many of Greece's most important poleis were ruled by tyrants. Among the most noteworthy were Peisistratos in Athens, Pythagoras in Ephesos, Polycrates in Samos and Aristagoras in Miletus.

Cypselus

The earliest tyranny in Greece was established by Cypselus in Corinth, which had been ruled by the increasingly ineffectual Bacchiadae dynasty. Cypselus was a military leader, or polemarch, who used his influence among Corinth's soldiers to expel the Bacchiadae in c.657 BCE, encouraged by the Oracle of Delphi. He proved to be an enlightened usurper. He was not punitive in his treatment of his enemies, allowing them to set up colonies in north-western Greece. Corinth prospered as a major economic centre, trading with Italy and Sicily under his leadership. It was said that he did not need a bodyguard, which is probably evidence that he was able to remain secure in his position through demagoguery – appealing to the emotions of the populace. He died in 627 BCE, and his son Periander succeeded him. Under his rule, Corinth became one of the wealthiest poleis in Greece. Periander is thought to be one of the Seven Sages of Greece, a title given to seven philosophers, statesmen and lawgivers in the 6th century BCE – men who were revered for their wisdom.

THE GREEK ALPHABET

The Greek alphabet, which appeared in the 8th century BCE, was to transform literacy in the ancient world. The Greeks adapted the Phoenician phonetic writing system, using individual signs that could denote both consonants and vowels to represent their own language. Today, even though the Greek alphabet is only used for the Greek language, it is the root script of most of the scripts used in the Western world.

THE PHOENICIANS WERE A SEMITIC-SPEAKING PEOPLE who originated in the Lebanon and were successful merchants who sailed and established trading posts all over the Mediterranean. The Phoenician phonetic alphabet only had letters for consonants, not vowels; the Greeks took letters from the Phoenician alphabet for sounds for which there was no Greek equivalent, and used these letters to represent individual vowel sounds. They became the Greek letters alpha, epsilon, iota, omicron and upsilon. For the first time, an alphabet could accurately convey speech.

It seems that the Greek adaptation of the Phoenician alphabet, with the introduction of letters representing vowels, was a single, revolutionary, innovation, as evidenced by the very earliest examples of Greek writing, all of which feature the signs for vowels. The place where this occurred is believed to be the port of Methone in the northern Aegean, which may have been a juncture where there were mercantile contacts between the Greeks and Phoenicians. Once the alphabet had been invented, it spread swiftly. In the 9th century BCE there was no writing system; by 725 BCE writing was even being used to tell jokes.

At first, the Greeks followed the Phoenician practice of writing from right to left. A period then ensued of bi-directional writing, when the direction changed from line to line, a practice known as boustrophedon (literally 'ox-turning', describing the movement made as an ox turns when it ploughs a field). In the 5th century BCE, the orientation changed from left to right. From the 8th to 6th centuries BCE, three local variations of the alphabet developed: Cretan, Euboean and Ionic. These variations were standardized in the early 5th century BCE.

The Greek alphabet had 24 letters and consisted of capital letters, ideal for monumental inscriptions. Three scripts better suited to handwriting evolved: uncial, cursive and minuscule, which developed into the modern Greek handwritten form. With its limited number of signs, the Greek alphabet was accessible, and it revolutionized literacy, taking it out of the hands of specialist scribes and making it available for all. Greeks used a variety of writing implements: papyrus (obtained from Phoenician traders); scraped hides of cattle or goat; wooden tablets coated with wax; and more durable materials such as stone, bronze or ceramics. These more permanent materials were used for official inscriptions – for example the laws of the city, treaty texts, war memorials or temple dedications.

The Earliest Texts

The earliest known remnants of the Greek alphabet are fragmentary inscriptions. The Dipylon inscription is scratched on a Greek pottery vessel dating to *c.*740 BCE and found in Athens: 'Whoever of all these dancers now plays most delicately, to him this....' The 8th-century BCE Cup of Nestor, discovered on the island of Pithekoussai off the coast of Italy, was found in the grave of a 10-to 14-year-old child. It was made in Rhodes and decorated in the geometric style, and reads from right to left: 'I am the cup of Nestor good for drinking. Whoever drinks from this cup, desire for beautifully crowned Aphrodite will seize him instantly.'

Phoenician and Greek Alphabets

Phoenician

≮	'aleph
⊴	bē th
⅂	gī mel
◁	dā leth
∃	hē
Y	wā w
I	zayin
⊟	hē th
⊗	tē th
⅂	yō dh
⅄	kaph
∠	lā medh
ᙗ	mē m
ꓤ	nun
⧧	sā mekh
○	'ayin
⊃	pē
ꙏ	sā dē
Φ	qō ph
◁	reš
W	sī n
X	tā w

Greek

A	alpha
B	beta
Γ	gamma
Δ	delta
E	epsilon
F	digamma
Y	upsilon
Z	zeta
H	eta
Θ	theta
I	iota
K	kappa
Λ	lambda
M	mu
N	nu
Ξ	xi
O	omicron
Π	pi
M	san
Ϙ	qoppa
P	rho
Σ	sigma
T	tau
Φ	phi
X	chi
Ψ	psi
Ω	omega

OLYMPIANS

The 12 deities of Mount Olympus together comprised an attempt by the ancient Greeks to explain the chaotic and unpredictable nature of the human condition and the forces that govern human destiny. The Olympian gods are by turn loyal, fickle, jealous, vindictive, angry, amorous, manipulative and petty. The stories of their conflicts, affairs, bickering and sexual intrigues form a mythology that has influenced subsequent language and narrative within the Western world.

GREEK RELIGIOUS PRACTICES are rooted in the Bronze Age, and their time-honoured observances owe much to their Minoan and Mycenaean ancestors. The Greeks were polytheists; the 12 gods of the Greek pantheon are supplemented by countless patron gods and goddesses, who represent feelings, attributes, places and abstractions, as well as many minor and foreign deities.

The relation between humanity and the gods was seen as primarily transactional: gods bestowed gifts on humanity; mortals made votive offerings, of various sorts, as a physical expression of thanks and appeasement. Gods were generally viewed as benign, though they could be spectacularly cruel, meting out harsh and inexplicable punishments. This notion of 'divine punishment' was particularly powerful at times of personal or collective crisis. The gods were worshipped in sanctuaries – sacred spaces that were set apart. Frequently located within cities, they were marked by a temple that featured an outdoor altar, statues and sacred precincts. Alternatively, they could be situated in the country, perhaps in places denoted by sacred trees or springs, or in prominent and dramatic locations, such as headlands or rocky outcrops.

Religious rites centred on animal sacrifice, usually of sheep, goats or cows. Sacrifices took place within the sanctuary, usually at the altar in front of the temple, and assembled participants consumed the blood and entrails of the victim. Liquid offerings, or libations, were frequently made. The year was marked by religious festivals and feast days, and the four most famous festivals, which comprised a procession, athletic games and sacrifices, were Panhellenic, and were held every four years at Olympia, Delphi, Nemea and Isthmia.

The Olympian pantheon accounts for only a small number of the gods and goddesses that thronged the Greek world. The Twelve Titans were the gods and goddesses that preceded the Olympians, the six sons and six daughters of the primordial parents, Uranus (sky) and Gaia (earth). The primordial deities – such as Aither, Chronos, Eros, Hypnos and Uranus, which represent light and the upper atmosphere, time, love and attraction, sleep and the heavens respectively – are gods that symbolize abstractions, emotions, the unknowable and the unthinkable. There were also countless gods that personified concepts and ideas, such as misery, guilt, sloth, perplexity, jealousy, hope and rivalry. The Chthonic 'subterranean' deities were the spirits of the underworld, who guarded the gates of Hades (Cerberus), acted as a ferryman (Charon), or were responsible for magic, witchcraft and necromancy (Hecate). Hundreds of other deities represented the sea, sky, rustic life, agriculture, crafts and health.

THE PANTHEON

Aphrodite (Roman Venus)
The goddess of love, beauty and pleasure, she is depicted as playful and catlike. She rose from the sea, where she was born from sea foam and the severed genitals of Uranus. She was married to Hephaestus but bore him no children. She was connected with many lovers, including Ares, with whom she had three children. Her symbols include myrtle, roses and the scallop shell. Her sacred animals include doves and sparrows.

Apollo
The model of youthful strength and the god of music, arts, knowledge, prophecy, manly beauty and archery. He is the son of Zeus, twin brother of Artemis, and is depicted as handsome and athletic. He is powerful, passionate and dangerously destructive. He is the god of ritual purity and thereby the god of oracles. His oracular shrine is located at Delphi.

His symbols include the bow and arrow, lyre and laurel wreath, and his sacred animals include swans, pythons and roe deer.

The Apollo Belvedere is a famous marble statue from classical antiquity, dating to the mid-2nd century CE, although it is considered to be a copy of an original bronze statue of 330–320 BCE. The posture of the god would seem to indicate that he has just released an arrow from a bow held in his left hand.

Ares (Roman Mars)

The son of Zeus and Hera, Ares is the rarest of the great gods with only one country temple dedicated to him, and in the *Iliad* Homer represents him as the most unpopular god on Earth and in Olympus. He is the god of war, bloodshed and violence, representing the chaotic unpredictability of war, rather than military strategy and skill, which is represented by Athena. His sacred animals include boars, vultures, venomous snakes and dogs.

Artemis (Roman Diana)

The twin sister of Apollo is a virgin goddess of the hunt, who lives in forests and remote mountains among her nymphs. She is the goddess of initiation. Her attributes include hunting spears, animal pelts, deer and other wild animals. Her sacred animal is the deer.

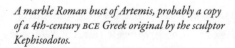

A marble Roman bust of Artemis, probably a copy of a 4th-century BCE Greek original by the sculptor Kephisodotos.

Athena (Roman Minerva)

The greatest goddess of Athens, of whom she is the patron, she is the goddess of wisdom, intelligence, peace, warfare, battle strategy, arts and crafts. According to tradition, she was born fully formed from Zeus' forehead. The Parthenon in Athens is her chief temple. She is usually depicted with a crested helmet, armed with a shield and spear. Her symbol is the olive tree and her sacred animal is the owl.

Demeter (Roman Ceres)

The goddess of grain, the harvest and nourishment, she is a sister of Zeus, by whom she bore Persephone. She is deeply enmeshed in rituals of death and rebirth, especially at Eleusis, where she was offered hospitality while searching for her stolen daughter, who was forced to spend part of the year in the underworld. The initiation rights into the cult of Demeter and Persephone were held every year in Eleusis, known as the Eleusian mysteries. Her mourning for her lost daughter causes winter; her recovery and reunion brings the spring. She is depicted as a mature woman, crowned and holding sheaves of wheat. Her symbols are the cornucopia, ears of wheat, the lotus staff and the winged serpent. Her sacred animals include pigs and snakes.

Dionysus (Roman Bacchus)

The god of wine, festivals, drunkenness, ecstasy, chaos and the theatre, he is said to be twice born, in that his father Zeus snatched him from his mother's womb and then stitched him into his own thigh until he was ready to be born. Before the 5th century BCE, he is depicted as a bearded man, and after that as a slender youth, accompanied by maenads and satyrs. His symbols include a drinking cup, a grape vine and a crown of ivy. His sacred animals include donkeys, dolphins, serpents and tigers. He is a very old god, worshipped since the earliest time, who supplanted Hestia as a member of the Greek pantheon.

Hephaistus (Roman Vulcan)

The blacksmith god, Hephaistus is the god of fire, metalworking and crafts. He is seen as a creative force. He is usually depicted as a bearded, crippled man with the tools of his trade, a hammer, tongs and anvil, sometimes riding a donkey, one of his sacred animals.

Hera (Roman Juno)

The wife and sister of Zeus, and his first and last love, she is the queen of the gods, and goddess of women, childbirth, heirs, kings and emperors. She is depicted as a regal woman, wearing a diadem and veil, and carrying a lotus-tipped staff. She has suffered from Zeus' many infidelities, which have driven her to jealousy and vengeance. Her sacred animals include the heifer, peacock and cuckoo.

Hermes

The messenger of the gods, he is the god of communication, trade, language, travel, thieves and writing. Anther son of Zeus, he is responsible for leading the newly deceased into the afterlife. His symbols include winged sandals and a traveller's cap, and his sacred animals include the tortoise.

Hermes Kriophoros, a late Roman copy of a Greek original from the 5th century BCE. The ancient Greek term kriophoros means 'ram-bearer', and this epithet is commonly associated with Hermes.

Hestia

The virgin goddess of the hearth, home and chastity, a sister of Zeus, Hestia is not often depicted in Greek art. She is said to have given up her seat as one of the 12 Olympians for Dionysos. Her symbols are a hearth and kettle, but she plays little role in the Greek myths.

Poseidon (Roman Neptune)

The god of the sea, rivers, floods, droughts and earthquakes. He rules the seas and the waters, and is depicted as a sturdy and bearded middle-aged man, who holds a trident. His sacred animals include the horse and dolphin.

Zeus (Roman Jupiter)

Zeus is the supreme ruler of Mount Olympus, the god of the sky, weather, thunder, lightning, law, order and justice. The master of the fates, he dispenses justice on Earth, as in heaven, by violence. Zeus seduced many mortal women, including Leda, when he appeared in the guise of a swan; Europa as a bull; and Danaë as a shower of gold. He is depicted as a regal and bearded mature man, and his symbols are the royal sceptre and lightning bolt. His sacred animals include the bull.

THE ORACLE OF DELPHI

With a history that dates back to 1400 BCE, Delphi was the most important shrine in all Greece, which became increasingly prominent in the mid-8th century BCE. Built around a sacred mountain spring, in a spectacularly remote and beautiful setting, it was considered the omphalos, 'navel of the world'. The Pythia, the priestess of Apollo, presided at Delphi and people came from all over Greece to hear her cryptic pronouncements.

LOCATED ON MOUNT PARNASSUS, near Corinth, the sanctuary was named Pytho ('python'), after the snake that Apollo was believed to have killed there. The cult that developed on this spot drew suppliants who sought the priestess's pronouncements on their future actions. A long process was enacted, including washing in a sacred spring, burning laurel leaves and drinking holy water. An animal, usually a goat, was then sacrificed before the procession into the inner sanctum of the temple, the *adytum*, where the priestess gave her pronouncements after entering an ecstatic trance. This may well have been drug-induced, or more likely was brought on by natural hallucinogenic gases, rising from an intersection of two geological fault lines adjacent to the temple, which emitted ethylene, a natural narcotic that induces feelings of euphoria.

The oracle was an older woman of blameless reputation chosen from the peasants of the surrounding region. At certain auspicious times in the year, determined on astrological and geological grounds, she sat alone in the inner sanctum on a tripod, a three-footed stand, with her head bowed over the chasm. On entering a trance, the Pythia 'raved', a form of ecstatic speech, and priests of the temple 'translated' her utterances into elegant hexameters. The oracle could not be consulted in the winter as this was the time when Apollo was away and Dionysos inhabited the temple.

The oracle's predictions were sometimes difficult to interpret. When Croesus, the fabulously rich king of Lydia who faced war with the

Persians, sought the oracle's advice he was told that if he went to war a great empire would surely fall. The Lydians were subsequently routed by the Persians, and it became clear to Croesus that the 'great empire' was not the obvious contender, Persia, but in fact Lydia.

The Pythian Panhellenic Games of Delphi began between 591 and 585 BCE, starting as a competition between solo singers, who sang a hymn to Apollo, but later hosting athletic competitions as well. Delphi, which was in effect an early tourist centre, was managed by the Delphic Amphictyony, a council of representatives from six tribes of Thessaly and central Greece who controlled Delphi and the Pythian Games and jointly administered the site, collecting offerings, raising taxes and initiating construction programmes.

The first major building at the shrine, the Doric temple of Apollo, was destroyed by fire in 548 BCE. A second Doric temple, endowed by the Alcemonid family of Athens, was completed in c.510 BCE. This was destroyed by an earthquake in 330 BCE, and it is the third temple built to replace it that stands today.

The tholos at the Sanctuary of Athena Pronaia at Delphi, Greece. The tholos, built of Attican marble, is a late classical circular building, constructed between 380 and 360 BCE, with an exterior that comprises 20 columns of the Doric order.

In addition, Delphi boasted a theatre that could seat 5,000 spectators, a temple to Athena, a huge stadium and about 20 treasuries, which housed the votive offerings from city-states all over Greece. The most impressive was the Athenian Treasury, built after the Athenian victory in the Battle of Marathon (490 BCE). Monuments were built to commemorate military victories and other events and Greek city-states sent notable monuments as offerings, such as the gold horse chariot from Rhodes, or the ten statues of the kings of Argos. Supplicants walked along the Sacred Way, which wound up past the treasuries of the various Greek city-states, and the monuments they had erected, to the oracle itself, which must have created an unforgettable and awe-inspiring spectacle in this remote mountain shrine.

KOUROI AND KORAI – THE HUMAN FORM

The human sculptures of the late Archaic period were votive offerings, which represented idealized youth. Their severe formality and symmetry was gradually alleviated as sculptors became more adventurous and began to experiment with more natural forms.

UNDOUBTEDLY INFLUENCED BY EGYPTIAN SCULPTURE, the marble statues of nude male youths (kouros, plural kouroi) that began to appear in the Archaic era (*c.* 800–480 BCE) reflect the anatomy within a strictly proportionate framework and artistic convention. The youths are depicted in a frontal pose, with arms touching the side of their thighs and the left leg slightly forward.

Life-size or larger, they were memorials to the dead, offerings to gods, or representations of heroes, which were placed in a temple or used to mark a tomb, partly explaining the restrained pose. The vast majority were sculpted in marble, but limestone, terracotta, wood, bronze and ivory were also used.

Their evolution over time is fascinating. The earliest kouroi were schematic, with the body rendered as a series of interrelated geometric planes, with the musculature 'drawn' on the surface of the body with a series of incisions. From the early 7th century BCE, a much more definitive realism began to emerge as the sculptures became more three-dimensional. Body proportions became more realistic with the head at a ratio of 1:7 to the body. Muscles gained volume and definition, and a smile, which became the stereotypical facial expression, mitigated their severity.

The female equivalent of the kouros, the kore (plural korai), always appear dressed, and are found mainly in the sanctuaries of female deities. Just as the male kouroi began to acquire a more naturalistic anatomy, the clothes of the korai began to acquire a more draped appearance, as the artists experimented with depth and the play of light and shadow.

The Archaic Smile

The 'smile' on the faces of kouroi and korai is a striking feature of Archaic sculptures. It began to appear in the 6th century BCE. The upturned lips are not particularly naturalistic, and it is possible that the smile was a symbolic representation of ideal health and well-being. It may also be the result of technical difficulties of describing the transition between the cheek and lips. Whatever the reason, the smile adds a sense of life and vivacity to later Archaic sculptures, in marked contrast to the more austere rigidity of the earlier forms.

The face of this Archaic kouros from Ptoon Sanctuary near Thebes (c.550–540 BCE) bears the strong imprint of the Archaic smile. The long face, with large eyes, conveys grace and nobility. It is framed by fine curls, which are gathered in a complex hairstyle that falls down the figure's back.

MAGNA GRAECIA

From the mid-8th century BCE, Greek poleis began to reach outwards, sending settlers to distant lands to found new colonies. Greek culture permeated the Mediterranean, leaving an enduring legacy and serving to reinforce a sense of Greek identity among the colonizers.

THE GREEKS WERE ALREADY EXPERIENCED SEAFARERS and inveterate travellers. In the Mycenaean age, settlers had already travelled to Sicily, southern Italy, Egypt and the coast of Asia Minor, and emigrants from the palace-states had settled in Cyprus in the 12th century BCE. The inhabitants of the island of Euboea were famously adventurous, and it is possible to trace their journeys to Asia Minor and the city of Tyre in the 10th century BCE. By *c.*780 BCE, Euboeans had occupied a small coastal settlement at Al Mina in northern Syria, and at the same time were exploring Sicily and the Bay of Naples. Many of these restless journeys were the result of the quest for copper and tin, and Greeks were beginning to follow the Phoenicians' example and set up permanent trading outposts (*emporia*).

It is probable that early travellers brought back reports of fertile land and territories that were ripe for exploitation to the Greek homeland. As population levels rose in Greece, it is likely that aristocratic families were burdened with more sons than they could comfortably accommodate, and it was these surplus offspring who spearheaded the move abroad, accompanied by a few adventurous or desperate members of the lower classes. Expeditions abroad were fully endorsed by the Greek gods, who were consulted at their oracle shrines and pronounced on whether journeys were auspicious. Once the settlements had been established, their founders were honoured and celebrated in founders' festivals.

The islands around Greece were the first places to be colonized by mainland poleis: for example, Corinth founded Corcyra (Corfu) in

733 BCE. From this point on, Greek settlements began to appear on the fertile eastern coast of Sicily, marking a new phase in Greek history, and from here they moved up the Italian coast and the coastline of modern Albania. They also travelled along the northern coast of the Black Sea. By 550 BCE, more than 60 Greek overseas poleis could be counted, with the most 'Greek' of all the colonies in southern Italy and Sicily. Greek settlement eventually stretched from southern Spain at the westernmost extreme to the Crimean peninsula in the east. Many of these settlements were simply trading posts populated by temporary residents, such as merchants and sailors.

The process of colonization meant that local populations frequently had to be subdued and co-opted as agricultural labourers or craftsmen. As time went on, colonists took native women as wives, and maintained their control through a complex process of inter-marriage, diplomacy, alliances and, sporadically, warfare.

New settlements retained links with their founding polis, which can be seen in social customs, religious cults and festivals, which all reflected their place of origin. But there was never any doubt that the foundation of a new settlement marked a decisive departure from the home polis, and some settlers were even banned from returning home for several years.

New settlements presented a *tabula rasa*: it was an opportunity to plan and lay out the site and to construct impressive public buildings and temples. As a result, some of the earliest examples of town planning are colonial. The Greeks exported all the attributes of their home cities: the agora, stadium, theatre, gymnasium, shrines and temples. Surrounding farmland was cultivated and locally available resources were traded through long-distance networks. The new territories provided a range of unknown goods and luxuries that were eagerly sought after at home: horses from the Black Sea steppes; linen from the Bay of Naples; and saffron from Libya. The Greeks brought their alphabet and language to the lands they conquered, introduced olives and vines, imported painted ceramics and initiated their new citizens in the rigours of athletics.

Some colonies became wealthy cities in their own right. Akragas (Agrigento) in southern Sicily, for instance, supported a population of 200,000 in the early 5th century BCE. Sybaris in southern Italy became the byword for luxurious living: with a population of 500,000, it is said that the Sybarites invented the Turkish bath and taught horses to dance to the music of a flute. Some colonies became extremely powerful: Syracuse in Sicily was a large polis which sought to expand its territory and create its own empire. Furthermore, some colonies created their own colonies and minted their own coinage, taking on all the traits of the founding Greek polis.

All over Magna Graecia (Greater Greece), Greek settlers, surrounded by foreigners, clung to their culture and traditions, remained loyal to the founding polis and valued their Greek identity. By 650 BCE, the word *Panhellenes* was in use, meaning 'all Greeks together'.

A coin from Tarentum on the southern coast of Apulia, Italy, c.500–480 BCE. The city of Tarentum, or Taras as it was first known in Greece, was founded in c.706 BCE by Spartans who had been instructed to settle by the Taras River in Italy by the Oracle of Delphi. Tarentum boasted a fine harbour and was therefore a strategically significant city throughout antiquity.

THE OLYMPIC GAMES

Thought to date to 776 BCE, the Olympic Games originated in the western Peloponnese as part of a religious festival in honour of Zeus, at the sanctuary of Zeus in Olympia. The region's young aristocrats originally came together in competition for physical fitness, and by the 6th century BCE the Games had become a pan-Greek event, and one of Ancient Greece's great legacies to the modern world.

WHILE THE GAMES WERE NOT EXCLUSIVELY restricted to the aristocracy, they were certainly initially dominated by members of the nobility, who had the leisure necessary to train and perfect their physical fitness. The main events were boxing, running, throwing and wrestling. Competition in all these events was unrestrained, brutal and intense, often resulting in serious injuries. The Games were restricted to men only, and they competed in the nude.

Heralds, who travelled to all the major Greek city-states, announced the four-yearly Games. Visitors came from all over Greece to witness them, and for a month before the event a truce prevailed, which meant that hostilities between city-states were temporarily suspended and it was safe to travel. Officials and judges, who swore that they would not take bribes, carefully moderated the event. They monitored the contests, carrying switches or sticks, and administering ad hoc beatings if they saw any evidence of cheating or malpractice.

The most spectacular contests, horse racing and chariot racing, were dominated by the aristocracy, who either excelled in their own right or had the resources to own and train horses and pay for dependents to ride them. Horse-racers hurtled down the length of the racing stadium, the *hippodrome*, bareback – stirrups and saddles had not yet been invented. Olympic chariot racing even gave wealthy women the right to win, simply by paying for the chariot and charioteer. This was the only way in which women could participate, and since they were also banned as spectators, they had to confine themselves to their own games in honour of Zeus's wife, Hera.

Wrestling and boxing were popular events, as was the *pankration*, a mixture of the two, which permitted almost any tactic, including eye gouging, stamping and kicking. In a time before boxing gloves, boxers protected their fists with leather thongs. Wrestlers were admired for their skill and agility, and wrestling formed part of the ancient pentathlon, which comprised discus, javelin, long jump, running and wrestling.

The most ancient, and prestigious, event was the running race, along the length of the Olympic stadium (192.28 m/210.29 yards), although there were also longer-distance races. Runners made a standing start, from a row of stone slabs set into the track. In the ancient long jump, athletes carried weights called *halteres*, which were swung forwards on take-off and back just before landing, to add thrust and momentum. Discus throwers did not spin around on the spot, and as a result the average throw was about 30 m (32.8 yards) – half the length achieved by the spinning throwers of today.

Winning athletes were awarded with the palm of victory, and bedecked with woollen ribbons around their heads, legs and arms. The final accolade was an olive wreath from the sacred tree of Zeus. In Greek mythology, Nike is the messenger of the gods and the personification of victory, and she was closely associated with Zeus, the god of the Olympic Games. Statues of Nike feature prominently at Olympia, and she is frequently depicted in flight, carrying a victory ribbon or wreath, ready to crown the victorious athlete.

An Attic Panathenaic amphora showing a charioteer racing to victory, c. 490–480 BCE. Racing with a quadriga, or four-horse chariot, was the most popular and prestigious event in the equestrian games. The driver perched on a wooden-wheeled, open-backed chariot, which rested on its own back axle.

LYRIC POETRY OF LESBOS

The term 'lyric verse' simply refers to a piece that was accompanied by a lyre. These pieces were generally short, personally felt and intense poems that were performed by both men and women. Lyric poems stand out because of their individualism; in this they represent their age, the late Archaic period, eschewing collectivism and bringing the artist and creator to the foreground.

LITTLE IS KNOWN ABOUT THE LIFE OF SAPPHO, the lyric poet who was born to an aristocratic family on the island of Lesbos *c.*620 BCE. Her life coincides with a time when there was a great flowering of lyric poetry on Lesbos, and she certainly corresponded with the poet Alcaeus, also from Lesbos. She was raised to learn the lyre, was exiled twice to Sicily because of her political views, and was famous enough to have statues raised in her honour and coins minted in her name.

It is known that she had several brothers, was married and had a daughter named Cleis. She was revered in antiquity as one of the greatest of the poets and hailed by Plato as the 'tenth muse'. Free from shame or guilt, she was unapologetically open about her sexuality, but even in antiquity she was denigrated and mocked for her unstinting honesty.

Her poems are technically accomplished (she gave her name to the 'Sapphic metre'), complex and innovative, but they are also simple, direct and honest. She became an inspiration to generations of Romantic poets, including Shelley, Byron and Tennyson, who admired her as a solitary voice of feeling who explored the overwhelming power of love. Her emotionally heightened emphasis on the individual consciousness, private feelings and subjective experience is in strong contrast to the epic, liturgical or courtly public poetry of the period.

Her work was written to be performed orally and was intended to be delivered to the accompaniment of the lyre to a small circle of friends and lovers rather than an impersonal text to be delivered to grandees and public figures. Sappho's work made her famous, and her poetry was sung, taught and recited long after her death, so much so that certain phrases of Sappho's have now entered the Greek language.

'If you forget me, think
of our gifts to Aphrodite
and all the loveliness that we shared
all the violet tiaras,
braided rosebuds, dill and
crocus twined around your young neck...'

SAPPHO, EXCERPT FROM:
'I HAVE NOT HAD ONE WORD FROM HER'

Alcaeus of Mitylene was also born on the island of Lesbos, in *c.*625 BCE, and was also a member of the aristocratic class. Lesbos had long been ruled by hereditary kings, but Alcaeus, along with his brothers, was involved in a doomed struggle to change the political order, which ultimately resulted in his exile – one ancient critic reports that he was exiled three times.

He lived on Lesbos at the same time as Sappho and it is quite likely that the poets met, perhaps at one of the festivals at which poets performed. Like Sappho, he wrote in the Aeolic dialect.

Alcaeus wrote in four main genres: drinking songs, political songs, hymns and love songs. While his work lacks Sappho's passionate intensity, it is praised for its deftness, vivacity and engagement. It describes the conservative milieu in which he was raised, and engages in political polemic, personal rancour, fierce joy and piercing insights. His love of wine permeates his work, and he is perhaps best remembered for his allegory of the 'ship of state'.

'Let's drink! Why are we waiting for the lamps?
    Only an inch of daylight left.
Lift down the large cups, my friends,
    the painted ones...'

ALCAEUS, EXCERPT FROM:

'A DRINKING POEM'

THE EMERGENCE OF DEMOCRACY

Democracy was one of classical Greece's most enduring legacies to the modern world. The process that led to the arrival of democracy in Athens at the end of the 6th century was protracted and episodic. It began with Solon's legislation and culminated in Cleisthenes' reforms.

FUNDAMENTAL CHANGES IN ATHENS' government were precipitated by a mounting agrarian crisis; landowners were responding to people who could not discharge their debts by selling them into slavery, which was leading to social unrest. By the 570s BCE, on the brink of a crisis, it was agreed that mediation was the only way forwards.

Solon, born in Athens *c.* 630 BCE, was an aristocrat and a businessman whose wealth came from trade rather than land ownership. He regarded the abuse of wealth as the root of all evil, and believed that freedom was something worth fighting for, especially for citizens within their own community. However, this did not mean that he was going to upset the status quo and embark on a radical programme of land redistribution.

Solon took the step of opening up magistracies to the rich as well as the aristocratic. He abolished the 'dues' that were payable to noble overlords by lesser landlords, as a kind of 'protection' levy. The payments were clearly unjust and even the nobles acquiesced in their termination, confident that Solon would not take the next radical step and redistribute the land from the rich to the poor. However, he did ban the practice of creditors demanding a debtor's person as security for debts, which could easily lead to the enslavement of the debtor. He declared all Athenians free, proclaiming that henceforth slaves within Attica (the region in which Athens was located) could only be foreign born. Solon believed in active citizenship, which was protected by abstract, impersonal justice, manifested in the written law.

Solon saw himself as 'a wolf hemmed in by a pack of hounds', conscious that his compromise, while defusing the present crisis, did not provide a long-term solution. But other reforms were crucial to Athens' future. He established a People's Court, the Heliaea, and gave every citizen the right to bring a prosecution. More significantly, he redefined the Athenian class structure, making wealth, not blood, the new criterion for rights and status. Eligibility for public office was restricted to the two top classes.

However, Solon was essentially a conservative and, although he redefined the class structure, it was then set in aspic. Much of his private legislation related to estates and adoption, and protected the rights of blood and property, so that the old tribal-aristocratic power structures remained. Once Solon had completed his reforms, he went abroad for ten years and chaos broke out as different factions fought for power in the Assembly. A strong man, Peisistratos (600–527 BCE) now stepped into the void. He was a tyrant who consolidated the power of Attica and greatly increased its prosperity. He accrued great personal wealth and invaded Athens three times, finally establishing himself as undisputed tyrant in 564 BCE when he launched a surprise attack on the Athenian army near Mount Hymettus. Peisistratos stripped power from local magnates by introducing travelling circuit judges, and encouraged small-time farmers to return to the land, with the help of loans. He also embarked on a magnificent programme of public works. Through his patronage of religion and art, he created a kind of pro-Athenian propaganda, which did much to define and shape the city. On his death, his rule was hailed as the age of 'Cronus', the golden age.

Peisistratos' legacy was his two ineffective sons: one was assassinated, the other was cruel and oppressive. Factionalism once again prevailed and the aristocrat, Cleisthenes, the leader of one of the Athenian clans, is said to have secured the elections of 508 BCE by offering the citizens 'rule of the state'. When his rival, Isagoras, invited the Spartans to Athens to suppress the newly enfranchised plebeians, an angry riot ensued. The Spartans were ousted and Cleisthenes returned in triumph.

Cleisthenes' reforms gave every free man, landless or not, the right to vote. Instead of the city being divided on tribal or clan lines, it was now subject to geographical divisions, with 170 'demes', or parishes, each with its own assembly, treasury and mayor. He created ten new tribes, each of which was allotted demes from the urban, coastal and inland regions. The new Council of Five Hundred was the de facto governing body, made up of 50 rotating representatives from each tribe, which changed on average every 36 days, ensuring that most citizens participated in government. Athenian democracy had come of age.

THE ATHENIAN BRAND

The 6th century BCE in Athens was a period of phenomenal growth, when monumental architecture began to adorn the city, and its unique ambience was created. Ironically, when Athens was hailed as the birthplace of democracy, much of this process took place under the tyrant Peisistratos (c.560–51 BCE) and his sons.

ATHENA WAS THE GODDESS of war and wisdom, who was born straight from the skull of Zeus and emerged fully grown and clad in armour. When she engaged with Poseidon in a contest to become the patron deity of the city, Poseidon struck his trident on the ground and created a saltwater spring; Athena responded by producing an olive tree. Athena thus became the revered patron goddess and namesake of the city.

In the 6th century BCE, the primitive shrines on the Acropolis were replaced with large stone-built temples. In about 580 BCE, a temple to Athena, the Hecatompedon ('hundred-footer') was built on the site that was later to be occupied by the Parthenon. In *c*.530 BCE, a new temple near the centre of the Acropolis was erected in honour of Athena Polias (guardian of the city), adorned with a marble pedimental sculpture showing a battle between gods and giants. Smaller buildings and treasuries clustered around these monumental structures, filled with votive offerings in marble, bronze and terracotta. The Acropolis had become a magnificent sanctuary, approached by a broad, ceremonial ramp.

In 566 BCE, Peisistratos reorganized the Panathenaic Games in honour of the goddess, which now were held on a four-yearly basis. This became a festival of religious devotion and national pride, which encompassed huge processions of infantry, craftsmen, priests, ordinary Athenians and foreigners, who witnessed sacrifices, religious devotions and athletic games. Victors were presented with special olive oil in an amphora that was decorated with the goddess on one side and the chosen discipline of the athlete on the other.

In these ways, the goddess Athena was incorporated into every aspect of Athenian life, inspiring a strong sense of loyalty and passionate patriotism, which imbued the Athenian population. She was seen as a protective guardian deity, but above all she was revered for her wisdom and her strategic skills. Her pragmatic gift of an olive tree would underpin the importance of agriculture and crafts to the growing city and its hinterland, Attica.

In c. 510 BCE, as Athens stood on the brink of a golden age, about to enact the reforms that would bring about the world's first democracy, a new silver coin, the 'owl' was minted, which depicted Athena's own symbol. These small silver coins were not just a way of facilitating commerce and trade, but also a means of projecting the image of Athens abroad. Like the US dollar today, the Athenian owl coin was widely recognized, easily exchangeable, and therefore become the world's first great trade currency, carrying Athens' unique 'brand' far and wide across the ancient world.

Parian marble relief of mourning Athena, c.460 BCE, built into the wall of a building to the south of the Parthenon. Athena is shown with her military helmet and spear. Her sorrowful, downcast gaze is directed towards a pillar, and it has been suggested that it perhaps represents a memorial to the Athenian dead, possibly the soldiers who died for the city.

THE WORLD ON A VASE

Painted pottery from Ancient Greece has survived in great profusion. The multiplicity of subjects that are depicted on these ancient vessels, and the naturalistic style and painstaking realism of many vase paintings, have given archaeologists a wealth of detailed information about everyday life, from clothes to dining, crafts, religious devotions and sex.

THE CLAY USED TO MAKE POTTERY was available all over Greece; the finest was the orange-red clay of Attica and the paler buff-coloured clay of Corinth. Pottery was fashioned on a potter's wheel, and was usually made in horizontal sections, from the base to the neck, which were then joined together with a clay 'slip', which was placed on the potter's wheel a second time for smoothing. At this stage, the pot was decorated. A popular method was to paint parts of the vase with back 'slip', a highly purified clay containing iron oxides. The vessel was then fired several times, a complex process that brought out the orange-red of the clay and fixed and darkened the paintwork. Individual forms were articulated by incising (scratching) the slip or adding white or purple enhancements.

This was clearly a highly skilled process, and painters and potters worked in partnership and sometimes even signed their work, although the majority of Greek pottery is unsigned. Like Renaissance artists' studios, painters commonly worked in a collective workshop under the supervision of a 'master' potter. Decorated vases were relatively cheap, costing about a day's wages for a manual labourer, and were in great demand. They were exported all over the Mediterranean world, and some potters relocated to other cities, particularly the Greek colonies, to set up workshops there, sometimes developing their own regional style.

Although these vases were highly decorative, they were primarily practical. They were used for holding olive oil, wine and perfumes.

Therefore, the shapes were fairly standardized: amphorae for storing and transporting liquid, large kraters – oversized vessels with handles used for mixing wine with water – jugs, cups with stems and handles, jars for holding perfumes and oils.

Decorative styles evolved over time. Early pottery, from about 1000 BCE, was decorated with geometric patterns, which developed from simple circles, semicircles and horizontal lines to more complex geometric shapes. From about the 8th century BCE, stylized figures of humans, birds and animals began to appear. In the 7th century BCE, Corinth, which traded extensively with the Levant and eastern Mediterranean, began to feature 'Orientalized' images, such as lotuses and palms. By the end of the 7th century BCE, the potters of Corinth had achieved new precision and depth in their engraving of black figures, and the black-figure style was born. The potters of Attica adopted this style and made it their own, dominating the Greek market for the next 150 years.

The fluid grace and poise of these figures, and the sense of life and motion, is outstanding, achieved by close attention to the fine details of musculature, which were engraved. Vase paintings were used to depict representations of mythological narratives, heroic tales, hoplites in phalanx formation, and elegant battle scenes.

In about 530 BCE, the potters of Athens invented the red-figure technique, whereby the decorative motifs remained the colour of the clay, while the background, filled in with a slip, turned black. Figures could then be articulated

A scene of young people gathering olives on an Attic black-figure neck amphora from Vulci, Italy, c.520 BCE. During the classical period, Greek olive oil was exported all over the known world. In the 6th century BCE, the great Athenian legislator, Solon, passed the first law that protected olive trees against uncontrolled felling.

with dilute washes of glaze, which were applied with a brush. This style, which initially coexisted with black-figure ware, persisted for the next 150 years. The use of the brush in red-figure style gave the artist much more scope for realistic detail: facial expressions, minute details of clothing, experiments with perspective and complex composition are all in evidence in red-figure ware. Everyday scenes included athletics, hunting, drinking, craftspeople at work, farmers labouring in the fields and women engaged in domestic activities. There is a strong sense of the time of day depicted, with lamps and torches being utilized to indicate night-time. By the late 5th century BCE, painters were skilled enough to evoke emotions, depicting poignant moments such as leave-taking, artistic activities such as music making, or moments of intense communication, such as symposia.

HEALERS

Healing was traditionally a realm of divine intervention, the province of the healer demigod Asklepios, where cures were sought through the intercession of the god. It involved a number of innovative thinkers and practitioners, each of whom transformed Greek medicine by using empirical observation to establish principles that are still respected and practised today.

IN A SOCIETY that placed a high premium on rational investigation and logic-based discussion, the obvious place to start to understand illness was to observe patients who were sick. An early medical school was established in Knidos, a city in south-western Asia Minor, in 700 BCE, where observations were made and recorded. Alcmaeon was a practitioner at the school who began to speculate about the internal causes of illness, looking at environmental problems, nutrition and lifestyle.

Once the link between natural causes and illnesses and disorders had been established, it was only logical to start investigating natural cures. Empedocles (495–435 BCE), a philosopher from the city of Akragas in Sicily, had proposed the theory that all matter consists of four elements: earth, air, fire and water. This idea prompted Greek doctors to establish a theory of four humours – blood, phlegm, yellow bile and black bile – which needed to be kept in balance in order to maintain good health. Later Greek thinkers linked each humour to an organ, a temper (such as melancholy) and a season, all of which needed to be kept in perfect balance. This theory persisted in western Europe up to the 17th century.

Perhaps the most important Greek doctor was Hippocrates of Kos (*c.*460–370 BCE), the founder of the Hippocratic School of Medicine. He established medicine as a profession and a discipline in its own right, rather than a branch of philosophy. The emphasis at Kos was on patient care and prognosis; the Knidian school was more focused on

The rod of Asklepios is a serpent-entwined staff that was wielded by Asklepios. According to myth, the whispering of snakes, which periodically shed their skin to emerge renewed, gave Asklepios his powers.

diagnosis, though it was hampered by the Greek taboo forbidding the dissection of humans.

Hippocrates wrote, with his assistants, the *Hippocratic Corpus*, which comprised about 60 medical texts promoting the practice of clinical medicine, studying disease by examining a living person. Perhaps his most important legacy was the Hippocratic Oath; the Oath is rarely used in its original form now, but it forms the foundation for other oaths that define good medical practice and ethics that are taken today by doctors and medical practitioners when they qualify. He left other legacies based on his observations: 'Hippocratic fingers' are clubbed digits, indicating a chronic lung disease, lung cancer or a heart condition; and the notion of the 'Hippocratic face' analyses the facial signs that indicate death is imminent. Hippocrates also coined a number of medical terms that are still in use today.

As Greek doctors abandoned magic and incantations, they began to search for natural cures and became expert herbalists. They also recognized that music and theatre could be a therapy, which soothed 'passion' and helped promote mental and physical well-being. Constant warfare, as well as sporting activities such as boxing and wrestling that could become violent, meant that Greek doctors became experienced surgeons, expert at setting bones, fixing dislocated limbs, removing arrowheads and carrying out amputations. They also stitched wounds and dressed them with linen soaked in vinegar, wine, oil, seawater or honey.

The Cult of Asklepios

The earliest centres of practical medicines were the Sanctuaries of Asklepios, and the cult of Asklepios probably originated in Epidaurus in the Peloponnese in the 4th century BCE, from which it spread throughout the Mediterranean. Asklepios was the demigod of medicine, who was generally portrayed holding a serpent-entwined staff. Sick patients came to temples of Asklepios, where after ritual purification and sacrifices to the demigod, they performed the rite of incubation, which meant sleeping in the temple and then reporting their dreams to a priest, who would interpret them and prescribe a cure.

A red-figure Attic aryballos (perfume-container), c.480–470 BCE, depicts a physician treating a patient. The seated doctor is concentrating on bleeding the arm of his nervous patient. A large container, presumably to receive the blood, is placed at the patient's feet.

SPARTA

Sparta was probably founded in the Eurotas valley of Laconia, in the south-east Peloponnese, in the 10th century BCE. It evolved into a highly militarized and communal society, which eschewed indulgence and revered duty. In contrast to the dynamism and creativity of Athens, it was a rigidly static society that adhered to tradition and custom. It is scarcely surprising that two such diametrically contrasting polities would oppose each other and ultimately clash.

SPARTAN SOCIETY WAS STRATIFIED and there was no social movement. At the top were the aristocratic Spartiates, the true Spartans; the *Perioikoi* ('neighbours', but in reality, conquered peoples) were beneath them, free but without political rights; at the bottom were the helots, ruthlessly suppressed serfs who served the entire community and laboured on the land, although they were conscripted into the army in times of war.

When, in the 8th century BCE the Spartans had found their territory was becoming over-populated, they did not become dependent on the usual Greek solution, founding colonies (although there are some Spartan colonies, such as Tarentum). Instead, the Spartans took the unusual step of conquering their neighbour, Messenia, annexing the territory and reducing the inhabitants to serfdom, thereby creating the largest city-state in Greece. The Spartans were able to do this because they had a standing army, supported by the labour of the helots. Even so, holding the territory of Messenia was a challenge, and it was only with difficulty that they were able to stamp out a Messenian revolt (685–668 BCE). At this point, the Spartans took measures to ensure that they would be prepared for any future insurgency.

Little is known about Lycurgus, who has a quasi-legendary status, but he is believed to have been the lawgiver of Sparta who, with the endorsement of the Oracle of Delphi, set about creating the highly militarized and communal Spartan society some time in the 7th century BCE. The Laws acknowledged that the citizen body was a dominant minority, which had to hold down a dangerous and restless population of serfs. Spartiates, the landed aristocracy, were therefore forbidden from engaging in agriculture and were forced to become soldiers. Helots worked the aristocrats' land, and every landowner was expected to contribute their produce to the communal soldiers' table.

Family life was extremely limited. Boys only lived with their mother to the age of seven, when they were taken away by the army for military instruction and lived in barracks. That said, women were allowed to hold property, obtained through dowries and inheritance, and enjoyed greater freedoms than were common in Greece – for example, they were permitted to take part in athletic contests. Girls were also given physical training. Discipline and courage were revered, but there was almost no intellectual education.

Great stress was laid on the necessity of making Spartans self-sufficient; trade was discouraged and foreign visitors barely tolerated. There were two hereditary kings who came from different families; the dual monarchy provided a check on autocracy. At home, the kings were overshadowed by the *Ephors* (overseers), five magistrates elected annually by lot. The Gerousia, which consisted of 28 men aged over 60, led the citizen assembly (*Ekklesia*), which met once a month and voted by simply shouting agreement or dissent. Abroad, on campaign, a king always commanded the army. The well-trained Spartan hoplite was feared and revered throughout Greece, and their military professionalism was widely respected.

The Spartan ideal was austere and rigorous. The helots may have been the labourers of Spartan society, but the Spartiates certainly did not rest on their laurels or luxuriate in comforts supplied by their servants. They valued personal heroism and sacrifice, and were prepared to renounce personal comfort and gratification for the communal ideal.

THE PERSIAN WARS

The allied Greek resistance to Persian invasion from 490–479 BCE was a defining moment in Greek history. It confirmed the Greeks in their belief that their free institutions were infinitely superior to Persian despotism and it reinforced a sense of Greek unity. Ultimately, the Persian Wars saw the emergence of the two great powers of 5th-century BCE Greece: Sparta at the head of the Peloponnesian League, and the growing naval power of Athens.

FROM THE 550s TO THE 520s BCE, the Persians had overrun the Near East from Egypt to the River Oxus. Hardy warriors, accomplished horsemen and skilled with bow and spear, they had a fearsome reputation. Their rule of conquered lands was savagely repressive and they accumulated booty and tribute from subject states all over Asia. They had no respect for the civic institutions and rights of the Greek world.

By 510 BCE, Emperor Darius I had gained the submission of the king of Macedonia. In 499 BCE, the Greeks of Asia Minor, who had been under Persian rule for 50 years, revolted. Eretria, on the island of Euboea, and Athens offered support to these eastern Greek communities. When the revolt was crushed in 494 BCE, retribution was inevitable.

In 490 BCE, the Persians sent an expedition against the two offending cities. They sacked Eretria and landed on the east coast of Attica, at Marathon. The Persians outnumbered the Greeks by more than two to one, but the 10,000 Greek defenders refused to be daunted. The Persians arrived in a flotilla of 600 ships and landed in a bay close to Marathon town. The Greeks formed a line, marched on the Persians and while the centre made a direct attack, the two flanks encircled the Persians. Marathon was a decisive defeat, and a defining moment in the formation of a confident and powerful Greece. According to legend, the Greek soldier Pheidippides ran approximately 40 km (25 miles) from the battlefield to Athens to announce the Persian defeat, a famous run that inspired the first Boston marathon in 1897.

For the next decade, the Persians were occupied with a revolt in Egypt and the death of Darius. Meanwhile, the Athenians used the wealth generated in silver mines of southern Attica to build a fleet; this fateful step would secure Athens' future as a commercial and maritime power. In 480 BCE, the Persians launched a full-scale land invasion under the leadership of Xerxes the Great, and this time an effective Greek unity was achieved. His huge army travelled south from Sardis, through Thrace and Macedonia. After crossing the Hellespont (the Dardanelles), Xerxes reached the narrow pass of Thermopylae. A Greek army of about 7,000 men, spearheaded by 300 Spartans, was guarding a gap in the cliff wall, making it difficult for Xerxes' troops to progress. After seven days, Xerxes' elite 'Immortals', who may have been 100,000-strong, massacred King Leonidas' Spartan army. Xerxes advanced southwards, capturing Boeotia and Attica. He then entered Athens and burned the temples of the Acropolis, watched by the Athenians, who had taken refuge on the island of Salamis.

Rejecting pressure to fight the Persians in Corinth, the senior commander Themistocles insisted that the allies should confront the Persians at Salamis. Tricking the Persian fleet with false intelligence of an allied naval retreat, he lured them into the narrow straits at Salamis, where the Greek fleet had formed a two-ship-deep wall blocking the Persians, who became scattered and disoriented. Three hundred Persian vessels were destroyed, compared to 40 Greek. The decimation of the Persian fleet was followed by their retreat from Athens.

The next summer, 479 BCE, the Greeks routed the retreating Persians at Plataea, north of Athens. Spartan hoplites snatched victory from retreat; the Persians had disrupted their supply lines and the cause appeared to be lost, but the Spartans turned round and engaged in hand-to-hand combat, forcing the Persians back. The final action of the war, at Mycale was a clearing-up operation; the Greek fleet, tipped off by the tyrant ruler of the island of Samos, sailed to the east coast of Asia Minor, landed their forces near Mycale, and routed the Persian camp. Retreating Persians were slain by local Ionians. The shadow of Persian invasion had been lifted.

PERSIAN WARS (BCE)

502	Unsuccessful attack by the Persians on the Greek island of Naxos.
c.500	First revolts in the Greek region of Ionia, Asia Minor.
498	Battle of Sardis is a minor victory for the Greeks against the Persians.
492	Persians invade the island of Naxos, the first invasion of Greece.
490	Marathon: Athenians defeat the Persian land invasion.
480	Thermopylae: 7,000 Greek troops attempt to hold a mountain pass against a Persian invasion of up to 100,000 men.
480	Salamis: Athenians and Corinthians defeat Persia in naval engagements.
479	Plataea: Spartan hoplites are crucial in the defeat of the Persians.
479	Mycale: Spartans and Athenians drive the remaining Persians from Greece.
478	Delian League is formed, under the leadership of Athens, to combine efforts against Persia.

HOPLITES

The backbone of the Greek army, hoplites were heavily armed foot soldiers, mainly ordinary citizens of the Greek city-states, who were called up to serve when necessary. Hoplites fought in tight formation; individual warrior heroes had made way for the communal good. Each soldier relied on his neighbours for mutual protection, and loyalty and reliability were highly valued.

THE PRINCIPAL WEAPONS OF A HOPLITE were a long wooden thrusting spear, up to 2.5 m (8.2 ft) in length and topped with a bronze or iron blade, and a short iron sword. The hoplites were heavily armoured. They wore a leather-lined bronze helmet, a breastplate of bronze or leather, bronze greaves (shin guards) and sometimes arm guards. In addition, they carried a large circular shield, up to 80 cm (2.6 ft) in diameter, which was made of wood or stiff leather, faced with bronze, and gripped using a strap that was attached to the shield rim. Breastplates and shields were sometimes decorated with emblems or designs; the gorgon from Greek mythology was popular. A fully armoured hoplite was required to carry about 20 kg (44 lb) of equipment, and since individuals were required to invest in their own armour and weaponry, being a hoplite indicated a certain status within Greek society. It is thought that one-third to one-half of the able-bodied male population served as hoplites.

Hoplites fought in regiments comprising several hundred men. In battle, they fought in ranks that were eight or more men deep: the phalanx. It was the weight and compactness of the hoplite phalanx that won battles. Since the shield was held on the left arm, each man's shield offered some protection to his neighbour on his left-hand side. Phalanxes advanced at a walk, accompanied by rhythmic music and war cries. On engaging with the enemy, they wielded their spears, which they held overarm. Swords were secondary weapons, used if spears were broken or lost or if the phalanx was separated. They fought at close quarters, battle only ending when one side broke ranks. Ideally, hoplites fought on terrain with high ground to either side, which prevented the phalanx from being flanked – this was the case at the famous Battle of Thermopylae (480 BCE), where the Spartans were able to hold off a huge Persian army in a narrow coastal pass for several days.

Hoplites were not professional soldiers, and lacked military training. However, some city-states did maintain elite units of professional soldiers, the *epilektoi* ('chosen'), who were picked from the ranks of the citizen infantry. Sparta maintained a professional standing army, manned by all male citizens over the age of 20.

Hoplite warfare probably developed towards the end of the 8th century BCE and it was closely linked to the rise and fall of the city-state. It was an effective means of conducting clashes between city-states, who engaged in a ritualized contest where both sides were following recognizable rules of engagement. As Greek civilization came into conflict with greater powers, for example the Persians, individual city-states had to form defensive leagues to confront huge numbers of enemy troops. With manpower pooled, the combatants were able to diversify, and increasingly conflict relied on navies, city walls, siege engines and mercenaries. By the time of the Peloponnesian War (431–404 BCE), large-scale wars of attrition were becoming the norm.

This depiction of a 5th-century BCE hoplite clearly reveals his equipment. Hoplites provided their own kit, so only the more wealthy could afford body armour, typically a bronze cuirass. Here, a helmet with cheek plates, decorated with a horsehair crest, sits on the floor, ready for use. The hoplite carries a large concave shield made of wood, bronze and leather, called an aspis, which was secured to the forearm by a leather fastening. The spear was the main offensive weapon, standing 2.4–4.5 m (7.9–14.8 ft) high. Hoplites also carried a short sword, called a xiphos.

TRIREMES

The triremes were the fast and manoeuvrable ships that formed the backbone of the navies of classical Greece, and were the source of Athens' maritime dominance in the Aegean in the 5th century BCE. In battle, the trireme became a deadly waterborne projectile, propelled by human muscle power.

IT IS THOUGHT THAT PHOENICIANS first invented triremes, which were possibly adopted by Corinthians as early as 700 BCE. The triremes were so called because they were powered by an arrangement of three banks of rowers, sitting almost on top of each other, in three lines of 30 each down the length of the ship, which could amount to 170–180 rowers in total. Each rower sat on a fixed seat, and wielded a 4-m-long (13-ft-long) oar, attached to a fixed vertical pin with a leather oar-loop. With this capacity of oarsmen, triremes could reach speeds of nine or ten knots (18 km/h/11.2 mph). On a good day, with oarsmen rowing for six to eight hours, a trireme could cover distances of 80–100 km (50–62 miles). In battle, the triremes wielded a bronze-sheathed battering ram, which was fixed to the prow. The ram was used to disable enemy ships, allowing soldiers who had been travelling on deck to board the ship.

Ships were up to 37 m long (121.4 ft), and weighed up to 50 tons, which meant that crews could beach the vessels overnight, if necessary. They were built using oak planks sealed with pitch and resin for the outer hulls, with softwoods in the interior – pine, fir and cedar. Ribs and tightened ropes were fixed inside to strengthen the structure. Reconstructions of triremes, built in the late 20th century, have proved that the ships could turn 90 degrees in a matter of seconds.

Two square sails, made of papyrus or flax, were used when cruising, but these were lowered during battle conditions. A single helmsman, who stood next to the ship's commander, controlled two steering oars on either side of the stern. A rowing master shouted instructions, while the crew rowed to the sound of a piper (aulete). The prow of the ship was frequently shaped like an animal head and was decorated with painted eyes. The purpose of decorations on the trireme was to strike fear into the hearts of the enemy.

In Athenian triremes, rich and poor rowed alongside each other. They trained rigorously in peacetime for this physically demanding task, which was an integral part of military service. *Thranitai* were the rowers in the top row, who utilized outboard oarlocks (outriggers), which made greater demands on their strength and synchronization. *Zygitai* were the middle-row oarsmen, named after the beams on which they sat. The lowest row were the *thalimitai*, who were positioned under their colleagues, and rowed blindly. They were just 45 cm (18 in) above the waterline. Perched on the deck, triremes could carry up to 30 hoplites. At the famous naval battle of Salamis (480 BCE), each Athenian ship was recorded to have 14 hoplites and four archers on board.

Triremes were designed for day-long journeys, and were not able to carry provisions or accommodate crews at night. For these reasons, they sailed close to the coast, landed each night for supplies and were dependent on local resources for their survival. When beached, the fleet was vulnerable and could be caught unawares when the crew was scavenging for supplies.

Attic black-figure ware depicting a Greek trireme, late 6th century BCE. The helmsman at the rear holds the steering oar, and is effectively in charge of the ship. The lookout (centre) was in charge of the foredeck. The rowers, sitting in three tiers, could see very little, and merely acted as the 'engine' of the ship.

ATHENS UNDER PERICLES

*Pericles was a populist leader who rose to power in the resurgent
Athens following victory in the Persian Wars. He pursued his
ambitions for Athens, helping to forge a spectacular city that was home
to the greatest philosophers and artists of the age. His expansionist and
territorial ambitions would lead Athens into its fateful conflict with
Sparta, although he would not live to see
Athens' downfall.*

THE PERSIAN WARS created a resurgence of patriotism in Athens.
In the wake of the naval triumph at Salamis, the Athenians created an
alternative to Sparta's land-based Peloponnesian League. The Delian
League was a maritime alliance of the Aegean city-states, but Athens, as
the primary maritime power, was dominant. Over time, the Athenians
became dedicated regulators, controlling everything from weights and
measures to religious observance. League members were increasingly
subjects rather than allies.

In the peaceful period that followed the Persian Wars, public opinion
in Athens sprang back to aristocratic traditionalism. The dashing new
hero of Athens was Cimon (510–450 BCE), the son of the victor at
Marathon, Miltiades (554–489 BCE). Cimon took a fleet to the eastern
Mediterranean in 469 BCE and routed Persia's forces, reopening trade
routes to the Levant and Egypt, an exploit that was greeted with much
acclaim.

However, Cimon and his circle of aristocratic friends were not as
secure as might appear. A new generation of young populists, led by
Ephialtes (*d.*461 BCE) and Pericles (*c.*495–429 BCE), launched an
attack against the privileges of the aristocratic Areopagus Council, and
by 461 BCE the radicals were in control and Cimon had been ostracized.
Under the guidance of Pericles, Athens now embarked on a programme
of imperial aggression, engaging in conflicts in Egypt and Cyprus, as

well as intermittent conflicts closer to home with Sparta and her allies, Aegina and the Megarid, the land that lies between central Greece and the Peloponnese.

In 458 BCE, construction of the defensive Long Walls, between the city and the new port of Piraeus, was begun. In 454 BCE, Pericles led a successful military campaign in Corinth, an ally of Sparta, and sponsored the establishment of Athenian colonies in Thrace and on the Black Sea coast. This First Peloponnesian War ended with a treaty in 446/5 BCE, which established limits to the reach of both Athens and Sparta. Athens also negotiated a peace with Persia (449 BCE), so the defensive Delian League lost its *raison d'être*. But by now the Delian League had become a virtual Athenian Empire. The city had been through precarious times, but now it stood, poised and ready, for its Periclean heyday.

Pericles was a ruthless politician who was ambitious for his city and aspired to Athenian greatness: he wanted a city that was splendidly ostentatious, backed up by a sound economy based on tribute, with Athens taking a leading role in Aegean affairs, reinforced by its fleet. In 449 BCE, he set these dreams in motion by declaring a Panhellenic Congress at which the restoration of shrines destroyed by the Persians was discussed. Pericles argued that League funds should be used to restore Athens' monuments, since his own city had suffered the greatest depredations from the Persians.

The Parthenon was a monument to civic pride; the public works building programme, which also included the Temple of Athena Nike and the Erechtheion, was also an effective way of wiping out unemployment and pre-empting any mob discontent or violence. It wasn't all bombastic building projects: Pericles introduced subsidized theatre admission for poorer citizens and promoted art, literature and philosophy. He also introduced a number of social reforms, paying for citizens to undertake jury duty and various civic duties to encourage full citizen participation in Athens' government. His intellectual clarity and open-mindedness meant that Athens attracted great artists and thinkers from all over Greece.

Pericles was also a famous orator: his stirring funeral oration at the end of the First Peloponnesian War held up the model of Athenian democracy and personal freedom, which set the city apart. But the peaceful interregnum he oversaw was not to last; in 431 BCE, Athens embarked on a second Peloponnesian War with Sparta. Pericles, the great Athenian statesman, did not live to see its conclusion, dying of plague in 429 BCE. A fierce defender of Athenian values and a master of realpolitik, he had also helped to create a culture where freedom of thought flourished and architecture, sculpture, theatre, literature and philosophy were all able to thrive.

Roman copy of a Greek bust of Pericles bearing the inscription 'Pericles, son of Xanthippus, Athenian', c.430 BCE. Pericles (495–429 BCE) was a prominent statesman, orator and general, who led Athens through the aftermath of the Persian Wars into its 'Golden Age'.

THE PARTHENON

This Dorian temple, of fine Attican marble, which was constructed on Athens' Acropolis in 447–433 BCE, has become the symbol of both Athens under Pericles, but also of the quintessential classical 'spirit'. It still dominates the modern city of Athens, a magnificent testament to the city's renown.

THE PARTHENON WAS DESIGNED to honour Athens' city goddess, but also to celebrate the city's leading role in the conquest of the Persians. The work was the inspiration of the great Athenian statesman Pericles, but much of the work was carried out by his friend, the sculptor Phidias. The decision to build the Parthenon came in the wake of the Persian attack on the city in 480 BCE, when many of the buildings on the Acropolis were damaged. It was funded by the surplus funds in the war treasury of the Delian League; during the wars, the Greek allies had sworn to leave all damaged buildings untouched, as a memorial to Persian vandalism. However, the peace treaty at the end of the war was held to invalidate that oath, and Pericles was able to assert Athens' dominance within the League to obtain the necessary funds for his building projects.

Set on the highest part of the Acropolis, the Parthenon is some 30.8 m (101 ft) long by 69.5 m (228 ft) wide, and utilizes 22,000 tons of honey-coloured marble from nearby Mount Pentelikon. It was the largest Greek Doric temple, named after Athena Parthenos, meaning 'virgin'. Because of the sheer scale of the building, it would appear slightly curved from a distance, so the architects compensated for this optical illusion by leaning the columns slightly inwards, which makes them appear perpendicular. The columns are slightly wider in the middle, and the narrowing towards the top adds to an uplifting sense of soaring height and grace.

Flanked by these Doric columns, the building was entered through large wooden doors decorated with bronze, gold and ivory. Two interior rooms housed the city's treasury and the cult statue of Athena. The temple roof was constructed of cedar and marble tiles. The complexity and beauty of the interior reliefs and architectural sculptures of the Parthenon are unprecedented in Greek temple architecture. The Parthenon frieze runs round all four sides of the building, with monumental sculptures adorning both pediments.

The Parthenon frieze was carved in low relief around all four side of the building inside the colonnade. It presents a total of 16 m (52.5 ft) of sculpture, featuring 380 human figures and 220 animals, mainly horses. It depicts the Panathenaic procession, which was held every four years, and culminates in a reception of assembled Olympian gods and Athenian tribal heroes. The main part of the procession is made up of warriors, cavaliers and chariots, reflecting the turbulent war-torn times that the temple commemorates. The depictions of mortals – heroic defenders of Athenian civilization – on a sacred building is highly unusual.

The metopes are square panels in high relief that were placed above the architrave (the lintel above the columns) on the outside of the temple. They are decorated with episodes from Greek mythology, including the battle of the Centaurs and the Lapiths (youths).

The pediments are the triangular upper part of the temple, below the roof. The western pediment sculpture is a masterpiece of the Greek sculptor's art, depicting musculature and drapery with life-like intensity. It is a representation of the struggle between Athena and Poseidon for the land of Attica. In the east pediment, the Three Fates lounge and recline in position of languorous abandon. Reclining figures were brilliantly adapted to fit into the awkward corner shapes of the pediment.

The cult statue of Athena, the work of Phidias, is now lost, with only miniature Roman copies remaining. It was a colossal figure, standing more than 12 m (39.4 ft) high, of gold and ivory, wrapped around a wooden core. Athena was depicted fully armed, with a helmet that was surmounted by a sphinx and two griffins, carrying a shield that depicted the battles between the Amazons and the giants. A shallow basin of water placed before the statue reflected the light that came through the door, creating a dazzling image of power and divinity.

Lord Elgin

Over the centuries, the Parthenon was desecrated and damaged. It was turned into a Christian church in around 500 CE, became an Ottoman mosque in the 1460s, and its roof was blown up in 1687 when the Venetians, who were besieging the Ottoman-held city, used it as a gunpowder store. By 1800, when European aristocrats were visiting Athens, the birthplace of democracy, as part of their European Grand Tour, only about half the Parthenon sculptures remained. From 1801, Lord Elgin, the British ambassador, removed about half these sculptures, with Ottoman permission, and brought them back to London. In 1816, the government purchased these sculptures for the British Museum, where they have remained ever since. The collection, known as the Elgin Marbles, comprises 14 metopes, some of the best slabs from the frieze, and some of the figures from the pediment. The sculptures that remained in situ suffered severe damage from Athens' air pollution, but in 1993 they were moved to a purpose-built exhibition space in full view of the Parthenon, and are now treated with the reverence that their creators, Pericles and Phidias, would expect.

Cavalcade from the west frieze of the Parthenon, c.447–433 BCE. The west side is the first side approached by the visitor to the Acropolis, and it depicts the beginning of the cavalcade of horse and riders, many not yet mounted, before they divide and move up the long north and south sides of the temple.

GREEK ARCHITECTURAL ORDERS

An architectural order describes a style of building, most readily recognizable by the type of column used, as well as by its proportions, profiles and various aesthetic details. The three classical orders – Doric, Ionic and Corinthian – are descriptive labels but also a reflection of the ways in which architecture in classical Greece developed.

COLUMNS CONSIST OF A BASE (not always present), a shaft and a capital. They support the 'entablature', which comprises three horizontal sections, separated from each other by mouldings and bands, comprising the architrave, frieze and cornice. The ancient Greek temple clearly drew on inspiration from other cultures – the 7th century BCE is known as the 'Orientalizing' period, when inspiration came from cultures to the East, especially Egypt, where stone temple architecture dates back thousands of years. However, the basic structure of the classical orders, with their columns supporting an architrave, is basically a variation of the post-and-lintel system, which had been in use in Greece since the Bronze Age.

Doric order

This is the earliest of the three classical orders, and is characterized by plain, unadorned capitals and fluted (grooved) columns, which are sturdy and imposing. The columns reach a height that is only four to eight times their diameter, and each column is channelled with 20 flutes. They sit directly on the floor, without a base. The column tapers in from the bottom, which contributes to its squat, earth-bound appearance. The frieze of the Doric entablature is divided into triglyphs and metopes. The triglyph is a vertically channelled tablet. Metopes are the plain or carved reliefs between the triglyphs.

The Doric order dates back to the Greek mainland in the late 7th century BCE and it is thought that this style developed in the Doric-speaking trade centre of Corinth, and was widely deployed until the early 5th century BCE. The Doric order finds its full artistic expression in the Parthenon Temple, Athens (447–433 BCE).

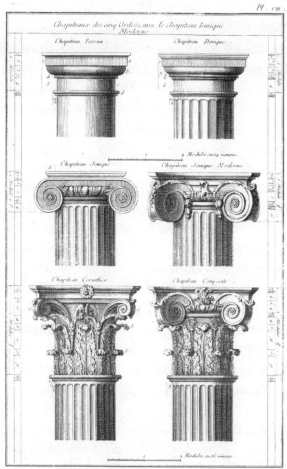

An illustration of the Five Architectural Orders engraved for Diderot's Encyclopédie, vol. 18, showing the Tuscan and Doric orders (top row); two versions of the Ionic order (centre row); Corinthian and Composite orders (bottom row). Diderot's monumental reference work, published 1751–66, embodied the thinking of the European Enlightenment, reflecting a growing interest in the classical world.

Ionic order

Originating in Ionia, a coastal region of central Turkey, in the mid-6th century BCE, the columns of the Ionic order are much more elegant and graceful than their sturdy Doric counterparts. Tall and slender, Ionic columns reach a height that is nine times their diameter, with 24 flutes. Unlike the Doric column, a base supports the column. The Ionic capital is distinguished by 'volutes', scroll-like ornaments resembling rams' horns. The Ionic frieze, which dispenses with the Doric triglyphs and metopes, is continuous. The Ionic order, which reached mainland Greece by the 5th century BCE, can be clearly seen in the construction of the Erechtheion in Athens c.421–405 BCE.

Corinthian order

The earliest evidence for this most elaborate of the classical orders comes from the Temple of Epikourios Apollo at Bassae in the Peloponnese and dates to the late 5th century BCE, although the name would suggest a Corinthian origin. Corinthian columns are distinguished by their elaborate carved capitals, which feature stylized acanthus leaves. This style was never as popular among the Greeks as the Doric and Ionic orders, but was much appropriated by the Romans.

In the 4th century BCE, Greek architects departed from a strict adherence to one architectural style and began to experiment with the orders, perhaps using one order for the interior and one for the exterior. The Parthenon in Athens, for example, is basically a Doric temple, but it features a continuous sculpted frieze, which is an Ionic feature, as well as four Ionic columns which support the roof of the 'opisthodomos', or treasury.

THE PELOPONNESIAN WAR

The Peloponnesian War, which extended over the last three decades of the 5th century BCE, was a bitter struggle between Greek city-states, which killed tens of thousands, and was only resolved with the help of Persia. This came at a price, forcing the abandonment of all the Greek cities in the Persian sphere.

THE STARTING POINT OF THE WAR was the expansion of Athenian power, especially as it began to extend into the Greek west and Sicily. Corinth, strategically placed on the route north-west, was feeling increasingly vulnerable, and when the Athenians and Corinthians clashed diplomatically over the island of Corcyra (Corfu), the spark was ignited. The Corinthians threatened to leave the Peloponnesian League unless the leaders of the League, the Spartans, were willing to go to war against Athens.

It had long been Spartan practice to maintain its security with a cordon of loyal oligarchies. Sparta viewed Athens, a newly formed democracy where culture and philosophy flourished, with absolute distrust. The final straw was when Athens sought to destabilize Sparta's ally, Megara, by introducing an embargo on Megaran trade. In 431 BCE, the Spartans took up the Athenian challenge when Thebes, a Spartan ally, attacked Plataea, an ally of Athens. The conflict that now unfolded would be fought all over the Greek world, and would cause widespread death and devastation.

The Athenians retreated behind their Long Walls, and a war of attrition began. The Spartans, with their dogged commitment to discipline and warfare, adopted an effective policy of invading Attica on an annual basis and laying waste to Athens' agricultural hinterland. Sparta's allies, however, were unsupported by a helot slave population and could not linger on campaign: they had to return to their home territories to gather in the harvest. Meanwhile, the Athenian fleet roamed the Aegean, striking at will, and causing severe supply problems for several of the city-states in the Peloponnesian League.

Pericles died in a plague (probably typhus) epidemic, in 429 BCE, which had devastated the overcrowded city of Athens, packed with refugees from the Spartan destruction of Attica. Following his death, the policy of sitting out the hostilities that he had promoted began to falter. His successors began to engage in more active strategies, for example raiding Sicily (427–424 BCE), which supplied grain to both Sparta and Corinth, and launching an expedition against Megara and Boeotia in 424 BCE, which ultimately failed. In 421 BCE, a truce and a 50-year peace were agreed, which effectively returned the situation to the pre-war status quo.

In 416 BCE Athens embarked on a brutal campaign against the island of Melos, which arguably owed her no allegiance at all, and genocide ensued. A year later, the Athenians, intent on exploiting the island of Sicily for its grain and timber, launched a huge naval expedition under the pretext that the small polis of Segesta had asked for protection from Syracuse. When the well-trained Syracusan cavalry confronted the Athenian navy, their assault collapsed – a disaster for Athens and her navy, which lost 200 triremes. A rash of revolts by Athens' Ionian subject allies (412 BCE) and an anti-democratic coup in 411 BCE divided Athens and rendered it vulnerable, but the Spartans failed to press home their advantage.

The Spartans' eventual victory in 404 BCE was partly due to Persian funding of their new fleet, and also can be attributed to the aggressive tactics of the Spartans' new leader, Lysander. By contrast, Athens had lost some of its finest military leaders in the coup, and was now being defended by a second-rank military command. When the Athenians lost the naval battle of Aegospotami near the Hellespont, they lost control of a vital trade route, on which their import of Black Sea grain depended. The Athenians had no choice but to surrender and accept short-lived rule by a Spartan oligarchy. But Athens was no longer a dominant player in the Mediterranean, and the Golden Age of Athenian democracy had come to an end.

PELOPONNESIAN WAR (BCE)

445   Peace treaty between Athens and the Peloponnesians.

435   War between Corinth (a major ally of Sparta) and Corcyra (Corfu).

433   Athenian alliance with Corcyra brings her into conflict with Corinth.

432   Potidaea, a Boeotian city in the northern Aegean, revolts against the Athenian Empire with Corinthian help (Potidaea finally surrenders in 430 BCE).

431–421   Archidamian War (Archidamos was king of Sparta).

430   Plague at Athens decimates the population.

429   Peloponnesians lay siege to Plataea, which they capture in 427 BCE.

428   The cities of Lesbos, an island off the west coast of Turkey, revolt against the Athenian Empire, led by Mytilene.

425   Athenians trap 120 Spartan 'Equals' and 170 allies on the island of Sphakteria off Pylos (south-western Peloponnese); Spartans sue for peace.

423   Truce to allow for peace negotiations.

421   Peace of Nikias, named after chief Athenian negotiator.

416   Athenians attack and capture Melos.

415–413   Major Athenian invasion of Sicily.

413   Peloponnesians establish a fort at Dekeleia in north-eastern Attica as a base for harassing the countryside, making farming mostly impossible.

412   Spartan fleet begins regular operations in the Aegean. The Spartans form an alliance with Persia, which provides them with subsidies. Athenian allies in the Aegean begin to revolt.

411   *Coup d'état* in Athens produces a mild oligarchy (the 'Four Hundred', followed by the 'Five Thousand').

406   Athenian naval victory at Arginousai, where generals are tried and executed for failing to collect the dead after battle.

405   Spartan naval victory at Aegospotami; with the loss of its fleet, Athens is now defenceless.

404   Athens surrenders; a Spartan oligarchy takes power in Athens (the 'Thirty Tyrants').

403   Democracy in Athens is restored.

GYMNASIA

More than merely a place in which to train the body and hone athletic skills, the Greek notion of the gymnasium was that it was a venue that catered for a sound body and a stimulated mind, combining physical training with philosophical discussion and study.

IN THE 6TH CENTURY BCE, the gymnasium was a simple gathering place, often in a sanctuary or a site that was famous for its games, which was normally located in the shade with access to water, such as a stream. The gymnasium provided a place where young Greeks could improve their fitness and train for warfare or for peacetime competitive games. In time, they evolved into purpose-built structures which could be found in major cities. By the 5th century BCE, they were no longer just dedicated to physical health; they were also places for intellectual exertion, discussion and education. In effect, they were a kind of university where members could listen to lectures, join stimulating discussions or simply train. Sports that were practised at gymnasia included: wrestling, running, jumping, armed combat, archery, and discus and javelin throwing. Many of these sports would have taken place to the accompaniment of rhythmic music.

The word 'gymnasium' comes from the Greek word for nudity (*gymnos*) because sports were always undertaken, by men only, in the nude. Plato discusses the fact that gymnasia were often places in which an important homoerotic relationship in Greek society was enacted: between a young boy (*eromenos*) and a young man (*erastes*). The two would become lovers, and the older man would become a mentor to the younger one.

Athens boasted three public gymnasia: the Cynosarges, the Lyceum and the Academy. The Athenians wisely held that there could be no health of the mind unless the body was cared for, and also viewed exercise as a powerful remedy against disease. In general, an ancient gymnasium faced east; its principal entrance led to an open quadrangle which contained two inner courts. The eastern court, the *peristylium*, was surrounded by a row of columns. This was the main training area. The western court was also bordered by porticoes; it contained plane trees for shade, benches and seats, and was probably the place where the studious or the contemplative met and conversed. To the north lay the stadium, which was where athletes trained for foot races; it was sometimes outside the gymnasium precincts. To the south was an outer area with trees and walkways, which formed a quiet retreat.

Gymnasia also provided rooms for washing. In the dressing room, athletes anointed their skin with oil, preferably olive oil; this may have been to massage the muscles, or simply for aesthetic purposes. Dust was sprinkled on the oil to avoid slipperiness. After training, when the athletes were slick with sweat and oil, they scraped off the dirt using a bronze or iron scraper (*xyston*), which also massaged tired muscles. They then washed themselves in cold water in simple washing basins – the luxurious wallowing in communal baths so enjoyed by the Romans was not a Greek practice. Finally, the athletes finished their routine by anointing themselves with perfumed oil.

Marble relief showing Greek wrestlers and their handlers.

GREEK THEATRE

The tragedies and comedies that emerged in Athens' heyday, the 5th century BCE, were innovative, challenging, stimulating and thought-provoking. They were also harbingers of a new form of mass entertainment, and the foundation upon which all modern theatre is built.

THE MAIN FESTIVAL DEDICATED TO THE GOD Dionysos had been introduced in Athens in the 530s BCE, where 'dithyrambs', songs sung in praise of Dionysos, were performed. These evolved into tragedies (literally 'goat songs', perhaps referring to sacrifices made to the god), which became part of that festival, where they were performed as part of a theatrical contest. The music, dance and intoxication of the Dionysian ritual are all present in the role of the chorus and music in Greek theatre. Athens transmitted these festivals to its allies to encourage cultural cohesion, and they became enduringly popular, spreading throughout the Mediterranean world. They are the precursors of modern theatre.

Tragedies explored the moral and religious conflicts through tales of a mythical 'royal' past. They explored family and community, sexual morality, religion and the characters of heroes, accompanied by the complex singing and dancing of the chorus. The ultimate object of the tragedy was 'catharsis' (emotional cleansing) for the audience, who had lived through the characters' experience and suffering.

Early tragedies were performed by just one male actor, who wore a mask which allowed him to impersonate the gods. From the early 6th century BCE, he was joined by a chorus of up to 15 male actors, who sang and danced but did not speak. Eventually, plays may have been performed by up to three actors, each of whom had to take on many roles, so changes of mask, costume, voice and gesture were required. In the vast theatres of Ancient Greece, exaggerated costumes and masks, which showed leering or tragic faces, were necessary because it was difficult for audiences to make out the details of facial expression. Masks also amplified the actor's voice. The combination of recitation in metrical verse and the chorus, who danced and sang meant that Greek tragedies appeared more like operas than plays.

Three great dramatists dominated Greek tragedy: Aeschylus (*c.*525–*c.*456 BCE), Sophocles (*c.*496–*c.*406 BCE) and Euripides (*c.*484–407 BCE). Aeschylus was responsible for the introduction of a second actor, and also for integrating the chorus more closely into the action of the play. His tragedies, which explored the great themes of religion and morality, were performed in groups of three, such as *The Oresteia* and *The Persians*. Sophocles, who lived through Athens' golden age, is credited with introducing the third actor and abolished the 'trilogic' form, meaning that each of his plays could be performed on its own. The shorter form greatly increased dramatic tension and plot development. Sophocles also began to focus more clearly on the plight of individuals and the hubris and fate that shaped their actions. Famous plays include: *Antigone, Electra, Oedipus at Colonus* and *Oedipus the King*. Euripides, the youngest of the three dramatists, flourished towards the end of the 5th century BCE, during a period of great intellectual exploration and scientific discovery. Euripides brought these insights to his tragedies, focusing on the thoughts and experiences of ordinary individuals rather

The classical Greek theatre at Epidaurus, Peloponnese, is considered to be the most perfect Greek theatre in terms of both acoustics and aesthetics. It was built at the end of the 4th century BCE by the architect Polykleitos the Younger, and had a seating capacity of 14,000. It was located to the south-east of a sanctuary to the Greek god of medicine, Asklepios, and it is thought that theatre performances were used as a means of healing patients and stimulating mental health.

than the legendary figures of the heroic past, portraying the more fallible, human sides of heroes and gods in plays such as *Medea* and *The Bacchae*.

In the early Dionysian competitions, each dramatist produced three tragedies and one satyr play – a burlesque parody on a theme from mythology, performed by satrys, the followers of Dionysos. These plays opened with a spectacular song and dance routine by a chorus of up to 24 actors, often dressed in outlandish costumes, called the *parodos*. The second part of the show, the *agon*, comprised a witty verbal contest or debate between actors, often accompanied by fast scene changes. The third part of the play, the *parabasis*, consisted of a direct address to the audience by the chorus. The play ended with the *exodus*, when the chorus made a dramatic exit, performing another song and dance routine.

Little is known about the origin and early development of ancient Greek comedy, but it certainly emerged later than tragedy, receiving official recognition and state support in the City Dionysian festival in the early 480s BCE. Its origins would appear to stem from the bawdy and ribald songs that were performed at fertility festivals. Athenian comedy is dominated by Aristophanes (active from the 420s to 380s BCE), who blended wordplay, sexual allusions, parody, invective and satire. His famous plays include *Lysistrata*, a drama about the women of Athens imposing a sex strike on their men to bring about peace, and *The Clouds*, which offers an irreverent and buffoonish portrayal of the great philosopher Socrates. Aristophanes' successors include Menander, Philemon and Diphilus.

The Form of Greek Theatres

Theatres were typically built on the slope of a hill, and were cleverly constructed to ensure excellent acoustics. There were three main parts. The orchestra was a large circular or rectangular area in the centre of the theatre, where the play, dance and religious rites took place. The skene was a rectangular building behind the orchestra, which was the backstage area, where actors could change their costumes and masks. Violent deaths always occurred

---

offstage, and often an *ekkyklema*, or cart, was wheeled out from the skene to display the tragic aftermath. Initially, the skene was a tent or hut, but it evolved into a stone structure, which was sometimes painted to serve as a backdrop. The 'audience', which may well have been men only, rose in a semicircle around the orchestra, with steeply raked seating on stone steps. Theatres were built to a large scale, and could seat a large number of people, up to 14,000.

GREEK PHILOSOPHY

Greek philosophers posed thought-provoking questions, challenged traditional beliefs and prejudices, and even endangered their own lives for their beliefs. Ranging from mystics to hard-nosed realists, their insights are still considered important today.

THE CRADLE OF GREEK PHILOSOPHY was the ancient region of Ionia, with its cosmopolitan cities and wealthy trading centres. The first group of Greek philosophers – Thales (*c.*624–*c.*528 BCE), Anaximander (610–546 BCE) and Anaximenes (*c.*586–*c.*526 BCE) – came from the area's southernmost city, Miletus, in the late 7th/early 6th century BCE. They were interested in a cosmological theory that was based on the study of natural phenomena, unobscured by dogma, myth and superstition. Pythagoras (*c.*570–*c.*495 BCE), who came from the Ionian island of Samos, departed from purely scientific deduction, combining science with mysticism, such as his belief in the transmigration of souls. He proposed the doctrine that 'all things are numbers', meaning that the structure and essence of all things can be determined by finding the numerical relations they express. He is credited with being the inventor of the first known mathematical formulation. Leucippus (dates unknown), probably from Miletus, and Democritus (*c.*460–*c.*370 BCE), who was born in Thrace, believed that everything is composed of atoms, and he developed a determinist philosophy based on natural laws in the 5th century BCE.

In Athens, the emergence of democracy brought debate and rhetoric to the foreground. All free citizens took part in the discussions of the assembly, or represented themselves in court, and skilful speech, argument and rhetoric was much valued. This period saw the beginning of the 'Sophist' school, and education in the arts of rhetoric and argument was central to its purpose. Socrates (469–399 BCE), a major figure in Greek philosophy, was also an educationalist who lived a life of austerity

Portrait bust of Aristotle, 1st or 2nd century CE, a Roman copy of a lost bronze sculpture made by Lysippos in the 4th century BCE. Aristotle (384–322 BCE) wrote on a huge variety of subjects, including: physics, biology, zoology, metaphysics, economics, politics, linguistics, aesthetics, poetry and theatre.

Copy of the portrait of Plato (c.428–c.348 BCE) made by Silanion in c.370 BCE for the Academia in Athens. Plato, the pupil of Socrates and teacher of Aristotle, is seen as a pivotal figure in the history of Western philosophy. He is also one of the founding philosophers of Western religion and spirituality.

Marble portrait of Socrates (469–399 BCE), possibly a 1st-century CE Roman copy of a lost bronze statue made by Lysippos. Socrates is credited as the founder of the Western ethical tradition of thought, and his work is known chiefly through the writings of his pupils Plato and Xenophon.

and turned his enquiring mind away from the physical world to moral and psychological questions. He taught by posing thought-provoking questions to his students, and challenging their underlying assumptions. His agnosticism and intolerance for lack of intellectual clarity earned him powerful enemies. He was put on trial for the corruption of youth and condemned to death: a sentence he opted to perform himself, by drinking hemlock, rather than by following the more conventional option of escaping.

Plato (*c.*428–*c.*348 BCE), a student of Socrates, left Athens in disgust following the death of his teacher. He returned several years later to open his famous Academy. Plato was fascinated by ethics and politics, but is most famous for his focus on metaphysical and epistemological ideas. His most famous work of ethical and political philosophy, *Republic*, draws the outlines of an ideal state ruled by an elite that governs exclusively by reason.

Aristotle (384–322 BCE) was, in turn, a student of Plato, and he was the tutor of Alexander the Great for almost 20 years. Aristotle was a polymath, interested in physics, biology, astronomy, psychology, politics, rhetoric, ethics and metaphysics. He is perhaps best known as the first thinker to systematically develop the study of logic, creating a system that comprised five treatises, known as the *Organon*. He also wrote major works: *Ethics*, *Politics*, *Poetics* and *Rhetoric*.

After the death of Aristotle, the Greek city-states began to fall apart and they became pawns in the power games of rival Hellenistic kings. Out of this environment, two dogmatic schools of philosophy emerged: stoicism and epicureanism. The stoics, led by a Syrian, Zeno of Citium (*c.*335–*c.*263 BCE), proposed that to live 'in agreement with oneself', in possession of virtue that is based on self-control and denial of the passions, is at the root of happiness.

Zeno's contemporary, Epicurus (341–270 BCE), created a philosophy that took an opposing view, putting pleasure at the very centre of a person's happiness, and warning against participation in public life. He was not an advocate of dissolution or debauchery, arguing that the simplest pleasures make life happy. He taught that the gods were much too superior to trouble themselves with the affairs of mere mortals.

The final major Hellenistic school of philosophy was Scepticism, promoted by Pyrrho of Elis (*c.*360–*c.*270 BCE), who was convinced that nobody can know anything with any certainty, or even be sure that the things that are perceived with the senses are real, and not illusory. He was so convinced of his beliefs that he is said to have walked along the road with no regard for the dangers from vehicles or other pedestrians; his devoted disciplines had to guide him so that he escaped injury.

The Symposium

This was a gathering in a private house when men came together to eat, drink, sing and converse. Topics that were discussed included politics, philosophy and poetry recitals. The only women who were permitted were high-class prostitutes, trained in music, dance and gymnastics. The guests reposed on cushioned couches that were arranged around the walls of the room so that every guest was visible. After eating, drinking and libations, drinking continued throughout the evening and a shared cup or *kylix* was passed around.

THE RISE OF MACEDONIA

The era of Greek city-states and democracies came to an end with the rise of the kingdom of Macedon, which was situated on the periphery of the Greek world. When Macedonian military power was ruthlessly unleashed in a series of conquests in the 4th century BCE, individual freedoms were curtailed and personal power was asserted though conquest and extravagant displays of wealth and luxury.

MACEDON HAD NEVER BEEN A TRUE PART of the Greek world. It stood on its northern edge, a wild and mountainous country, ruled by a royal family that claimed descent from the Greek hero, Achilles. Philip II ascended to the Macedonian throne in 359 BCE, following the ruthless assassination of various members of his family. His predecessors mainly stood out for their feats of drinking, feuding and debauchery, although there had been intermittent, and largely unsuccessful, attempts at Hellenization – for example the playwright Euripides was invited to live and write in Macedon in 408 BCE.

Philip II was ambitious, ruthless and intelligent. In his youth, he had spent some time in the city-state of Thebes, which had shocked the Greek world in 371 BCE by winning the Battle of Leuctra against the Spartans. Following the Theban example, Philip had pioneered a new hoplite formation. The phalanx was 16 ranks deep, rather than the usual eight, and armed with the fearsome Macedonian pike (the 5.5–6 m/18–20 ft-long *sarissa*), and was able, by sheer weight of numbers, to break through the opposing line. He also created an elite cavalry corps, the so-called 'Companions'. As Philip began to conquer the rich lands to the east of his borders, he brought war captives back to Macedon as slaves, which enabled Macedonian landowners to join the standing professional army, which had a 24,000-strong infantry, with 3,400 cavalry. Each soldier swore an oath of loyalty to the king.

Philip's deadly Macedonian phalanx became the terror of the Greek world. He made short work of the Illyrian tribes, who were threatening Macedon from the north-west. In 357 BCE, he seized the Athenian colony of Amphipolis, which was blocking his way to the south, thereby acquiring its gold and silver mines. He went on to conquer towns throughout the Chalcidic peninsula. Next, he turned his attention to Olynthos, at the head of the Gulf of Torone.

As the fate of the city stood in the balance, the great Athenian orator Demosthenes, who understood that Philip posed a threat to Athenian civilization, tried to warn his fellow citizens, imploring them to make a stand in a series of impassioned speeches, known as *The Philippics*. But for too long they chose to believe Philip's false assurances, agreeing to the Peace of Philocrates (346 BCE), which endorsed the status quo and legitimized Philip's new territorial acquisitions. Ultimately, the Athenians realized that their policy of appeasement would lead to their annihilation and made a belated stand, forging an alliance with Thebes, and confronting Philip at the Battle of Chaeronea (338 BCE). After a Panhellenic Congress at Corinth, peace was finally established and Philip, an absolutist monarch, was established as Head of the Congress. The League of Corinth resolved to launch a war against Persia, with Philip in command.

Philip married seven times. Most significantly, his marriage to Olympias led to the birth of Alexander, who would eventually succeed his battle-hardened father and fulfil his ambition to conquer Persia. Philip was murdered by his friend and former lover, Pausanias, in 336

A bust of Philip of Macedon (r. 359–336 BCE), from the Hellenistic period. A skilled military tactician and diplomatist, Philip followed the polygamist customs of Macedonia and married seven times. He was shot by an arrow in the eye and blinded, and walked with a limp following a devastating injury.

BCE and Alexander ascended to the throne, but not before his mother Olympias had ordered the murder of Philip's newest young wife and child. The ruthlessness and savagery of the Macedonian court still prevailed.

THE RISE OF MACEDONIA (BCE)

371   A Spartan army is overwhelmed at Leuctra by a smaller number of Thebans under Epaminondas.

359   Philip II succeeds his father Amyntas III on the throne of Macedonia, the northernmost kingdom of Greece.

356   Alexander the Great is born in Pella, the capital of his father Philip II, at the heart of the expanding Macedonian kingdom.

348   The citizens of Olynthos abandon their homes when their city is attacked by Philip of Macedon.

343   Aristotle is employed in Macedon as tutor to the 13-year-old heir to the throne, Alexander.

c.340   Alexander the Great, at the age of 16, conducts his first successful military campaign – against the Thracians.

338   Philip of Macedon defeats Athens and Thebes at Chaeronea, giving him control of Greece.

337   Philip of Macedon persuades most of the Greek city-states, brought together in Corinth, to agree to a military alliance with himself as leader.

336   Following Philip's murder, the League of Corinth elects Alexander to take his father's place as leader of the campaign against Persia.

335   Before departing for the east, Alexander destroys Thebes and enslaves the Thebans for rebelling against the League of Corinth.

334   Alexander the Great marches east with some 5,000 cavalry and 30,000 foot soldiers. At the River Granicus, near Troy, Alexander defeats a Persian army.

333   At Issus, close to the Turkish border with Syria, Alexander defeats the Persian emperor Darius III.

332   Alexander moves south through Syria and Palestine, arriving in

Egypt, where the Persian governor surrenders.

331   Alexander moves north-east into Mesopotamia, and defeats Darius III (at Gaugamela), leaving Persia open to his advances.

*c.*330   Alexander destroys the great palace of Xerxes at Persepolis.

327   Alexander marries Roxana after subduing the territories of her father, a Bactrian chief in the modern region of Afghanistan.

325   Alexander's Greek troops threaten to mutiny unless he turns for home.

324   Alexander and his companion Hephaestion marry daughters of Darius III. When the army reaches Ecbatana, Hephaestion dies of a fever.

323   Alexander the Great, still only 33, dies in Babylon following a banquet.

Alexander's generals decide that the joint heirs to his throne shall be his half-brother (Philip III) and his posthumous son by Roxana (Alexander IV).

The ruins of the Philippeion at Olympia, built by Philip II to celebrate his victory at the Battle of Chaeronea in 338 BCE, which was fought between Macedon and an alliance of Greek city-states. It was a decisive victory for the Macedonians.

VERGINA

The royal Macedonian tombs discovered at Vergina in northern Greece are a testament to the enormous power and wealth of the Macedonian kings. The gold and ivory grave goods are sumptuous and ornate, while vivid frescoes depict royal hunts and mythological scenes.

IN 1977, THE GREEK ARCHAEOLOGIST Manolis Andronikos discovered a pair of spectacular royal tombs. These contained a wealth of gold, silver, bronze and iron objects, two caskets of human bones and several wall frescoes. The tombs were found buried 5 m (16.4 ft) underground in Vergina, a village in northern Greece, and dated to *c.*350–320 BCE.

Vergina was the site of Aigea, which was the original capital of ancient Macedon before it was replaced by Pella. The site of Aigea has yielded a great deal of information about the ancient Macedonians. Remains include a monumental palace (*c.*340 BCE), a theatre, the sanctuaries of Eukleia, city walls and a royal necropolis, containing more than 500 tumuli. It is thought that Aigea was never a substantial royal city, but rather a collection of villages, which represented the assorted aristocratic tribes of ancient Macedon. Even after the Macedonian capital was transferred to Pella on the central Macedonian plain in the 4th century BCE, Aigea remained the sacred city of Macedon, where dynastic marriages took place, and where members of the royal family were buried.

There is ongoing controversy about the occupants of the tombs. Tomb II was conventionally believed to be the burial place of Philip II, although the latest research, which has analysed the skeleton for signs of Philip's notorious leg wound, inflicted by a lance, did not find any evidence of it. It has been suggested that in fact Philip and his wife are buried in Tomb I. If this is the case, Tomb II may belong to his son, Philip Arrhidaeus, the half-brother of Alexander the Great, and his wife Eurydice, who were murdered in 316 BCE.

Tomb II is subterranean and temple-shaped. The facade is decorated with a painting of a hunting scene in a royal game park with exquisitely preserved colour. The tomb was separated into two rooms. In the main room, a marble chest enclosed a golden coffin (*larnax*), embossed with the Vergina Sun (or Macedonian star) symbol, which contained cremated bones and a finely wrought golden oak leaf wreath. Inside this room were a panoply (a ceremonial burial bed on which the body was laid before cremation), ivory head sculptures that once adorned the bed, and silver utensils that were used for the funeral feast. The tomb also contains gold suits of armour and weapons. In the antechamber there is another golden coffin, containing the body of a woman, probably a queen who, by tradition, sacrificed herself at the funeral.

Gold wall lamp shaped as Medusa's head, from the Royals Tombs at Vergina, Greece, mid-4th century BCE.

ALEXANDER THE GREAT

Aristotle, Alexander the Great's tutor, advised him to be 'a leader to the Greeks and a despot to the barbarians, to look after the former as after friends and relatives, and to deal with the latter as with beasts or plants'. Alexander's pride, thirst for military glory and determination to succeed were all palpable as he set out to conquer the Persian Empire, but it was his ability to discard his tutor's ruthless precepts that led to his ultimate triumph.

ALEXANDER SUCCEEDED HIS MURDERED father in 336 BCE, at the age of 20. Endorsed by Philip's Macedonian army, he set out at once to subdue rebellious tribesmen and secure the loyalty of the more recalcitrant Greek states. He annihilated troublesome Thebes and enslaved the population, then left for Asia in spring 334 BCE. He would never return to Macedon.

His march of conquest was spectacular. Three major battles – Granicus (334 BCE), Issus (333 BCE) and Gaugamela (331 BCE) – shattered the once-mighty Achaemenid Empire and left Alexander with a vast and subjugated domain. He conquered Egypt in 331 BCE and was proclaimed a son of the god Zeus-Ammon at the Oracle of Siwa. Alexander's armies fought using the formations and tactics developed by his father, Philip II, and pragmatic engineering solutions; he used siege towers for assaults on city walls and was a supremely successful besieger. When he was attacking the island city of Tyre, he built a causeway across the sea to carry attacking troops. He burned Darius' city of Persepolis to the ground. He was hardy and audacious, a cool strategist and an impulsive risk-taker. He was ruthless, and could be brutal, ordering the murder of entire city populations whose resistance was particularly stubborn. His hero was Achilles, and he worshipped the word of Homeric Greece.

Alexander redrew the map of the Greek world. He founded at least 16 new cities, possibly more, which were placed strategically on key trade routes. Many were named after him; one was named after his beloved horse Bucephalus, which carried him for more than 17 years. His new cities were essentially Greek, with Greek settlers and Greek language, but conquered peoples also lived there, and nomadic warriors were transformed into settled cultivators.

Having liberated the Greek cities of Asia Minor, he restored them to democratic self-rule. He was not interested in imposing his own ideas of religion or behaviour on conquered peoples and was happy to grant them 'autonomy', as long as they continued to feed and supply his troops. In reality, for most people this was simply a subtle change of master; Alexander took over the Persian apparatus of tribute payments, and his troops and governors maintained the peace. His conquests brought him unparalleled wealth and luxury. He hosted vast banquets, his 'Companions' (the elite cavalry of the Macedonian army) lounged on silver couches, and huge amounts of alcohol were consumed, sometimes resulting in bouts of intemperate violence.

His quest for the so-called 'Outer Ocean', which he believed encircled the world, took him to the foothills of the Himalayas in India. In the process he had amassed an army of some 120,000 men, mostly comprised of Indians, Iranians and assorted barbarians. But in the middle of an Indian monsoon, his troops mutinied and forced Alexander to turn back towards home. En route, he held a mass marriage service at Susa, in which he married members of his senior staff to Persian noblewomen. Many troops objected to this forced cultural merger, and were feeling increasingly resentful of his adoption of Persian dress and manners. When he reached Babylon in 323 BCE, he died, probably of malaria, although his squabbling Companions spread rumours, almost certainly false, of poisoning. At the time of his death, he was planning fresh campaigns and, suffering from increasing megalomania, he was demanding to be worshipped as a god. His empire immediately collapsed following his death, and his surviving senior officers fought bitterly over his legacy. Classical Greece expired with Alexander the

Great, ushering in the Hellenistic Age.

Alexander spread Hellenic civilization to an area that stretched beyond the Hindu Kush. Scientists and surveyors who travelled with his army laid down the foundations of knowledge relating to Eastern geography, flora, fauna and different cultures. He changed the shape of the known world and became an almost mythical figure, the pioneering conqueror who recognized no boundaries.

Detail of a mosaic from the House of the Faun, Pompeii, c.100 BCE, depicting Alexander the Great defeating the forces of Darius III at the Battle of Issus (333 BCE). The heroic figure of Alexander the Great is shown riding into battle on his horse Bucephalus, while the Persian king flees from his nemesis, his forces in disarray. This extraordinary mosaic captures the chaos and dynamism of the battle scene with naturalistic skill.

PART III
Transitions

Late 4th-century BCE Hellenistic Alexander sarcophagus from the necropolis at Sidon, Lebanon, showing Alexander the Great at the Battle of Issus (333 BCE), in which the Hellenic League, led by Alexander, was victorious against the army of the Achaemenid Empire, led by Darius III.

HELLENISTIC GREECE

On Alexander's death, his empire was divided and split between his warring generals, the 'diadochi'. Centralized kingdoms now supplanted city-states throughout the Greek world and personal power and authority became paramount. Cultural life was cosmopolitan, eclectic and exuberant, and philosophy, drama and architecture all flourished during this period.

IN THE IMMEDIATE AFTERMATH of Alexander's death, Macedon was ruled by two figureheads: Philip's mentally impaired son Philip III Arrhidaeus (*c.*358–317 BCE); and Alexander's own son, from his union with the Persian princess Roxana, Alexander IV (323–*c.*310 BCE). Antipater (*c.*397–319 BCE), one of Alexander's leading generals, became the regent and was the actual authority figure in Macedon and Greece, who asserted his control by fending off usurpers and stamping out an Athenian-led revolt.

Elsewhere, decades of conflict ensued as Alexander's generals vied for power. The most stable legacy was Egypt, and some neighbouring parts of the Middle East, where Ptolemy I Soter ('Saviour') (*c.*366–282 BCE) held sway, establishing a secure dynasty. Elsewhere, the situation was much more confused. Perdiccas (*c.*360–321 BCE), an ambitious general who exercised wide authority in Asia, raised the suspicions of his fellow regional governors, Ptolemy in Egypt, Antigonus (382–301 BCE) in Phrygia, Craterus (370–321 BCE) in Babylon and Antipater in Macedonia. This suspicion culminated in an out-and-out conflict between Perdiccas and Ptolemy, when mutinous officers murdered Perdiccas.

At this stage, Seleucus (*c.*358–281 BCE) was the governor in Babylon, and Lysimachus (*c.*360–281 BCE), one of Alexander's Macedonian bodyguards, now ruled in Thrace. When Antigonus, ruler of Phrygia, began to nurse overweening ambitions, a coalition of Cassander (son of Antipater), Ptolemy and Lysimachus took up arms against him from 320–311 BCE. Eventually, Seleucus joined the alliance against Antigonus, who was defeated at the Battle of Ipsus in 301 BCE.

Further disputes led to a confrontation between Lysimachus and Seleucus, in which Seleucus was the victor. Three main kingdoms had now emerged from the chaotic disintegration of Alexander's empire: Ptolemy ruled in Egypt, Seleucus ruled in Syria and the remnants of the Persian Empire, and Antigonus (succeeded by his son Demetrius) ruled in Macedonia, Thrace and northern Asia Minor. In addition, smaller kingdoms were established at various times, most notably Pergamon in Asia Minor, which was ruled by Attalus I Soter (269–197 BCE). Pergamon had grown wealthy on agriculture and silver, and became a major centre of art, literature and philosophy. Most of the Greek cities south of Thessaly remained independent. City-states formed into defensive leagues, such as the Aetolian League, Achaean League and Boeotian League.

In 280 BCE, the endless internal power struggles in the Hellenistic kingdoms were compounded by a new external threat: a Celtic invasion from the north. Warring Hellenistic rulers united against the Celtic interlopers, winning decisive victories, and the invaders eventually settled in Serbia, Thrace, Galatia and Central Anatolia.

Against this background of conflict and disruption, new cities emerged as centres of new kingdoms: Pergamon, Ephesus, Antioch, Damascus and Alexandria. These grand new foundations were adorned with public buildings and monuments on a heroic scale, which reflected the wealth, exuberant ambition and confidence of the Hellenistic rulers.

HELLENISTIC TIMELINE (BCE)

323	Alexander the Great dies.
322–320	FIRST DIADOCHI WAR.
321	Perdiccas is assassinated.
320–311	SECOND DIADOCHI WAR.
317	Philip III of Macedonia is assassinated.
301	Battle of Ipsus; Lysimachus and Seleucus I defeat Antigonus I

and Demetrius I of Macedon.

295–168	Antigonid dynasty rules Macedonia.
281	Formation of the Achaean League in Greece. Seleucus is assassinated.
280–275	Pyrrhic War; Pyrrhus, king of Epirus, assists the Greek people of Tarentum in Sicily against the Roman Republic.
280–277	Celtic invasions.
276–239	Antigonus II Gonatas becomes king of Macedonia.
267–262	Chremonidean War; a coalition of Greek city-states and Ptolemaic Egypt rises up against Antigonid Macedonian domination. Macedonia is victorious.
262	Victory of Eumenes I against the Seleucid Antiochus I. Beginning of the Pergamon Empire.
260	Rebellion of Diodotos against Antiochus I, creating the Graeco-Bactrian kingdom.
221	Philip V becomes king of Macedonia.
239–229	Demetrius II becomes king of Macedonia.
229–221	Antigonus III becomes king of Macedonia.
221–179	Philip V becomes king of Macedonia.
214–205	First Macedonian War. Rome allies with the Aetolian League and Attalus I of Pergamon against Macedonia, ending in a stalemate.
200–197	Second Macedonian War between Philip V of Macedon and Rome, allied with Pergamon and Rome. Philip is defeated.
192–188	Seleucid War between the Seleucid Empire and the Roman Republic ends in Roman victory.
c.190	Beginning of the Indo-Greek kingdoms.
179	Third Macedonian War ends in Roman victory.
149	Greece becomes a Roman province.
148	Macedonia becomes a Roman province.
133	Attalus III, last king of Pergamon, bequeaths the empire to Rome.

THE SELEUCIDS

The empire established by Seleucus I Nicator ('Victor'), which eventually stretched over a vast territory from the Mediterranean Sea to the Indus River, was multinational and multi-ethnic and had an efficient bureaucracy and highly lucrative trade-based economy. Ultimately, its multiculturalism would be its downfall as, under pressure from Rome, it began to fracture and unravel.

EARLY ON IN HIS RULE, Seleucus (*r.* 312–281 BCE) launched a war (305–303 BCE) against Chandragupta Maurya (*r.* 321–297 BCE), which gave the Punjab to Chandragupta in return for various trade agreements and 500 war elephants. These were to prove decisive when he fought in the Battle of Ipsus (301 BCE) against his former colleague Antigonus. By 300 BCE, he controlled Mesopotamia, Syria, Armenia and Cappadocia and had established a new city, Antioch, which would be the capital of the western part of his realm. His son Antiochus I Soter ruled the eastern part from the new city of Seleucia. When Seleucus intervened in a dispute against another of the diadochi, Lysimachus, he added Anatolia to his empire.

Silver tetradrachm of Seleucus I from Pergamon, 305–281 BCE. Elephants are a prominent motif on the coinage of Seleucus I, where they serve as symbols of kingship and victory.

In the mid-3rd century BCE, the Seleucids lost territory to Parthian nomads in northern Iran and the satrapy of Bactria claimed independence. However, the Seleucid king Antiochus III 'the great' reconquered these territories between 209–204 BCE, and it was in his reign that the empire reached its greatest extent. In 196 BCE, he crossed the Hellespont, adding Thrace to his empire just two years later. For the first time, the Seleucids came into conflict with the growing power of Rome. A defeat at the hands of the Romans at the Battle of Magnesia (189 BCE) by Jewish forces (the Maccabean Revolt, 167–160 BCE), who eventually drove the Seleucids out of Palestine, and by the Parthians, who captured Seleucia in 141 BCE, led to the gradual diminution of Seleucid power, and to Rome's eventual conquest of the Seleucid kingdom in 64 BCE.

The Seleucid Empire was a Hellenistic civilization, and Greek language and customs were pre-eminent. Following Alexander's precedent, a Greek-speaking aristocratic class, the so-called 'Friends of the King', dominated the cities. Greek was the language of commerce among the traders who moved between the oasis cities of central Asia and the urban centres of the Near East. Nevertheless, intermittent Seleucid attempts to force indigenous peoples to adopt Hellenic customs met with disaster: when a statue of Zeus was raised in the Jewish temple, for example, it led to the Maccabean Revolt. The Seleucid royal family claimed descent from the god Apollo; as a gesture towards local sensibilities, Apollo and his twin sister Artemis were equated with the Sun and Moon gods worshipped in the polytheistic empire.

The many cities founded by the Seleucids were the cornerstones of their empire, and the wealth generated by military conquest and tribute was immense. Huge mercenary armies, up to 80,000 strong, and war fleets helped to maintain power. In addition, military colonies were founded and garrisoned by Macedonian soldiers, who received land in exchange for military service. The Seleucids dominated overland trade between the Mediterranean and Asia through strategic control of mountain passes. The army was on hand to deal with sporadic raids from the nomadic horsemen of Central Asia: Antiochus I even built a wall nearly 160 km (100 miles) long to protect the city of Merv.

The main impact of the Seleucids on Iran, the heartland of their empire, was a coin-based economy, an ideology of kingship, and the military and economic structures of the Seleucid Empire. Their cultural impact was not destined to last.

The city of Apamea, founded in 301 BCE by the Seleucid Empire, was one of the most important cities in north Syria, and was a prominent military and commercial centre. The Great Colonnade, which extended for 2 km (1.25 miles), is the longest in the Roman world.

PTOLEMAIC EGYPT

*From Alexander to Cleopatra, the three centuries of Greek rule in
Egypt saw the Greeks emerge as pharaohs, rather than as conquerors.
The Ptolemaic dynasty was pragmatic; it did not seek to impose Greek
culture, but instead instituted an innovative, and largely successful,
experiment in multiculturalism.*

PTOLEMY I SOTER FOUNDED the Ptolemaic dynasty of Egypt
in 305 BCE. The Ptolemaic hegemony did not go undisputed and the
Syrian Wars, in which the Ptolemies and the Seleucid Empire battled
over territories in the Near East, dominated much of the 3rd century
BCE. Nevertheless, the dynasty survived and remained intact until the
Roman takeover in 30 BCE.

The Ptolemaic rulers remained completely Greek throughout the
three centuries of their rule, maintaining their cultural and ethnic roots
by intermarriages between siblings, or uncles and nieces. In this, they
followed existing Egyptian customs, and they emphasized their link to
the Egyptian triad of gods, the brother and sister Osiris and Isis, and
their offspring Horus.

Ptolemaic rule was based in the newly founded cosmopolitan city
of Alexandria on the north-western delta coast. Alexandria was very
much a city on Greek lines, with a street grid, palaces and temples. The
massive library and museum built at Alexandria in around 295 BCE were
intended to be the repository of all the knowledge in the known world,
and it became the cultural centre of the Mediterranean, housing as many
as 700,000 scrolls. The scholars known to have been in residence there
included luminaries such as the mathematicians Archimedes (*c.*287–212
BCE) and Euclid (325–265 BCE), the geographer Erastothenes (*c.*276–
194 BCE) and the astronomer Claudius Ptolemy (*c.*100–170 CE).

The Ptolemaic rulers created a synthesis between their own deities and the Egyptians' ancient gods. Temples were dedicated to the chief god Serapis, a Graeco-Egyptian god of the Sun, whose cult was celebrated in association with the Egyptian bull god, Apis. Egypt's long-established traditions and practices were resilient, and the Ptolemaic rulers actively supported Egyptian cults and the priesthood. Temple-building projects that were in train at the time of Alexander's conquest were taken to completion, and as time went on, the Ptolemies enlarged and embellished existing temples. Ptolemaic kings even established their own ruler cults in Egyptian temples. Outside the delta region, Memphis remained an important second city, and its High Priests of Ptah held an influential role. At Hermopolis, the Ptolemaic rulers built a Greek-style temple in honour of the royal cult of Thoth.

Fragment of a black basalt statue of Ptolemy I portrayed as a pharaoh of Egypt, c.305–283 BCE. The melding of Greek and Egyptian cultural traditions in the portraits of the Ptolemies helped to legitimize them as true rulers of Egypt and advance their ideology.

There was an influx of Greek settlers, especially in the delta region in the north. The Greeks were a privileged minority, who lived under Greek law, received a Greek education and were tried in Greek courts. New immigrants were granted estates in the fertile Faiyum basin, where they set about transforming the landscape through irrigation and intensive cultivation. Greek became a major language, which was used for government and commerce, but other languages were spoken and no official language was imposed.

The Ptolemies appropriated the monumental grandeur of Egyptian imagery, having themselves depicted as colossal pharaohs in ancient Egyptian style. Clearly, the Ptolemies adopted the pharaonic sculptural style as a political weapon, asserting messages of continuity and respect. Gradually, as their rule became more established, they began to produce images that synthesized a Greek appearance with Egyptian attributes and pose.

When the Romans finally declared Egypt a province in 30 BCE, following the death of Cleopatra VII, their overriding interest in their new colony was in its grain, on which the city of Rome was dependent. They did little to alter the administrative and cultural life of the region, which remained largely managed by Greeks. Like the Greeks, the Romans protected Egyptian religion and cults, while subtly introducing their own deities, perpetuating the Hellenistic policy of pragmatic multiculturalism.

PERGAMON

Pergamon in north-west Anatolia was the capital of the Attalid dynasty (281–133 BCE), which transformed it into one of the Hellenistic world's most outstanding cultural centres. The city occupies a 335 m (1,100 ft)-high rocky outcrop, which physically dominates the surrounding plain, a beacon of Hellenistic opulence and self-confidence.

AT THE TIME OF ALEXANDER'S DEATH, Pergamon was little more than a hilltop fortress, which came under the territory controlled by Lysimachus, one of the Macedonian generals. When Lysimachus became involved in conflicts with the Seleucid Empire, he was killed and Pergamon fell under Seleucid control, but under the semi-autonomous rule of Philetaerus, a trusted lieutenant.

By the time Philetaerus died, in 263 BCE, Pergamon had become a substantial city-state. His nephew, whom Philetaerus had adopted as his heir, became the ruler Eumenes I (*r.* 263–241 BCE), and the Attalid dynasty was born. Attalus I (*r.* 241–197 BCE) reinforced Pergamon's power in Asia Minor with his victory over the Galatians, a Celtic tribe who settled in central Anatolia in the 3rd century BCE. When Attalus I's son Eumenes II (*r.* 197–159 BCE) formed an alliance with the Romans, who had expelled the Seleucids from Anatolia, the Attalid dynasty secured its position, although it was distrusted by many Greeks who felt that the alliance with Rome had betrayed the Hellenistic cause.

Pergamon, located in the Aegean region of Asia Minor, stood at the crossroads of the ancient Hellenistic world, strategically poised between Europe and the Middle East. Its location high on Kale Hill meant that the Attalid city dominated the surrounding plains; it was seen as, literally and symbolically, the protector of the surrounding Aegean cities. Eumenes II and his brother Attalus II (*r.* 159–138 BCE) sought to make Pergamon a cultural hub, supporting the foundation of new towns in their domain, allowing Greek cities to retain nominal independence, and sending gifts to cultural centres such as Delos and Delphi.

They secured Pergamon's reputation as a regional cultural capital by establishing a library and centre of learning that was second only to Alexandria in the Hellenistic world. Pergamon also became famous as a centre for the production of parchment (the word is a corruption of *pergamenos*, meaning 'from Pergamon'). The acropolis was remodelled on Athenian lines and the Great Altar of Pergamon, a masterpiece of Hellenistic art, was commissioned. The Altar flanks a grand staircase and its famous frieze, 120 m (394 ft) long and 2.3 m (7.5 ft) high, is surmounted by a colonnaded gallery. The frieze depicts, in high relief, the victory of the Olympian gods over the Giants – a monumental assertion of Greek power and prestige.

When Attalus III died without an heir in 133 BCE, he bequeathed the city of Pergamon to Rome, and ultimately the bulk of its territory became part of the new Roman province of Asia. The city enjoyed a brief period of freedom, and was even the short-lived capital of the province, but this role was transferred to Ephesos. Pergamon nevertheless remained a

A view of the temple of Trajan at the Pergamon acropolis, near Bergama, modern Turkey. The acropolis of Pergamon was the capital of the Hellenic Attalid dynasty, founded in the 3rd century BCE. It was a major centre of learning in the ancient world, endowed with theatres, temples, a stoa and a library, surrounded by an extensive city wall.

famous city, so much so that an ambitious 'new city' was created at the base of the Acropolis, under the Emperor Trajan (*c.*113 CE). A shrine to the god Asklepios, which was transformed into a lavish spa, turned Pergamon into a celebrated health resort, and it continued to thrive until an earthquake and subsequent sacking by Goths led to its final collapse in the late 3rd century CE.

INDO-GREEK KINGDOMS

Hellenistic Greece's most remote outposts lay in central Asia and the north-western Indian subcontinent, where the legacy of Alexander the Great and his conquering army still permeated the Indo-Greek kingdoms that succeeded him. The Greek language and calendrical system remained for many centuries, and the sophisticated Indo-Greek coinage transformed Indian currencies.

ALEXANDER THE GREAT CONQUERED Bactria, located in modern-day Uzbekistan, Tajikistan and Afghanistan, between 329 and 327 BCE. Following Alexander's death, it became part of the Seleucid Empire, but in about 255 BCE Diodotus, the satrap of Bactria, rose up against Seleucid rule and declared independence. Diodotus went on to conquer Sogdiana, an area of Central Asia between the Oxus and Iaxartes rivers, and founded the first Indo-Greek kingdom.

In *c*.230 BCE, Euthydemus, a satrap of Sogdiana, overthrew the Graeco-Bactrian king Diodotus II and founded a dynasty. In about 190 BCE, the Graeco-Bactrian king Demetrius (*r. c*.190–167 BCE) took his armies into the Punjab and down the Indus valley. He was accompanied by Menander, a great Bactrian general, who extended the Graeco-Bactrian domain as far as Pataliputra (modern Patna), which he conquered briefly. Following a civil war, the Greeks' vast Asian realm divided into two kingdoms: the Graeco-Bactrian and the Indo-Greek.

Menander became king of the Indo-Greeks in 165 BCE and expanded his realm to the south, with the help of a huge army. He ruled from his capital at Sakala in the Punjab (present-day Sialkot). From 130 to 180 BCE, numerous Greek kings ruled dynastic polities in India, making frequent – and failed – attempts to unite the disparate kingdoms. Meanwhile, the incursions of the nomadic Iranian Scythians in Bactria led to the downfall of the last Graeco-Bactrian king in about 130 BCE. Ultimately, the Indo-Greek kingdoms also fell to the Scythians, finally

Gautama Buddha in Graeco-Buddhist style from Gandhara in north-western Pakistan and eastern Afghanistan, 1st–2nd century CE. Gandhara, one of the major centres of Buddhism in the Indian subcontinent from the 3rd century BCE onwards, was a cultural crossroads, and the art of the region fused Graeco-Roman, Iranian and Indian styles. Hellenistic influence is apparent in the idealistic realism of the Buddha statues, as well as naturalistic details, such as the folds of draped fabric.

succumbing to the Indo-Scythian king Rajuvula in *c.*10 BCE, although pockets of Greek populations probably persisted in the region for several centuries.

These kingdoms, thousands of miles from the Greek homeland, were lost to the Greek world, and developed autonomously, drawing in elements of Indian culture and exerting a strong influence on their neighbours. It is unknown whether the greatest Indo-Greek king Menander was Buddhist, but he was certainly a patron of Buddhism. He is famous for the *Milinda Pañha* (*Questions of Milinda*, or Menander), a Socratic dialogue between Menander and the Buddhist monk Nāgasena, which explores profound metaphysical questions.

Despite their distance from the homeland, the Indo-Greeks followed the Hellenistic model of governance, with Greek-style city-colonies and a standing army to ensure stability. At its height, the army could field 60,000 infantry, 1,000 horsemen and 700 war elephants. The kingdoms were divided into administrative zones, or provinces, led by *strategoi* (generals), who acted as governors with both military and civil responsibilities. Greek was the language of the educated elite and aristocrats. The kingdoms minted high-quality coins, which are now an indispensable guide to the complex succession of rulers and dynasties. They were used in inter-regional trade with Bactria, China and the southern Indians, which was vital for the Indo-Greek economy.

The Hellenistic artistic legacy is clearly seen in the enigmatic smiles, subtle draperies, and elegant postures that characterize the later masterpieces of Graeco-Buddhist art, the Buddhas of Gandhara. Before the Greeks arrived in India, Buddha was depicted symbolically. However, when the Indo-Greeks arrived, and many converted to Buddhism, it is thought they used the inspiration of statues of Greek gods such as Apollo and Hercules to depict Buddha as a human. The 'Gandharan' Buddhas, which are attributed to the direct successors of the Indo-Greeks, were highly influential in the early centuries CE, and Graeco-Buddhist art spread as far as China, Korea and Japan.

HELLENISTIC ART

Under the Hellenistic rulers, the artistic centre of Greece moved east, to cities such as Alexandria and Pergamon, and artists now found themselves commissioned by kings and private citizens who vied to outdo each other with their splendid royal courts, grandiose buildings and magnificent sculptures. The old ideals of religious reverence and civic pride that had characterized classical Greece had given way to unrestrained propaganda and uninhibited display.

ROYAL FAMILIES LIVED in grand palaces with elaborate banquet halls and gardens. They displayed their wealth and luxury at court festivals and symposia, and were prominent patrons of the arts, commissioning everything from grandiose public monuments to ornate jewellery, which proclaimed their wealth and taste. Hellenistic art was vibrant, flamboyant, opulent and naturalistic. It was also innovative and expansive, exploring new cultural horizons. Museums and libraries, such as those founded at Alexandria and Pergamon, consolidated a strong sense of history and cultural pride.

Much of Hellenistic sculpture was designed to be viewed in the round. Draped figures, which demonstrated the sculptors' virtuosity, were increasingly common. Fabrics were depicted as taut and clinging or voluminous and weighty. There was a new interest in the female nude: popular sculptures of a nude Aphrodite reflected the increasing secularization of traditional religion and an open fascination with eroticism. A new spirit of internationalism and curiosity allowed artists to break free from traditional expectations and explore unorthodox subjects, such as children and elderly people, nymphs, satyrs and grotesques. They also began to reflect a wider range of emotions, such as agony, kindness, cruelty or wisdom, ushering in an era of realism when sculptors were no longer obliged to depict ideals of physical beauty.

Relief sculptures, such as the Alexander sarcophagus and the friezes on the Pergamon altar, depict actual historic events in realistic detail. Writhing intertwined figures and animals, coiling snakes and floating drapery create a dynamic, struggling, turbulent maelstrom, which seems to be barely held in check by the background stone.

Wall paintings and mosaics made prominent use of naturalistic landscapes, which frequently introduced mythological or sacro-idyllic elements. The wall paintings that have recently been uncovered in the Macedonian royal tombs at Vergina provide an unprecedented opportunity to study Greek painting, revealing that Greek artists had a clear understanding of perspective, used light and shade to render form, and frequently experimented with *trompe l'oeil* realism.

Laocoön and His Sons, *a marble copy of a Hellenistic original from c.200 BCE. Laocoön is a Trojan priest, and the group is shown being attacked by sea serpents. The contorted faces of all three figures are vividly expressive of agony and despair, and the sculpture is seen as the finest example of Hellenistic 'baroque' style.*

In Hellenistic buildings, the rules of the two architectural orders – Doric and Ionic – were relaxed, and the two orders were also brought together in the same building. The flamboyant Corinthian order became increasingly popular and its florid, naturalistic-style capitals can be found all over the Hellenistic world. Increasingly, columns were used in a non-structural role within buildings, serving a simply decorative function. The new foundations established in Hellenistic Greece were notable for their unified and harmonious design. Many were laid out on a rectangular grid and the architects were keen to relate buildings to each other in a pleasing manner, frequently using the stoa (colonnade) as a framing device. Architects were also adept at utilizing the terrain creatively; at Pergamon, the city seems to grow organically out of the landscape on a series of fan-like terraces.

SEVEN WONDERS
OF THE WORLD

As the horizons of the Hellenistic world expanded, the travellers of classical antiquity began to explore these new lands and were captivated by various landmarks and monuments. The 'wonders' are what the ancient Greeks called theamata *(things to be seen), and were brought together in a list, which served as a kind of travel guidebook, by Diodorus Siculus (91–c.30 BCE), whose epic universal history* (Bibliotheca historica) *was compiled between 60 and 30 BCE. Of the seven monuments listed, only the pyramids of Giza still survive.*

PYRAMIDS AT GIZA

Described by the Greek epigrammist Antipater of Sidon as 'the great man-made mountains of the lofty pyramids', the monumental pyramid complex at Giza rises up to 147 m (482 ft) above the sandy desert plains near modern Cairo. Constructed between *c.*2550 and 2490 BCE, it was a burial place for pharaohs that was built to endure for an eternity. The pyramids are massive tombs, fully equipped with everything the pharaohs would need for their afterlife. The first pyramid to be built, the Great Pyramid of Khufu, is constructed of an estimated 2.3 million stone blocks, a back-breaking labour for the workers who lived nearby in a temporary builders' city. The second pyramid, started some 30 years later, was for his son, Khafre. The third and smallest pyramid, built by Pharaoh Menkaure, *c.*2490 BCE, features a complex mortuary temple. By making elaborate provision for an afterlife, the ancient Egyptians preserved an encyclopaedic record of their civilization on decorated tombs, where wall paintings depict everyday life, and inscriptions and texts provide written records.

A heliogravure of the Pyramids of Giza, 1893, reproduced from an original print. Heliogravures are the oldest procedure for reproducing photographic images.

HANGING GARDENS OF BABYLON

As described by Diodorus Siculus, the Hanging Gardens of Babylon were built by Nebuchadnezzar between 605 and 562 BCE as a gift to his wife, Amytis, who missed the mountains and greenery of her Iranian homeland. The site of the Gardens has never been conclusively established and is much disputed by archaeologists. It is theorized that they were, in fact, a collection of roof gardens, which were laid out on a series of ascending ziggurat terraces. They would have been irrigated by pumps from the Euphrates River, and irrigation water would have been prevented from seeping through the terraces by an ingenious lining of reeds, bitumen and lead.

STATUE OF ZEUS AT OLYMPIA

Constructed by the celebrated sculptor Phidias, who also worked on the Parthenon, the statue of Zeus depicted the god seated on his cedarwood throne, which was decorated with gold, precious stones, ebony and ivory.

With a skin of ivory and robes of hammered gold, the 12 m (39.4 ft)-tall statue was said to strike worshippers with awe and wonder as they entered the temple of Zeus at Olympia. On his outstretched right hand was a statue of Nike (Victory), while his left hand held a sceptre, on which an eagle was perched. It is thought that this magnificent statue dated to about 430 BCE. The statue was lost in the 5th century CE. It may have been destroyed by a fire that severely damaged the temple in 425 CE. Alternatively, it may have been carried off to Constantinople, after the Roman emperor Theodosius I banned pagan cults, where it could have been destroyed in the great fire of the Palace of Lausus in 475 CE.

An illustration of the statue of Zeus in gold and ivory in Olympia's main temple, as visualized by the French archaeologist and architectural historian Antoine-Chyrsostome Quatremère de Quincy (1755–1849).

THE TEMPLE OF ARTEMIS AT EPHESOS

This magnificent temple at the Greek colony of Ephesos in Asia Minor was completed in 550 BCE. The building replaced an earlier temple, which had been destroyed by a flood, and was sponsored by King Croesus of Lydia, whose wealth was legendary. The grandiose reconstruction was an imposing marble building 115 m (377 ft) long, supported by 127 columns, some of which were decorated with relief carvings. But this elegant structure fell prey to an arsonist named Herostratus, who set fire to the temple in 356 BCE, in order to achieve lasting fame. According to tradition, Alexander the Great was born on the fateful night on which the temple burned to the ground. He offered to rebuild the temple, but the Ephesians preferred to fund their more modest reconstruction, which was eventually destroyed by invading Goths in 268 BCE. Rebuilt again for a third and final time, it was closed in the early 5th century CE by Christians and fell into disrepair.

THE MAUSOLEUM AT HALICARNASSOS

Mausolus was a Persian satrap, or regional governor, who chose Halicarnassos (present-day Bodrum in Turkey) as his new capital city. When he died in 353 BCE, his wife Artemisia created a final resting place that would be worthy of the great king, and she was also interred there two years later. The tomb was 41 m (134.5 ft) tall and ornately decorated with fine sculptural reliefs. It was erected on a hill overlooking the city and stood on a stone platform in the centre of an enclosed courtyard. A stairway flanked by sculptures of lions led to the top of the platform, where the tomb was guarded on each of its four corners by stone warriors mounted on horseback. The upper section of the tomb comprised 36 slim columns, which supported the tomb's massive pyramidal roof. The roof was surmounted by a quadriga – four magnificent horses pulling a chariot in which rode Mausolus and Artemisia. It is unclear precisely when the tomb was destroyed; it was probably reduced to ruins by an earthquake some time between the 12th and 14th centuries CE. It is from the name of Mausolus that the English word 'mausoleum' is derived.

LIGHTHOUSE OF ALEXANDRIA

One of the tallest man-made structures in the ancient world, the lighthouse was commissioned by Ptolemy I Soter. Completed in *c.*280 BCE, it was built on the island of Pharos in the western Nile delta and stood more than 110 m (360 ft) high. The island of Pharos and the city of Alexandria were connected by a mole more than 1.2 km (0.75 miles) long, called the 'Hepstadion'. The lighthouse could be seen 50 km (31 miles) away; its light source was a mirror that reflected the sun's rays during the day and a furnace that burned at night. The elegant lighthouse was built in three sections, probably of pink granite, each of which tapered inwards. The lowest base was square, the middle section was octagonal and the top was cylindrical. The latter part, where the fire burned at night, was reached by a broad spiral ramp. In 1994, marine archaeologists found a large amount of statuary in the waters off Pharos Island, including two monumental statues of Ptolemy and his wife, Arsinoe, which were probably placed below the lighthouse, facing the harbour entrance. The lighthouse was repeatedly damaged by earthquakes between 946 and 1323 CE, and by the year 1480 it had fallen into ruins.

COLOSSUS OF RHODES

This monumental statue of the god Helios, the patron god of the island of Rhodes, was constructed between 292 and 280 BCE. It stood on a white marble pedestal, was more than 33 m (108 ft) high and dominated the island's main port, in much the same way as the Statue of Liberty in New York. The statue was raised as the result of a famous victory, when the Rhodians defeated the invading army of Demetrius I of Macedon in 305 BCE. Demetrius abandoned most of his siege equipment, which the Rhodians were able to sell, providing funding for the statue, and they reforged his abandoned bronze and iron weapons for use in the construction. It is believed that the following words were used in the dedication text: 'To you, O Sun, the people of Dorian Rhodes set up this bronze statue reaching to Olympus, when they had pacified the waves of war and crowned their city with the spoils taken from the enemy. Not only over the seas but also on land did they kindle the lovely torch of freedom and independence.' But the colossal statue only stood for

56 years before it was hit by an earthquake in 226 BCE and fell to the ground. Even the broken remains were impressive enough to make the fallen statue a tourist attraction, which it remained until the 7th century CE, when the statue was melted down and sold to a Jewish merchant from Edessa, who transported the bronze away on 900 camels.

The Colossus of Rhodes, *as visualized in the 16th century by Martin van Heemskerck (1498–1574), part of his series on the Seven Wonders of the World.*

PART IV
Republic

A bronze sculpture depicting the legendary she-wolf who suckled the mythical founders of Rome, Romulus and Remus, after they were cast into the River Tiber by their usurping great-uncle. The statue was long thought to be Etruscan, but scientific analysis reveals that the wolf figure was created in the 11th–12th centuries CE, while the figures of the twins were added in the late 15th century CE.

THE ETRUSCANS

The brilliant Etruscan civilization of central Italy set the stage for the rise of Rome, and the Etruscan influence on Rome was profound. They founded hilltop cities, established wide-ranging trade networks, and were master craftsmen and artists, yet they remain enigmatic, since their writing has not been fully deciphered. Much of what we know about Etruscan life is derived from their tombs, or 'cities of the dead'.

ETRUSCAN CIVILIZATION AROSE in Etruria in central Italy, between the Arno and Tiber rivers, eventually reaching the Po valley in the north and Campania in the south in the 8th century BCE. It thrived until the 3rd century BCE when the Romans absorbed Etruscan culture, in particular clothing, religious practices and architecture.

Etruscan origins are much disputed, and while it has long been believed that they are an indigenous Italian people, recent DNA analysis and studies of the Etruscan language indicate that the Etruscans may, in fact, have come from the Near East in the Bronze Age, possibly the Lydian coast of Anatolia. For a long time, it has been thought that Etruscan civilization evolved from the Villanovan culture of central Italy in the 12th century BCE, which was an Iron Age village-based society that thrived on the region's rich natural resources, farming and trade. Eventually these early villages would develop into major Etruscan cities: Cerveteri, Chiusi, Tarquinia, Veii and Vulci. These prosperous settlements exploited fertile lands and utilized rich mineral resources, in particular iron, to manufacture metal tools. The Etruscans were part of a Mediterranean commercial network, trading with Greeks, Phoenicians and Carthaginians and exporting iron, pottery, wine, olive oil and grain.

Inevitably, trade led to cultural contact, and the Greeks and Phoenicians who settled in emporia on the Italian coast 'Orientalized' Etruscan culture, introducing their religions, clothing, food and alphabet. The Etruscans were skilled mariners who dominated the seas and maritime trade along the Italian coast. This led to conflict and, in 474 BCE, the tyrant of Syracuse in Sicily inflicted a naval defeat on the Etruscans. The Syracusans continued to target their Etruscan rivals, attacking and destroying many of their ports in the early 4th century BCE.

Initially, the Etruscan cities were ruled by monarchies, which later developed into ruling oligarchies. The cities were autonomous and self-governing, and the 'Etruscan League', which comprised 12 of the most major cities, met annually. Relations were not always harmonious, and there is evidence that there was frequent conflict between the cities. Women enjoyed an unusual amount of freedom in that they were able to inherit their own property and participate fully in social life; but, as in every ancient culture, they did not take part in public life.

The Etruscans were polytheists with a pantheon of gods, headed by a deity named Tin, or Tinia, the sky god. There were gods of the sun, moon, love, war and so on, and various Greek gods were also co-opted into the Etruscan pantheon, for example Artemis and Dionysus. Augury – the reading of omens from natural phenomena, such as bird flights and lightning strikes – was central to the religion. The Etruscans were also practitioners of haruspicy (examining the entrails of sacrificed animals to divine the future). Religious rituals, such as sacrifices and libations, took place outside temples, where votive offerings, such as food, pottery vessels and bronze statuettes, were left to propitiate the gods.

Etruscan temples, originally modest wooden structures, had become monumental structures by the 7th century BCE, utilizing non-fluted Tuscan columns. The Etruscans' greatest architectural legacy is their tombs, where several generations of the same family were buried, indicating the emergence of a hereditary aristocratic elite. Tombs could be small square buildings or large circular buildings with corbelled or domed ceilings, as much as 40 m (131 ft) in diameter. Tombs contained niches for funerary urns and life-size sarcophagi, whose lids were surmounted by extraordinary terracotta sculptural portraits of the deceased, who were portrayed in a supine position. Tombs contained grave goods for the afterlife, which testify to the great wealth of the period: gold pectorals, bracelets and brooches, silver and bronze vessels, and furniture such as beds. The magnificent paintings that decorated the walls of the tombs, dating to the mid-6th century BCE, are a vibrant and naturalistic reflection of daily life, conjuring up vivid scenes of music-making, dancing, hunting, processions and dining.

The Etruscans are also well known for their distinctive 'Bucchero' pottery, which has a dark, glossy finish; Bucchero bowls, jugs, cups and utensils were exported throughout Europe. Etruscan bronze-working is highly skilled, and finely engraved bronze mirrors were thought to be part of the Etruscan bride's dowry. Bronze figurines were a common form of votive offering, and large-scale metal sculptures, such as the Minerva of Arezzo and the Mars of Todi, are outstanding works of art.

Detail of two dancers from the Etruscan Tomb of the Triclinium, from the necropolis of Monterozzi, c. 470 BCE. The Monterozzi necropolis contains some 6,000 graves and about 200 of them are decorated with frescoes. The Tomb of the Triclinium (meaning 'dining room') is named after the formal banqueting scene it depicts. It comprises a single room, showing a banquet on the back wall, and lively scenes of dancing and music-making on the two facing side walls.

ROME:
FROM VILLAGE TO CITY

The succession of three Etruscan kings who ruled the independent city of Rome from the 8th century BCE brought well-established ideas of government, culture and religion to Rome, profoundly influencing its future development. They also attacked traditional privileges and extended the franchise to wider groups, paving the way for the Republic.

ROME IS LOCATED on the River Tiber, 24 km (15 miles) from the sea. The site was a bridge between two worlds: to the north lay the Etruscan civilization of Etruria; to the south were the thriving Greek colonies of Campania and Sicily. Rome is made up of seven compact hills, with marshy land lying between them. In about 1000 BCE, a cluster of shepherds' huts appeared on the Palatine Hill, the nucleus of an Iron Age settlement that gradually spread to the other hills, which were cleared of woodland, then terraced and cultivated. The Palatine, site of the first settlement, eventually became its acropolis, crowned by a temple of Jupiter. The marshland was drained and became the Roman Forum.

The first legendary king of Rome was Romulus. He and his twin brother, Remus, were believed to be the sons of the god of war, Mars, who were abandoned in the wilderness of Latium and rescued by a she-wolf, and later raised by shepherds. Romulus killed Remus in an argument over who should rule their new city-state, and became king of Rome. It is said that after Romulus there were six more kings of Rome, but it is certain that, from 753–510 BCE, Rome's last three kings were Etruscans: the immigrant Tarquinius Priscus (*r.* 616–578 BCE); Servius Tullius (*r.* 578–535 BCE), who was the son of a slave; and Tarquinius Superbus (*r.* 535–509 BCE), who was a warlike king who used violence and intimidation to exert his control. All three Etruscan monarchs based their position on popular support and challenged the power of the aristocrats. In particular, Servius Tullius was a reformer who introduced a new constitution and founded the Comitia Centuriata, a new citizen assembly.

At this time, Rome was divided into three main tribes: the Ramnes, Tities and Luceres. The patricians were the descendants of the 100 original citizens whom Romulus chose to advise him: the Senate. The patricians were representatives of the most important social group, the gentes, or clans. These were Roman families who could trace their history back for generations to one common ancestor. Each of these aristocrats had a retinue of relatives, retainers and dependants, known as 'clients', who would play a major role in the politics of Republican Rome. At this point, absolute authority was invested in the king, who could expect unquestioning obedience from his subjects and had the power to make all official appointments, act as a presiding magistrate and raise a conscript army. This power, referred to as imperium, was symbolized by an Etruscan device, the fasces – a bundle of elm and birch rods and an axe, 1.5 m (4.9 ft) in length, tied together with red leather thongs.

Under the kings, the Senate and the Curiate assembly of ordinary citizens had little power, acting merely as a rubber stamp for legislation that was handed down by the king. The monarchy was not hereditary and the Senate, which at this time had 300 members representing the three main tribes of Rome, was responsible for nominating and appointing the new king during the interregnum, the period following a king's death. As the king would also serve as the High Priest of Rome, an augur was consulted, whose job was to interpret the divine will of the gods in relation to the king's appointment.

The Etruscan kings greatly extended Rome's control of the region and were responsible for many grandiose public works. Tarquinius Priscus drained the Roman Forum and constructed the Cloaca Maxima (the main sewer) and the Circus Maximus. Servius built the Temple of Diana, the Forum Boarium and constructed a new city wall. Tarquinius Superbus built the Temple of Jupiter Optimus Maximus. By c.500 BCE, there were probably as many as 35,000 male Roman citizens, and Roman rule extended southwards along the coast to Terracina, about 65 km (40 miles) from Rome.

The Romans now sought freedom from the despotic rule of the king. In 509 BCE, four aristocrats initiated a revolt that would lead to the deposition of the much-hated Tarquinius Superbus, whose son had raped Lucretia, the wife and daughter of powerful Roman nobles. The era of the Roman Republic was about to begin.

The Forum Romanum was the centre of everyday life in Rome for many centuries. Rome's oldest and most important structures were located there, including the royal residence, the Regia (the residence of Rome's earliest kings) and the Temple of Vesta. The Senate House, government offices, statues, temples and memorials were gradually added after the establishment of the Republic.

BIRTH OF THE REPUBLIC

When the Roman patricians mounted a revolt against the king in 509 BCE, they ushered in the Republic, a new kind of government. Initially the preserve of a small aristocratic elite, the demands of the ordinary people (the plebeians), who fought for their rights and their political voice, transformed the Republic into a more representative government, which aimed to serve the public good.

FOLLOWING THE NOBLES' *coup d'état*, the power of imperium was now exercised by two 'consuls', who were elected annually by a public vote; the idea being that one man could exercise restraint on the other. The consuls were patricians drawn from the aristocracy, and – in the fashion of the Roman clans – were accompanied at all times by 12 attendants who acted as bodyguards and heralds, carrying the consuls' rods and axe of office (*fasces*). In times of peril, the Romans could appoint a dictator, one man who could use executive action to restore order to the affairs of state, before control was handed back to the consuls. As government grew more complex throughout the 5th century BCE, a series of subordinate magistrates were appointed, whose job was to take charge of some of the consuls' duties. Together with the consuls, they formed the ruling hierarchy. The Senate represented the political elite, not the Roman citizens; it comprised patricians and former office-holders and did not have the power to make laws, simply to debate legislation and act as an advisory body for the elected office-holders.

The Republic was a system that effectively melded together several different traditions of government. It incorporated elements of democracy (elections and the passing of bills in public assemblies), oligarchy (the Senate) and monarchy (the consuls). This structure was dynamic, flexible and effective, but it begged a very important question: was public office-holding to be restricted to the patrician class? Or would the ordinary people (the plebeians) be allowed to participate? Unsurprisingly, the wealthiest plebeians were keen to wield power within Rome, and they began to agitate for reform. But prospective candidates for elections or magistracies needed a great deal of money, and only a tiny percentage of Rome's citizenry could possibly access the inner corridors of power. In addition, wealthy plebeians who managed to achieve powerful positions tended to close ranks with the aristocrats to form a new, exclusive 'aristocracy'.

The ordinary plebeians – craftsmen, peasants, shopkeepers, traders – had to fight hard for their own rights. In 494 BCE, the situation came to a head. Weighed down by debt and arbitrary repression, the plebeians set up an alternative 'state within a state' on the Aventine Hill. They created their own magistracies, called 'tribunes of the people', and only ended their protest when the patricians – a tiny minority of the Roman population who survived through the support and protection of their clients – recognized this office in a series of laws enacted in 471 and 449 BCE.

Sacrifice during a census, depicted on the left part of a plaque from the Altar of Domitius Ahenobarbus, known as the 'Census frieze', marble, late 2nd century BCE. The relief may have been created during the construction of the Temple of Neptune on the Field of Mars. Domitius Ahenobarbus attained his consulship in 122 BCE.

This was a radical departure. The plebeians could now elect ten tribunes a year, and each tribune was responsible for protecting his own constituency from abuses of power, such as wrongful arrest or unjust punishment. They held wide-ranging powers, and were permitted to impose fines, order imprisonment or even sentence offenders to death. It was their responsibility to summon the *Concilium Plebis* (Plebeian Assembly), attended only by plebeians, where laws were passed. They were also able to intercede in the general business of the state, using their veto (*intercessio*) to bring government to a standstill. The ultimate weapon of the plebeians was secession; if all else failed, they could simply down tools and withdraw once again to the Aventine Hill. This happened five times between 494 and 287 BCE, and the Aventine became a hub of plebeian activity.

The ways in which the aristocratic elite and the popular assemblies worked together to rule Rome were highly unusual and, initially, very successful. This formula was recognized in the initials SPQR (*Senatus Populusque Romanus* – the Senate and the Roman people), which were emblazoned on the military standards that Roman legions brandished as they marched out from Rome to conquer new lands.

THE SENATE AND
ROMAN LAW

The great dynamism of the Roman Republic is reflected in its range of representative bodies and assemblies, and its growing body of law. In all these areas there was a tension between tradition and innovation, patrician and plebeian, citizen and foreigner. Challenges to the status quo led to a huge array of senatorial decrees, magisterial decisions and assembly votes, which created a flexible society that was able to adapt to changing circumstances, the more representative government, aimed to serve the public good.

THE VOICE OF THE PEOPLE of Rome was represented in a number of assemblies: the Roman Senate was a consultative body which proposed laws but did not enact them. However, it controlled the states' finances, civil administration and foreign policy. The power to enact laws lay in the hands of two popular assemblies: the Comitia Centuriata, which also elected consuls and declared war, and the Concilium Plebis, which represented the plebeians through their elected tribunes. The Assemblies were divided into blocks, and voted in blocks. As well as these two major legislative assemblies, there were also a number of smaller tribal assemblies.

Members of the Senate were originally appointed by the consuls; former serving magistrates were usually automatically appointed to the Senate. From 318 BCE, the censor, one of the magistrates appointed to the Senate, was given the power to appoint senators, and also remove them if they had transgressed in any way. Since senators were not paid and were banned from engaging in banking, public contracts or commerce, it was inevitable that they were independently wealthy.

The Senate had ancient origins and its procedures were based on long tradition and precedent. The Senate always met at the beginning of the year, usually at the Temple of Jupiter Capitolinus, although other venues were used, and some Senate meetings took place outside the city boundaries. Whatever the location, the Senate was only allowed to meet in a building of religious significance. Before any meeting began, a sacrifice to the gods was made, and a search for divine omens (auspices) was conducted.

It was in the Senate that the art of Roman oratory was forged and refined. Meetings usually began at dawn. Once the senators had been summoned, the doors were left open, allowing members of the public to observe proceedings, but only senators could speak. Proceedings were conducted by a consul or presiding magistrate. After an opening statement by the presiding official, every senator was expected to speak, in order of seniority, starting with the *princeps senatus* (leader of the Senate). It was only after everyone had spoken that a vote could be held, and since all Senate meetings were expected to end by nightfall, there was ample opportunity for filibustering – prolonging a speech in order to prevent a vote. Heckling, booing and applause could also hold up the debate, and the Senate was frequently a rowdy place. A quorum was required for a vote to be held; in 67 BCE, a quorum was held to be 200 senators. Any motion could be vetoed by the plebeian tribune, the magistrate who represented the people, but this usually required him to be present at the debate.

The Republic was also the period when the foundations of Roman law were laid down. In 451 BCE, ten legislators (*decemvirs*) were appointed, and the resulting 'Twelve Tables' codified Roman law as it related to family, marriage, divorce, property ownership, inheritance, debt and slavery. This body of law applied only to Roman citizens. In practice, this meant that the laws applied only to the male head of the family (paterfamilias) as they held great power over everyone under their care, including relations, servants and slaves. An initial prohibition on marriage between patricians and plebeians led to a storm of public protest, and was repealed in 445 BCE. For the most part, however, the Tables gave equal rights to free citizens, although it was the plaintiff's responsibility to get his opponent to court and to execute judgement. In these circumstances, it was likely that for most ordinary people the law offered little protection, and they remained dependent on the protection of the rich and powerful.

Times were changing and new areas of law were required that were not covered by the Twelve Tables. Rome's increasingly complex commercial activities, which were bringing Roman citizens into contact with foreigners, needed legal protection and from *c.*242 BCE a special magistrate (*praetor peregrinus*) was appointed, whose specific concerns were legal disputes involving foreigners and relations with foreign states. On the domestic front, the emphasis was on the ad hoc adaptation of existing laws by magistrates, rather than a wholesale repeal of the legal system.

LIFE IN REPUBLICAN ROME

Republican Rome was the capital city of a growing power, but for all its grandiose buildings and monumental public works, its narrow streets were cramped and seething with life, and large numbers of the plebeians lived in slum conditions, far removed from the elegant streets, piped water and clean air of the Palatine Hill.

SPACE WAS AT A PREMIUM in walled cities like Rome, and the solution was to create six- or seven-storied apartment buildings or *insulae*. As early as 150 BCE, it is recorded that there were more than 46,000 *insulae* in the city of Rome. These were basically ramshackle tenements, built of timber and mud-brick, which were overcrowded and dangerous. Residents lived in perpetual fear of fire or collapse, and these risks were compounded by extremely narrow streets, which could be as little as 2 m (6.6 ft) wide.

The lower floors of the *insulae* were the most luxurious, and apartments there boasted several rooms, natural light and even glazed windows. They had access to running water and even, in some cases, indoor toilets – Rome had a sewerage system that dated to the 6th century BCE when the Cloaca Maxima was constructed. The upper floors were cramped and hot, with families living together in single rooms. People had no access to running water or to a latrine, relying on public troughs and fountains, and human waste was regularly dumped into the streets, which stank and were a breeding ground for disease. Since they also had no kitchens, they spilled out on to the crowded streets, where bars and cheap eating-houses flourished. Carts, horses, wagons, litters and manure added to the noise and confusion.

The wealthy residents were comfortably distant from the stinking, congested city streets. They lived in single-family houses (*domus*) on the Palatine Hill. While the ground floor might contain a shop or business premises at the street front, the home was built around the open atrium that lay behind, where rainwater was collected in a rectangular pool to be used elsewhere in the house. The atrium was surrounded by an array of rooms: bedrooms, offices, a kitchen and *triclinium* (dining room). At the rear of the house was a garden, surrounded by a columned passage, the *peristylium*. Very wealthy people frequently abandoned the city altogether, taking refuge in elegant villas in the countryside, where they enjoyed central heating provided by the underfloor hypocaust system, and running water. Frequently, villas were self-sufficient, with a farm that supplied produce and supported a large number of farm labourers and slaves.

Romans in the early Republican era admired rugged austerity and did not indulge in luxuries; this was to change gradually. Ordinary Romans ate very simple food, comprising bread, salad, olives, cheeses, fruits and nuts. Wine was neither mass-produced nor widely available until around 250 BCE, when it became a cheap, staple drink, although Romans always drank it mixed with water. It has been estimated that on average each Roman citizen drank a bottle of wine a day, though manual labourers and soldiers would certainly have drunk much more than ladies of leisure.

*The Via Diana in Ostia, the port of Rome, which is lined with brick-built tenements (*insulae*). Ostia, founded in the 3rd century BCE, was a city of high-rise apartments, generally up to four storeys high.*

Most Romans worked a six-hour day, starting at dawn and ending at noon. Some shops reopened in the evening. The afternoon was given over to leisure: gladiatorial competitions, chariot races, theatre performances and baths. Young men probably participated in various sports, including wrestling, boxing and racing. Chariot racing was a popular spectacle, and supporters often gambled on the results. Bars and brothels provided entertainment in the evenings.

Bathing was all-important to the Romans, who usually visited the baths once or twice a week. The bath complex contained a gym, health centre and swimming pool as well as three bathrooms; *tepidarium* (relaxation room), *caldarium* (hot room) and *frigidarium* (cooling room). Most baths, which were funded by wealthy patrons, were extremely cheap, and occasionally free to users.

These lifestyles were eventually replicated all over the Roman Empire, in towns and cities founded by the Romans, but in the countryside large numbers of Roman subjects continued to lead timeless existences, quite divorced from the amenities and deficiencies of Roman towns. They cultivated the land and lived in small villages, as their ancestors had done before them.

ROMAN DRESS

The clothes of Republican Rome were highly influenced by both Greeks and Etruscans. Initially, they were plain and practical, reflecting admired Roman virtues. However, as international trade brought wealth and luxury to Rome, clothing became more sumptuous and elaborate, and eventually laws were enacted to ensure that every Roman citizen wore the clothing appropriate to his or her age, role and social standing.

MOST ROMAN CLOTHES were made of wool, linen or flax. Cotton from India and silk from China were extremely expensive and became a much-sought-after mark of wealth. Certain colours, fabrics and styles were exclusive to Roman citizens and important people. The Romans made ceremonial use of the expensive Tyrian purple dye, which came from small glands in the mollusc *Purpura* (hence the word 'purple'), and was exported from Tyre and Sidon in the Levant. Most workaday clothes used dyes made from cheap and plentiful sources, such as indigo, lichen, madder and woad.

The basic universally worn item of Roman clothing was the linen tunic, which was secured at the waist with a belt. Men and boys wore their tunics short-sleeved or sleeveless and knee-length, while women and girls wore a longer tunic, usually sleeved. On more formal occasions, men wore a woollen toga draped over their tunic. In cold weather, both sexes wore a soft under-tunic under a thicker over-tunic. Men and women both wore loincloths under their tunics, and women wore a band across their breasts, a *strophium*.

The toga may have evolved from a practical woollen blanket that was worn by the Romans' hardy and rugged ancestors, who were peasants and herdsmen. It became the recognized symbol of a freeborn male citizen of Rome. By the time of the Republic, it had evolved into a semi-elliptical

In Rome, there was a marked difference between the clothing of the common people and that of the upper classes, both in terms of the style and in the materials used. Women usually wore clothes in different colours. The most common dress was a long tunic, or stola, worn over another tunic, known as the tunica interior. Most men's clothing was white, comprising a tunic (the only item of clothing for the lower classes and slaves) and a toga, which was reserved for free Roman citizens.

woollen cloth, which was up to 5.5 m (18 ft) long, and was draped over the body and the left shoulder and arm, leaving the right arm free. The voluminous material fell into heavy pleats and pouches, and could also be drawn up over the head to create a kind of hood. Commoners' togas were off-white, undyed wool. Senators' togas were more voluminous and a more pristine white. Magistrates and priests wore togas that were edged with purple bands. The mourning toga was made of dark dyed wool and the rarely worn *toga picta* and *tunica palmate* were purple, embroidered with gold, and awarded to Roman generals on the day of their triumph, as well as consuls and emperors. Only emperors were allowed to 'take the purple', referring to the *trabea* toga, which was entirely purple.

The wealthier the wearer, the more voluminous the toga – heavy drapes of folded wool were highly impractical and not suitable for manual work. They befitted men who were engaged in oratory, or seated in formal processions or the Senate, or on display at events like the theatre or gladiatorial combats. For practical reasons, most citizens avoided wearing the toga on any but the most formal occasions.

As well as tunics, married women wore the sedate and modest *stola*, which originated as a garment for patrician women, but eventually became acceptable wear for plebeian matrons. Typically, it comprised two rectangular segments of cloth that were fixed at the shoulder and sides by a *fibulae* (brooch) and buttons so that it hung in heavy folds. The outermost over-garment for women was the *palla*, a rectangular shawl up to 3 m (9.8 ft) long and 2 m (6.6 ft) wide. It was either wrapped around the body or worn as a hooded cloak. In public, women wore their hair bound up in woollen bands and were veiled.

Outdoor shoes were flat-soled, with leather uppers that were sometimes semi-openwork. Workers' shoes were often hobnailed, as was the standard military marching boot. Thin-soled sandals with elaborate thongs and straps that created decorative patterns, were used for more formal wear and special occasions.

Sumptuary laws

As private wealth began to grow in Republican Rome, lawmakers enacted legislation that would restrain unbridled luxury and regulate private consumption. The Roman sumptuary laws tried to control spending on funerals, banquets and festivals. They also put a check on the extravagance that was manifested in dress and personal adornment. The *Lex Oppia*, which was enacted in 215 BCE, ruled that women could not wear more than half an ounce of gold upon their person and that their tunics should not be in different colours. Other laws made further stipulations: only the emperor was allowed to wear a toga coloured entirely in purple; only augurs were allowed to wear saffron togas; only members of the Senate and their sons were allowed the privilege of the broad purple stripe on their tunic; magistrates and young men up to the age of 17 were allowed to wear a toga that was bordered by a broad purple stripe (the *toga praetexta*). The number of stripes on the universally worn tunic (*clavus*) was also dictated by social rank. In this way, the Roman legislators sought to rein in profligate display, assert the traditional prerogatives of the ruling class, and ensure that the social status of every Roman citizen was openly proclaimed.

PROPITIATING THE GODS

The primary motivating force behind Roman religious worship was to harness good fortune from the gods; it was not about the forgiveness of sins, nor did it provide any insurance policy for the afterlife. Roman polytheists were intent on propitiating the gods – by worshipping them, making sacrifices and honouring them, it was believed that they would avert their anger.

THE ROMANS SHARED many of the myths and traditions that underpinned Greek worship. The Roman pantheon, which was headed by Jupiter, had Latin names, but could be clearly equated with the Greek pantheon (see pages 39–43). The Romans also worshipped deities that protected them in their everyday life: from crop failure, disease and financial failure to unhappy marriages, childlessness and bad luck.

The city of Rome was presided over by the greatest god and goddess. Jupiter, the Roman equivalent of Zeus, was the king of the gods and the sky god, who controlled weather and natural phenomena. As the city grew, a temple to Jupiter was dedicated on the Capitoline Hill. On the Esquiline Hill, a temple was dedicated to Juno; the supreme goddess of the light and the moon, she embodied the virtues of Roman matronhood, and was the patron of childbirth and fertility.

As in Greece, the main act of religious worship was the sacrifice of an animal to a deity. Entrails of the sacrificed animal were studied closely for omens by professional diviners, or haruspices, as were other signs in the natural world, such as the flight of birds, the birth of a deformed child, or an extraordinary weather phenomenon. The Romans sought auguries that would validate their endeavours, and it was common for presiding magistrates to take the auspices before public meetings or military campaigns. Any signs of ill omen were taken with the utmost seriousness.

Public adherence to a rigid set of rituals, an annual calendar of cults and the public rites associated with them ruled Roman society. These

Bronze lar from Roman Spain, c.1–50 CE, height 22.5 cm (9 in). Lares familiares ('family guardians') were domestic guardian spirits that looked after the welfare and prosperity of each household. The household's larium was the shrine to the god, normally comprising a wall niche where the small statue stood, or a free-standing statue.

were dictated by long tradition and presided over by male priests (*pontifices*), supervised by the high priest, the head of state religion (*pontifex maximus*), and combined long processions with chanted prayers and hymns. The calendar reflected annual cycles that were rooted in the farming year, as well as the traditional spring and summer military campaigning season. For this reason, March was the month when Mars, the god of war, was honoured with processions, dancing and a chariot race on the Field of Mars. There was a festival for the dead (Parentalia) in February, a festival of fertility in April (Flora), and a carnival of misrule, when slaves briefly became masters, in December (Saturnalia).

The main female religious officials were the Vestal Virgins, the attendants to the cult of Vesta, the goddess of the hearth. They were chosen from the patrician class at the age of six, served the goddess and adhered to their vow of chastity – on pain of death – for the next 30 years, when they were eventually allowed to marry.

Away from public life, gods permeated everyday life; there were gods of crossroads, boundaries, rivers, springs, hills and households. It was the duty of the paterfamilias to perform various rites that would propitiate the gods of the household, such as Vesta or Janus (the gods of gates and doorways). Panes and Penates were the sprits of the pantry and the kitchen, while Lares were the spirits of the ancestors. Umbrae (shades) were ghosts of the departed to be placated by charms and amulets. The Romans believed that the smooth running of the household, and the good fortune of its inhabitants, was maintained by honouring its spirits.

The Romans revered the Sibylline Books, Greek oracular verses reportedly spoken by a prophetic female Sybil, a priestess of the god Apollo, who came to Rome from the Greek colony of Cumae during the time of the Etruscan king Tarquinius. They were guarded by a board of 15 prominent Romans and consulted during times of emergency. Pronouncements from the Sibylline Books often led to the introduction of Greek cults to Rome; in the 290s BCE, a famine in Rome led to the introduction of the Greek healing cult of Asclepius.

Cults to various gods – Bacchus, Cybele, Isis, Serapis – were an important part of Roman religion, which were adopted at various times and sometimes followed with frenzied devotion. On occasion, this could make the authorities nervous. In fact, the cult of Bacchus, which led to intoxicated and anarchic celebrations on 17 March, proved alarmingly popular among Roman youth and was suppressed in 186 BCE.

A bronze model, the so-called 'Liver of Piacenza', of an animal liver engraved with the Etruscan names of the deities connected to each part of the organ, 2nd century BCE. It was created for the purposes of performing haruspicy – divination through the inspection of the entrails of sacrificed animals.

ROMAN EXPANSION

The Romans, who gained control of the Italian peninsula within a span of 200 years, were relentless conquerors. They were merciless and brutal in conflict, but generous in victory, ultimately consolidating control by an enlightened diplomatic policy of military alliances, with Roman citizenship being offered to many conquered peoples to take away the bitter taste of defeat.

THE FIRST YEARS of the Roman Republic were a time of social tensions, famines and hostilities within the Italian peninsula. Rome was a member of the Latin League, an ancient defensive confederation of the tribes and villages of Latium (central western Italy). In this capacity, in 496 BCE, Rome defended Latium against assaults by various hill tribes – the Volsci, Sabines and Aequi. In 396 BCE, when the Latin League turned its attention to the region of Etruria, it seized control of the territory ruled by Rome's former overlords, the Etruscans. However, Latium's rapid territorial expansion was held back by the migration of other groups on the Italian peninsula, such as the Samnites of southern Italy, who had access to the fertile plains and western coast.

In c.390 BCE, disaster struck when Gallic invaders from southern France surged southwards down the Italian peninsula and sacked Rome itself. There were many legends surrounding this event; the most famous is the story of the geese on the Capitoline Hill, whose cackling alerted the Roman defenders to the Gallic attack. Despite its guardian geese, the Gauls left Rome in complete disarray, and the city was hastily rebuilt. By the 360s BCE, however, the Romans had regrouped, resolved their internal tensions and were ready to assert their dominance.

In 346 BCE, Rome turned on its former allies, efficiently eviscerating the political leagues of its Latin neighbours and imposing a series of settlements on their member states. Rome then extended its control into the rich bay of Naples, finally taking Naples (Neapolis) itself in 326 BCE.

Despite a disastrous Samnite ambush in 321 BCE, Rome rebounded and eventually conquered its main regional rivals. In 295 BCE the Romans were victorious in a battle at Sentinum in Umbria, consolidating their control of the north. Over the course of this ruthless Roman campaign, many leading citizens of conquered towns surrendered. Rome frequently conferred citizenship on these conquered people, absorbing them into the Roman commonwealth and effectively reinforcing its control.

Part of the Romans' success is attributable to their reform of military tactics. They abandoned the traditional hoplite formation and introduced three main ranks of infantry, who were combined in a flexible formation and equipped with heavy throwing-spears and swords. Roman soldiers were tough and resilient, fighting for the honour of their families. New citizens and allies constantly swelled their ranks, and the Roman army continued to march relentlessly forwards.

In the far south of Italy, the cities of Magna Graecia were notable for their wealth and the luxurious lifestyles of their citizens, which the pugnacious Romans despised as effete and enervating. These cities were beset by attacks from non-Roman barbarians and internal disputes. When Rome became involved in these disputes, it came into a direct confrontation with Tarentum, an ancient Spartan foundation which was now an established democracy. The Tarentines felt that the Romans, who were sailing in waters off the south-east Italian coast that were forbidden to them, were infringing on their territory, and they regarded them as barbaric and illegal troublemakers. The Romans responded to the 'insult' by attacking Tarentum and winning a decisive victory.

The Tarentines reached out for assistance to King Pyrrhus of Epirus, on the north-west mainland of Greece. In spring 280 BCE, he travelled to southern Italy and confronted the Romans, confounding them by bringing some of the descendants of Alexander the Great's war elephants, an animal they had never encountered before. Pyrrhus was a heroic figure, a brave soldier and an acknowledged expert on military tactics. He rallied the discontented Greek citizens of southern Italy, won a victory at Tarentum's colony, Heraclea, and set off northwards for Rome, despatching a diplomat ahead to discuss terms, which the Romans bluntly refused. Pyrrhus went on to win a second victory in

Apulia in 279 BCE, but sustained heavy losses. A third bloody encounter took place at Beneventum in 275 BCE. Pyrrhus was again victorious, but at a heavy cost. With the words: 'With another victory like this, we will be finished!' (hence the phrase 'Pyrrhic victory'), he withdrew to Greece, where he was eventually killed in battle at Argos in 272 BCE.

The Romans soon capitalized on Pyrrhus' departure by consolidating control of the Greek cities of southern Italy. They took Tarentum in 272 BCE and then made a step that was to prove momentous – they crossed the Strait of Messina into Sicily. Roman interference in Sicilian affairs was a provocation to Carthage, and the two great powers of the western Mediterranean – Rome and Carthage – were now destined to clash.

THE PUNIC WARS

The mighty Mediterranean powers of Rome and Carthage were on a collision course in the 3rd century BCE. A Roman incursion into Sicily in 264 BCE was seen as an intolerable invasion of Carthage's sphere of influence and hostilities inevitably erupted. The ensuing Punic Wars ended in the annihilation of Carthage and the foundation of Rome's Mediterranean empire.

ACCORDING TO LEGEND, the Phoenician city of Carthage ('Punic' is Latin for 'Phoenician') was founded on the North African coast in 813 BCE. A small trading outpost, Carthage grew into the most powerful city in the Mediterranean before the rise of Rome, a place of legendary wealth and luxury that controlled a trading empire extending to Iberia, Sicily and the eastern Mediterranean.

The First Punic War (264–241 BCE) started as a war by proxy in Sicily, with the Romans defending Messina, while the Carthaginians supported Syracuse. This local war blew up into a direct conflict when the Romans persuaded Syracuse to defect to their side and the Carthaginians were obliged to send a large fleet to protect their colony. The war over the control of Sicily was to last 20 years. The Romans soon realized that driving out the Carthaginians would involve engaging with their fleet, and up to this point Roman military strength had been firmly land-based. It is said that the Romans built a war fleet of 330 ships, modelled on a captured Carthaginian warship that ran aground on the southern coast of Italy, within just two months. The incipient Roman navy, which relied on the help of south Italian and Greek allies, won its first naval victory at Mylae in 260 BCE.

Many disasters struck in the following years. Storms wiped out the Roman fleet on no less than three occasions – the Romans doggedly rebuilt their ships – and an ill-advised invasion of North Africa was defeated. Finally, the Romans won a decisive naval battle off the Aegates

Islands, northern Sicily, in 241 BCE. The unbeaten Carthaginian general, Hamilcar Barca (276–228 BCE), who was conducting a successful guerrilla campaign in Sicily, was forced to come to terms. The Carthaginians evacuated Sicily, with the exception of Syracuse, and the rest of the island became Rome's first overseas colony. Crippled by extortionate war indemnities, the Carthaginians were in no position to defend their island territories of Corsica and Sardinia, and Rome was now in possession of three wealthy Mediterranean islands.

The Carthaginians, defeated to the east, now turned their attention to the west, to the potential of the Iberian peninsula, where Hamilcar and his two sons began to construct an important power base. Rome, alarmed, sent envoys to New Carthage in Spain, and extracted an agreement from the Carthaginians that they would not expand beyond the Ebro River. At the same time, the Romans established an alliance with the independent city of Saguntum on the Mediterranean coast.

In 221 BCE, Hamilcar's younger son, Hannibal (247–c.183–1 BCE), assumed command of Carthaginian forces in Spain. Enraged by Saguntum's aggressive raids on Carthaginian territory, Hannibal crossed the Ebro and unilaterally took control of the city, without the endorsement of the Carthaginian authorities. This was the event that ignited the Second Punic War (218–201 BCE).

Contrary to everyone's expectations, the war was not fought in Spain; Hannibal took the extraordinary decision to lead his troops across the Alps and invade Italy. He set out in spring 218 BCE with 40,000 troops, 12,000 cavalry and 37 war elephants. His route was a daunting 1,600 km (1,000 miles), and involved taking the elephants across the River Rhone on rafts, and leading his huge entourage through the snow-bound mountain passes of the Alps. Hannibal was a born leader who marched alongside his men, shared their privations and encouraged them to persevere. Not only did he succeed in reaching Italy, albeit with a depleted army and very few surviving elephants, but he also then went on to win three major battles against his Roman enemies at Ticinus (218 BCE), Trebia (218 BCE) and Trasimene (217 BCE). Finally, at Cannae in southern Italy in 216 BCE, Hannibal surrounded a huge Roman army with both flanks of his cavalry, closed in on the enemy, and butchered 47,000 Roman infantry and 2,700 cavalry. The battle effectively decapitated the Roman army, extinguishing an entire elite aristocratic officer class.

Many of Rome's southern Italian allies defected to the Carthaginian side, but Hannibal could not capitalize on his victory, because the Carthaginians refused to send him the reinforcements and supplies he needed. The Roman policy in the ensuing months was to employ delaying tactics, devastating the countryside and destroying the Carthaginian supply lines.

Out of the terrible defeat of Cannae, a great Roman leader emerged: Publius Cornelius Scipio Africanus (235–183 BCE). He managed to rally the terrified and scattered Roman troops and remind them of their loyalty to the Roman Republic. Under Scipio's command, the Roman army – with its seemingly inexhaustible supply of manpower – rose again. Instead of engaging with Hannibal as he attempted to raise a coalition of new forces in southern Italy, the revived Roman army invaded Spain, taking New Carthage and driving the Carthaginians out of the peninsula.

The victorious Scipio now turned his sights on Carthage itself and Hannibal and his army were recalled to help deal with this threat. The two great generals finally met at Zama, along the coast from Carthage, in 202 BCE. This time Scipio turned the tables, enveloping the Carthaginian troops, to win an extraordinary victory that ended the Second Punic War. Under the terms of the peace, Carthage retained its North African territory but forfeited its overseas empire and surrendered its navy. Carthage was required to pay a war debt of 200 talents annually for 50 years.

Carthage adhered to its debt repayment obligations, but considered that when the 50 years of debt had been paid, that marked the end of any treaty with Rome. Following a failed Carthaginian invasion of Numidia in 150 BCE, the Romans sent an embassy to Carthage in 149 BCE, which proposed that the city should simply be dismantled and moved inland. When the Carthaginians refused, the Third Punic War (149–146 BCE) began – effectively a three-year siege of the city of Carthage. When it finally fell, it was burned to the ground. Having comprehensively eradicated their enemy, the Romans emerged from the hostilities as the pre-eminent power in the Mediterranean Sea.

PUNIC WARS (BCE)

264   A clash in Sicily, between Rome and Carthage, leads to the First Punic War.

260   A Carthaginian quinquereme, captured by the Romans, is used as the model for the first Roman fleet. The new Roman fleet wins a decisive victory over the Carthaginians at Mylae.

241   A Roman naval victory at Trapani, off the north-west tip of Sicily, ends the First Punic War. Sicily becomes Rome's first overseas province.

228   The Carthaginian general, Hamilcar Barca, dies fighting in Spain, after establishing a strong Carthaginian presence in the peninsula.

227   Sardinia and Corsica are annexed by Rome, becoming the second Roman overseas province.

c.225   A treaty defines the Ebro River as the Spanish boundary between Carthage and Rome.

221   Hannibal succeeds to the command of the Carthaginian forces in Spain, on the death of his brother-in-law Hasdrubal.

218   Hannibal crosses the Alps with his elephants, beginning the Second Punic War.

217   Hannibal surprises and traps a Roman army on a narrow plain beside Lake Trasimene.

216   Hannibal destroys a Roman army at Cannae, in the most severe defeat ever suffered by Rome. He threatens the city of Rome but cannot take it because of lack of supplies and reinforcements.

213   Syracuse, a Carthaginian ally, is besieged and sacked by the Romans.

210–07   The Roman General Publius Cornelius Scipio Africanus captures New Carthage in southern Spain for Rome.

204   Scipio sails to Africa and invades Carthage.

202   Hannibal suffers his first decisive defeat by a Roman army, at Zama.

201   Carthaginian Spain is handed over to Rome to become two new provinces at the end of the Second Punic War.

150 Carthaginian army invades Numidia, breaking the 50-year peace treaty.

149 Rome picks a quarrel with Carthage to begin the Third Punic War.

146 Carthage is destroyed by the Romans at the end of the Third Punic War.

A hand-cut woodcut of a 19th-century illustration showing the Carthaginian general Hannibal leading his army across the Alps to invade Rome in 218 BCE. He led 40,000 troops and 37 elephants over the Alps in late October, probably crossing Mount Cenis via the 2,285 m (7,500 ft) Savine Coche pass. By the time he had descended to the plains above Turin, his army had halved in size.

ROME'S MEDITERRANEAN EMPIRE

Rome's assertion of power in the Mediterranean in the 2nd century BCE was the result of a succession of military victories. The Roman military machine was highly successful, but it could also be replenished by seemingly endless reserves of manpower, drawn from conquests and alliances. War had become an instrument of foreign policy, and Roman society was permeated with a military ethos.

ROME'S PUSH EASTWARDS began with the foundation of colonies on the eastern coast of Italy, which led to trade across the Adriatic Sea. Illyrian tribes were notorious for their piracy which disrupted maritime trade, and in 229 BCE Roman troops were sent to campaign against the barbarian Illyrians. In the course of two campaigns, the threat was eliminated, and the surrounding Greek states no doubt looked on in trepidation.

When the Romans learnt that Philip V of Macedon had offered his assistance to the Carthaginian general Hannibal, who was campaigning in Italy, war in Greece seemed inevitable. At that time, much of north-east Greece was under his control, while the independent city-states had formed into a series of defensive leagues; the Aetolian League in western Greece and the Achaean League in the east were especially powerful. The city-states were divided and quarrelsome. In 211/210 BCE, the Romans made an alliance with the Aetolians of central Greece. They returned to Greece in 200 BCE, on the pretext that Philip of Macedon was attacking friends of Rome in the east Aegean. Athens allied with the Romans, who won a decisive victory against Macedonia at Cynoscephalae in Thessaly in 197 BCE. At this point the Roman commander Titus Flamininus announced the 'freedom of the Greeks', at the Isthmian Games (196 BCE). The Aetolians who, despite their original alliance with Rome had received no special treatment, were disgruntled.

The Romans' view now turned further east towards Greek cities in Asia under the rule of the Seleucids. When the Aetolians invited the ruler of the Seleucids, Antiochus III – who had invaded Thrace in 196 BCE and was now alarmed by Roman threats – to cross into Greece with an army, the Romans met him at Thermopylae in 190/189 BCE, driving him back to West Asia where they won a decisive victory at Magnesia. The Seleucids paid the Romans the vast sum of 15,000 talents, and withdrew to beyond the Taurus Mountains. The territories they had captured in Asia Minor were returned to Rome's allies, Rhodes and Pergamon, and the Romans withdrew.

The Roman Senate was now responsible for arbitrating territorial disputes in Greece, and began to profit from Greek disunity and weakness. All over Greece, democracies were taken over by 'friends' of Rome: wealthy benefactors who stood for public order and firm rule. Rome was beginning to emerge as the policeman of the Mediterranean world.

Between 168 and 146 BCE, the Romans moved successfully against Macedonia, Seleucia and Dalmatia on the Aegean coast. The new king of Macedonia, Perseus, was a charismatic figure who offered a haven for Greeks who found themselves impoverished and disempowered by the new Roman imperium. The Roman army arrived in 168 BCE, and won a famous victory at Pydna that year, when 20,000 Macedonians were killed and 11,000 taken prisoner. Perseus was captured and taken back to Rome for ritual humiliation. The Macedonian palaces were plundered and Macedonia was divided into four republics. The peoples of Epirus in north-west Greece, who had aided the Macedonians, suffered terrible reprisals, with many being sold into slavery.

Rome had demonstrated that it would tolerate nothing less than complete obedience from its subjects, and the end game was inevitable. In 150 BCE, an uprising in Macedonia prompted Roman intervention, and two years later Macedonia became a regular province. In 149 BCE, following a futile revolt, the Romans dismembered the Achaean League and the city of Corinth was destroyed. Rome's control of the Mediterranean was now secure.

ROMAN LETTERING

The Roman alphabet is the most widely used alphabetic writing system in the world. The Romans perfected the shape, composition and symmetry of the Latin alphabet to create a model for all subsequent writing in the Latin West. The beauty, grace and clarity of the Roman letterforms have been revered for the last two millennia.

THE ROMAN ALPHABET, which evolved some time before 600 BCE, had Phoenician, Greek and Etruscan origins. The first known inscription in Latin is from a cloak pin from the 7th century BCE; just slightly later are inscriptions on a pillar in the Roman Forum and the Duenos inscription on a vase found near the Quirinal Hill in Rome.

Initially, the alphabet comprised just 20 upper case letters. The letter G was introduced in the 3rd century BCE, and Y and X, which were borrowed from the Greek alphabet, appeared in the 1st century CE. The letters J, U and W did not appear until the medieval period. In Roman times, there were two main types of Latin script: capital letters and cursive, the origin of the lower-case style, which probably originated in the 2nd century BCE for mundane handwritten letters.

The Romans used a variety of tools for writing. Everyday writing was usually done on a wax tablet, using a stylus (pointed stick). More important documents, such as legal contracts or literary texts, were written in pen and ink on papyrus or parchments. Inscriptions were carved in stone on buildings or other monuments.

It is thought that the characteristic Roman 'serifs' evolved when the Romans were creating lapidary inscriptions. Because it is difficult to end a chiselled stroke neatly when carving letters like 'I' in stone, it was easier to make horizontal strokes at the top and bottom, which were then cut to create the spaces between the letters. Alternatively, the stone-cutters may have followed the forms left by a square-cut writing implement,

The opening words of the inscription at the base of Trajan's column, erected in Rome in 113 CE, reads: 'The Senate and people of Rome [dedicate] this to the emperor Caesar, son of the divine Nerva'. Studies of the inscription on Trajan's column have helped us understand how the letters were formed. The letters were sketched using a flat square-tipped brush, using only three or four strokes; variations in thickness reflected the angle of the brush. The letters that had been traced out in this fashion were then engraved in the stone.

probably a stiff brush, which was held like a pen, and used to trace the letters before they were carved into the stone using a mallet and chisel.

Inscriptions proliferated during the imperial period. On the grandiose end of the scale, they were used to make large, formal statements, such as dedications to the gods, imperial decrees and official announcements. On the smallest scale, the names and titles of rulers were minted on coins. The largest body of Roman inscriptions can be found on funerary monuments, where they were used to record precise details about the deceased, as well as to articulate feelings of loss and grief.

Trajan

Trajan's Column, erected in Rome in 113 CE, is a victory memorial to the Emperor Trajan and his conquests in Greece and Macedonia. It is famous for its spiral bas-relief of battle scenes, but also for
its elegant incised inscription, a fine example of Roman square capitals. In 1989, Carol Twombly, working for Adobe, designed a typeface that was based on the inscription. She came

from a long line of typographers and craftsmen who had been inspired and fascinated by the classical letterforms. Predecessor designs include Rudolf Weiss's *Weiss* (1926), Goudy's *Goudy Trajan* (1930) and Warren Chappel's *Trajanus* (1939). Twombly used a full-sized rubbing of the original letters of the inscription. Elements of the typeface were modified for printing on paper; there were stronger serifs than in the original, and the stem and bowl weights were adjusted – for example the N was narrower and the S was wider. Twombly's Trajan was an instant success, used very widely wherever a sense of elegance and authority was required. It became the characteristic 'brand' typeface of the award-winning *West Wing* television series and has been used for numerous Hollywood movies, as well as being widely displayed on book covers, corporate branding and signage.

THE RISE OF JULIUS CAESAR

Julius Caesar, perhaps the most famous Roman, was a man of his time who emerged from a period of great instability and conflict. Ruthlessly ambitious and highly intelligent, he espoused the populist cause, which brought him into conflict with the Senate, and used his military genius to build a daunting power base in Gaul, from where he could launch his bid for personal glory.

THE PERIOD FROM 150–80 BCE was turbulent at home and abroad. Rome was beset by social unrest, including the Spartacus slave revolts in southern Italy and Sicily, and the 'Social Wars' (91–89 BCE) with discontented Italian allies – offers of Roman citizenship helped to bring about the wars' end.

When Mithridates, king of the Pontic kingdom bordering the Black Sea, annexed the Roman province of Asia, a patrician noble named Lucius Cornelius Sulla commanded the Roman army that confronted Mithridates. The people's assembly had rejected his appointment and he had responded by rallying his troops and marching on Rome. Despite winning a crushing victory against Mithridates in 85 BCE, he was outlawed by his enemy in Rome, the consul Lucius Cornelius Cinna. On hearing of Cinna's death, Sulla marched on Rome in 83 BCE and declared himself dictator. He then proceeded to enact a series of traditionalist laws that reasserted the power of the Senate and neutered the populist assemblies and the powers of the tribunes.

After Sulla's death in 79 BCE, there followed a decade in which his reforms were dismantled. In 70 BCE, the last of the tribunes' powers were restored by a notable pair of consuls: the wealthy patrician and military commander, Marcus Licinius Crassus (*c.*115 BCE–53 BCE), who had distinguished himself against Spartacus and his slave revolt; and Pompey the Great (106–148 BCE), an outstanding and brutal military commander, who had emerged from a wealthy Italian provincial family. It was Pompey who resolved the situation in Asia; within four years he had conquered King Mithridates, and he then went south, winning famous victories in Syria, the Lebanon and Judaea. Tribute and booty poured into Rome on an unprecedented scale, and Pompey's legendary Eastern Triumph in Rome in 69 BCE proclaimed him as a military colossus who was rapidly establishing a personal power base.

Another great Roman figure was also coming to prominence: Julius Caesar (100–44 BCE) was a true patrician and a born soldier, who resisted Sulla's reforms and held fast to the populist line. Hugely ambitious, Caesar was not afraid of borrowing substantial sums of money, primarily from Crassus, to secure prestige and appointments. When he gained a command in Spain in 61 BCE, he was able to extract vast wealth from the colony to discharge his debts. When he became consul in 59 BCE, he supported a populist agenda by working with the Peoples' Assemblies and tribunes, while using a delicately balanced exchange of favours to ensure the loyalty of the two most important men in Rome: Crassus and Pompey. Together, these three men formed the unofficial first Triumvirate, and committed to use their power and influence to help each other. The scrupulous, conservative senator Cato the Younger (95–46 BCE) led a stalwart defence against the ambitious reformist; he remained Caesar's implacable enemy.

Secure in his alliance with Pompey, who had now married his only daughter, Julia, Caesar ended his consulship with provincial commands in Transalpine Gaul (Provence) and Illyricum (Dalmatia). Caesar was immensely successful in Gaul, where he picked off the warring tribes one by one, conquering new lands and creating a substantial new Roman province. As governor of Gaul, Caesar had not been given permission by the Senate to wage war but, ever the opportunist, he chose to do so. His troops' allegiance was to him personally, rather than any abstract notion of the Republic, and to the wealth and security his exploits brought them; elsewhere in Rome, landless veterans faced a bleak future.

In Rome, Caesar was acclaimed for his courage and bold ambition, and his reputation was stellar. But the tables turned when an uprising broke out following the murder of the popular tribune Clodius (93–52 BCE) and the Senate House was burned to the ground (52 BCE). The senators begged Pompey to restore order as the city's sole consul. Would he now eclipse his rival Caesar?

Back in Gaul, a greatly outnumbered Caesar defeated the Gallic leader Vercingetorix (c.82–46 BCE), who was besieged in the fortress of Alesia (52 BCE). His victory was a combination of tactical genius and bravery, which brought outstanding riches, unparalleled acclaim and lavish celebrations in Rome, with much of the bill footed by Caesar himself. Despite this triumph, Caesar was under attack from the traditionalist senators who wanted to deprive him of his command. Pompey, who had married into one of the great patrician families and achieved acceptance from the traditionalists, was increasingly ambivalent about Caesar, and in 51 BCE he took a stance, declaring that Caesar should surrender his command.

Pompey was implored to take to the battlefield to defend the Republic against the overweening power of Caesar. Meanwhile, Caesar presented himself as an advocate of peace, but the Senate repeatedly demanded that he lay down his arms rather than dictate conditions to the Senate, and his allies, led by the tribune Marcus Antonius (Mark Antony) (83–30 BCE), were forced to make a rapid escape from Rome. On 10 January 49 BCE, Caesar and his troops crossed the Rubicon, a small river between Italy and Gaul. This forbidden act was a declaration of war, and the fate of the Republic now lay in the hands of Pompey and Caesar.

CIVIL WAR

*Julius Caesar had waged unsanctioned wars in Gaul and was
threatened with criminal charges in Rome. He refused to step down
from his military command, and initiated a civil war against his old
rival Pompey that left him in control of the government. But when
members of the Senate assassinated the overweening autocrat, it was
his adopted son Octavian who set about capitalizing on Caesar's
legacy.*

HAVING CROSSED THE RUBICON on 10 January 49 BCE, Caesar
and his 13th Legion swept southwards through Italy, where towns
opened their gates with little, or no, resistance, and Caesar promised
clemency to his rivals. In Rome, the speed and effectiveness of Caesar's
advance was deeply shocking, and quarrels and recriminations broke
out between the alarmed senators. Pompey, whose overconfidence in his
troops had been humiliatingly shattered, proposed a tactical retreat, and
the majority of the senators fled the city. The Pompeian army retreated to
the port of Brundisium (Brindisi) in southern Italy, with Caesar in hot
pursuit. Requisitioned ships evacuated the army and Pompey escaped
by the skin of his teeth.

Caesar marched into Rome in 49 BCE, but he did not receive a hero's
welcome. The people of Rome were terrified by the unfolding civil war,
and their worst fears were confirmed when Caesar used violence and
threats to seize the gold reserves of the Republic. He then marched to
Spain, where he campaigned against Pompey's armies over the course
of three hard-fought months. Meanwhile, in Greece, Pompey was busy
recruiting troops. Caesar was determined to take the fight to Pompey so,
in the winter of 49/48 BCE, Caesar returned to Brundisium and his army
sailed to Durres on the Albanian coast, avoiding Pompey's blockades
en route. But Caesar's supply lines were overstretched, and Pompey
conducted a war of attrition, watching Caesar's weary and battle-

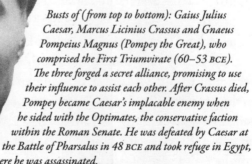

Busts of (from top to bottom): Gaius Julius Caesar, Marcus Licinius Crassus and Gnaeus Pompeius Magnus (Pompey the Great), who comprised the First Triumvirate (60–53 BCE). The three forged a secret alliance, promising to use their influence to assist each other. After Crassus died, Pompey became Caesar's implacable enemy when he sided with the Optimates, the conservative faction within the Roman Senate. He was defeated by Caesar at the Battle of Pharsalus in 48 BCE and took refuge in Egypt, where he was assassinated.

hardened troops gradually starve and refusing to engage with them. When Pompey finally met Caesar's forces at Dyrrachium in Albania, he won a decisive victory, but did not push home his advantage, allowing Caesar's troops to escape.

Once again, Caesar confounded expectations and marched his exhausted and depleted troops further into enemy territory, into the interior of Greece, with Pompey in pursuit. Caesar set up camp in a town called Pharsalus. Pompey did not immediately engage with his enemy, arguing to the increasingly impatient senators that his priority was to save Roman lives. Finally, on 9 August 48 BCE, Pompey responded to Caesar's baiting and battle began. Caesar's 22,000 infantry were outnumbered two to one, but he had a much better grasp of strategy. He created a fourth line of infantry, to be held back until the signal was given, when they advanced – with the advantage of surprise – to attack Pompey's cavalry. Caesar routed Pompey's army, stormed the enemy's camp and Pompey fled to Egypt. On arrival in Alexandria, where Pompey hoped to muster support, a eunuch at the court of the pharaoh assassinated him.

Caesar returned to Rome in triumph, and between 49 and 44 BCE he was voted four consulships and four dictatorships. With this power invested in him, he honoured his promises to restore the liberty of the people, initiated land reforms and supported the army veterans. But it was clear that, when Caesar accepted the title of dictator for life in February 44 BCE, he was in effect becoming an emperor. On the Ides of March (15th), members of the Senate finally took decisive action and stabbed Caesar 23 times, proclaiming that 'liberty' had been restored.

The young Gaius Octavius (Octavian) (63–14 BCE) was Caesar's adopted son. Claiming that it was his duty to avenge his father's assassination, he now made a bold bid for power. Uniting with Caesar's old ally Mark Antony, he went to war, finally defeating Caesar's assassins at the Battle of Philippi in 42 BCE. But how long would this pragmatic alliance last?

On 2 September 31 BCE, at Actium in north-western Greece, a momentous battle took place between the forces of Octavian and his old comrade Mark Antony, who was joined by his romantic and political ally, Queen Cleopatra of Egypt. The political tide was turning and Octavian, now a skilled military tactician, was in the ascendancy. He secured victory by firing volleys of flaming catapult balls at the enemy fleet, then surrounding them, trapping them with grappling hooks, boarding the ships and engaging in hand-to-hand combat. Cleopatra escaped with her fleet and Mark Antony's remaining ships were destroyed. Both Mark Antony and Cleopatra committed suicide in 30 BCE.

Characterized as the victory of rugged, virile Roman manhood over the enervating, louche laxity of the Orient, Octavian emerged from the conflict as much more than the victor. He now held the fate of the Roman Republic in his hands.

JULIUS CAESAR

65 BCE	Julius Caesar becomes an *aedile curule*, an elected official, in Rome.
60–53 BCE	First Triumvirate between Caesar, Pompey and Crassus.
58–51 BCE	Julius Caesar's conquest of Gaul.
55–54 BCE	Julius Caesar invades Britain twice.
52 BCE	After becoming trapped and besieged at Alesia, Vercingetorix surrenders to Caesar.
*c.*49 BCE	Caesar crosses the Rubicon. Civil war between Caesar and Pompey begins.
49 BCE	Julius Caesar besieges Massilia.
49 BCE	Julius Caesar captures Brundisium in southern Italy.
48 BCE	Caesar defeats Pompey (Battle of Pharsalus); Pompey flees to Egypt and is killed by courtiers of Ptolemy XIII.
48 BCE	Caesar arrives in Egypt and orders Ptolemy XIII and Cleopatra VII to disband their armies, but instead, war breaks out.
23 Jun 47 BCE	Birth of Cleopatra's son, named Caesarion; Caesar is said to be the father.
46 BCE	Julius Caesar celebrates a triple triumph in Rome.
15 Mar 44 BCE	Julius Caesar is murdered in the Senate.
44 BCE	Gaius Octavius Thurinus (Octavian), Caesar's great-nephew, is adopted posthumously by Julius Caesar.

43–36 BCE Second Roman Triumvirate: Antony, Octavian and Lepidus.

43 BCE Second Triumvirate, supported by Cleopatra, wages war against Brutus and Cassius, Caesar's assassins.

42 BCE Octavian and Antony defeat the Republicans under Brutus and Cassius at the Battle of Philippi (Greece).

36 BCE Octavian strips Lepidus of all power except Pontifex Maximus (supreme priest).

2 Sep 31 BCE The Battle of Actium. Octavian defeats Mark Antony and Cleopatra VII. Cleopatra flees to Alexandria.

Aug 30 BCE Cleopatra kills herself rather than be taken to Rome by Octavian. Mark Antony also commits suicide.

29 BCE Octavian celebrates a triple triumph in Rome.

27 BCE Octavian is given extraordinary powers by the Roman Senate, and the name Augustus.

PART V

Imperium

Frieze from the south side of the Ara Pacis Augustae (Altar of Augustan Peace), showing Augustus with his toga pulled over his head, the rex sacrorum (high priest), four priests and a lictor holding an axe. The altar was commissioned by the Roman Senate on 4 July 13 BCE to honour the return of Augustus after three years of campaigning in Hispania and Gaul. It originally stood on the west side of the Via Flaminia on the north-east of the Campus Martius, Rome.

AUGUSTUS AND THE RISE OF IMPERIAL ROME

Julius Caesar's adopted heir, Octavian, had won a famous victory at the Battle of Actium in 31 BCE. He went on to conquer Egypt, where Antony and Cleopatra, his erstwhile foes, committed suicide, and then returned to Rome, stupendously wealthy, for three sumptuous triumphs. Every Roman citizen received a cash bonus and his popularity knew no bounds. However, he lacked legitimacy. In 29 BCE, Octavian rebranded himself, adopting the name Augustus, which means 'sacred' or 'revered'. He had not explicitly declared himself a deity, but he had allied himself with the gods.

HIS FIRST MOVE, which assuaged the Roman senators' deep-rooted suspicion of autocracy, was to renounce all his powers and territories and hand them back to the Roman people. The grateful Senate duly granted Augustus the right to stand for the consulship. But more significantly, they granted him a province that embraced Gaul, Syria, Egypt and Cyprus. Because these territories bordered the frontiers of the Roman Empire, the majority of the Roman army legions were stationed there. The events of the civil war had proved that true power lay in an individual's right to command territories and armies. The Senate had effectively empowered Augustus.

Augustus held on to the consulship year after year, and this brought him into intermittent conflict with the Senate, but he retained his unrivalled popularity with the people. He capitalized on this by seeking the power that was accorded to a tribune of the people, which gave him the authority to propose and veto bills that were laid before the people's assembly. In this way, he was able to present himself as a champion of the rights of Roman citizens everywhere.

Augustus's power and legitimacy were now secure and it had become clear that debates within the Senate were mere window dressing; Augustus's word was law. He hand-picked an advisory body of consuls and senators who met in the Imperial Palace, much resented by the increasingly powerless senators. Augustus needed his inner circle to help him administer the ever-growing empire, but any transgression or suggestion that his own power base was under attack was suppressed with the utmost ruthlessness.

His final consolidation of power came with his reform of the army. The civil war had demonstrated that armies were loyal to their commanders, not the Republic, and were quite willing to slaughter their fellow Romans if they were promised land and booty. Augustus now nationalized the army: citizens were offered a professional career; wages were paid; promotions were regularized. While the legions continued to police the empire's borders, an elite 'Praetorian Guard' was stationed in Italy and Rome. Its 9,000 members were paid three times the salary of ordinary soldiers, and acted as the imperial bodyguard. These army reforms required tax revenues, and Augustus secured the smooth flow of revenue into the imperial treasury rather than the pockets of ambitious generals.

The new professional Roman army maintained peace within the empire and, increasingly, Augustus was revered for the 'Pax Romana'. In the eastern provinces, where Oriental cults of kingship were already established, he was worshipped as a god, and temples were built in his honour.

In 18 BCE, Augustus set about improving the morals of his empire with a series of laws that promoted marriage and family values and penalized sexual offences and adultery. The Games of the Ages in 17 BCE was a brilliantly stage-managed homage to Roman piety, chastity and morality. Augustus played a central role in the spectacular sacrifices and religious ceremonies, and rigorously upheld his edicts. When his daughter Julia transgressed against his new code of moral rectitude, he was pitiless in his condemnation, and had her exiled from Rome (2 BCE).

By the time of his death in 14 BCE, Augustus had established, through a mixture of ruthlessness, ambition, genius and improvisation, a new imperium. The Republic was dead. Soon after his death, Augustus was deified and his remains were placed in his mausoleum in the Campus Martius, crowned by a colossal bronze statue, 30 m (98 ft) high, of Rome's first emperor.

The 1st-century CE marble statue of Augustus of Prima Porta, a copy of a bronze original from c.20 BCE, height 2.4 m (7.9 ft), is a fine example of Augustan propaganda. Augustus, as well as projecting great power, is portrayed as youthful and virile, and is shown in full military regalia. At his right leg can be seen a cupid figure riding a dolphin. The dolphin symbolizes Augustus's naval victory over Antony and Cleopatra at the Battle of Actium (31 BCE). The cupid figure may also indicate that Augustus is the descendant of the gods; Cupid is the son of Venus, and Julius Caesar, his adopted father, claimed descent from the goddess of love. The highly decorated cuirass, or breastplate, shows a Parthian returning military standards to a Roman – a reference to Augustus's diplomatic victory in 20 BCE, when he negotiated their return. These figures are surrounded by gods and female symbols of Rome's conquered territories, indicating that the gods will look benignly upon the Roman Empire of Augustus and the Pax Romana that he introduced.

CITY OF MARBLE

Augustus wished to proclaim himself the pinnacle of Roman history, the manifestation of Rome's imperial destiny. By transforming Rome into a grandiose 'city of marble', he was creating a fitting capital city of his new empire.

MARBLE HAD TRADITIONALLY been a prohibitively expensive building material which had to be transported to Rome from Greece. However, the discovery of Italian marble at Carrara in Tuscany enabled Augustus to construct magnificent public buildings that would transform his city into a much more imposing capital, although most of the populace was still crammed into its rabbit warren of narrow streets and brick tenements. Among his famous additions were the Pantheon, the Temple of Apollo, the Ara Pacis (Altar of Peace), the Baths of Agrippa and Theatre of Marcellus, and the city's first stone-built amphitheatre. He also improved the city's water supply and sewerage systems.

His greatest achievement was the Forum of Augustus. Here, his genius for utilizing and aggrandizing Rome's historic past was on full display. The Forum was flanked by two porticoes, which were lined on one side with statues of historic figures, such as Romulus, Remus and heroes of the Republic. On the other side, he paid respect to his ancestors and descendants, asserting their impeccable aristocratic credentials. At one end stood the temple of Mars Ultor (Mars the Avenger), where the Senate met for declarations of war or peace, with statues of Venus, Mars and Julius Caesar. The restored standards of Crassus, which were captured by the Parthian Empire during his failed campaign in 53 BCE, were placed in the temple – a tribute to the Augustine peace treaty. In the centre of the Forum stood a statue of Augustus himself in full armour.

The Forum of Augustus is a magnificent piece of political propaganda, which not only honours the heroes of Rome's past, but also clearly places the figure of Augustus at the centre of that illustrious lineage.

AUGUSTUS

23 Sep 63 BCE	Octavian born Gaius Octavius Thurinus in Rome.
Mar 44 BCE	Octavian adopted posthumously by Julius Caesar.
43–36 BCE	Second Roman Triumvirate: Mark Antony, Octavian and Lepidus.
42 BCE	Octavian and Mark Antony defeat Republicans under Brutus and Cassius at the Battle of Philippi (Greece).
2 Sep 31 BCE	The Battle of Actium. Octavian defeats Mark Antony and Cleopatra VII.
29 BCE	Octavian celebrates a triple triumph in Rome.
29 BCE	Augustus builds the temple of Divius Iulius on the spot of Julius Caesar's funeral pyre in Rome's Forum Romanum.
27 BCE	Augustus creates the Praetorian Guard.
c.23 BCE	Augustus takes over most of the powers of the *tribuni plebis*.
20 BCE	Following a diplomatic agreement, Augustus receives returned legionary standards lost at Carrhae in the Parthian Empire (53 BCE).
19 BCE	Augustus is given supreme powers by the Roman Senate.
19 BCE	Arch of Augustus is built in Rome to commemorate victory over the Parthians.
c.10 BCE	Augustus rebuilds the Temple of Castor and Pollux in Rome's Forum Romanum.
c.10 BCE	Statue of Augustus as *pontifex maximus* is sculpted.
9 BCE	A massive altar, the Ara Pacis, is completed by Augustus in Rome.
2 BCE	Augustus appoints two prefects (*praefectus praetorio*) to command the Praetorian Guard.
c.2 BCE	Augustus is declared 'Father of His Country'.
2 BCE	Augustus inaugurates the Temple of Mars Ultor in Rome to

commemorate his victory at the Battle of Philippi in 42 BCE.

6 CE   Augustus creates the *aerarium militare*, a treasury drawn from taxes in order to fund a professional army.

*c.*13 CE   Augustus creates the *cohortes urbanae* in Rome to help maintain public order.

19 Aug 14 CE   Augustus dies at Nola of natural causes.

BREAD AND CIRCUSES

Rome was a martial society which enjoyed military spectacle, skilled horsemanship, combat and staged fights, and admired audacity and bravery in the face of death. For these reasons, gladiatorial and equestrian games were an enduringly popular spectacle. The author Juvenal (55–127 CE) observed that the people 'are only anxious for two things: bread and circuses'.

GLADIATORS WERE SLAVES, condemned criminals, prisoners of war, debtors or volunteers who fought to the death in front of bloodthirsty, baying crowds in huge amphitheatres. They fought each other and wild animals, and lived on the margins of society, segregated and subject to a strict and arduous training regime. Some gladiators survived and became celebrities, but the vast majority died prematurely. Enrolment in a gladiator school offered food and shelter, physical training and at least a chance of celebrity and prize money. From the mid-1st century CE, female gladiators presented an exotic new attraction. They were certainly a novelty, but were often greeted with ribaldry and mockery.

Gladiator games did not really emerge until the 3rd century BCE, and were thought to originate in Campania, southern Italy. By 105 BCE, state-sponsored gladiatorial combat was included in the state games that marked the major religious festivals. In the late years of the Republic, however, gladiatorial games became a means of self-promotion, and private citizens vied with each other to own gladiators and sponsor shows – a spectacular gladiatorial show could be a real vote-winner. Augustus ensured that the games came under imperial auspices; the most magnificent games were identified with the imperial cult, served to consolidate the emperor's public image, and were paid for by the emperor.

There was much anticipation before the games, which were advertised and promoted beforehand. Spectators were plied with food and drink, water sprinklers in hot weather, and an awning against the sun. Somewhat alarmingly, the gladiators were advised to put their personal and private affairs in order, and were given a banquet on the night before the games.

On the day of the games, as many as 50,000 spectators trooped into the amphitheatre. A procession entered the arena: magistrates, lictors (their bodyguards), scribes and trumpet-players and, last but not least, the gladiators themselves. Proceedings usually began with beast hunts or beast fights, which included animals such as lions, bears, elephants, giraffes, tigers and rhinos. Hungry animals fought each other, but sometimes they were turned against gladiators. This was followed by *ludi meridiani*, which involved executions, where the participants played doomed roles in re-enactments of myths and legends or took part in 'comedy fights'. The gladiatorial games proper began with warm-up

The Colosseum was commissioned c.72 CE by Emperor Vespasian as a gift to the Roman people, and was officially opened by his son Titus in 80 CE. This massive stone amphitheatre was built on the land near the centre of the city where Emperor Nero had built himself a golden palace after the great fire of 64 CE. Measuring some 190 x 155 m (623 x 508 ft), the Colosseum was the largest amphitheatre in the Roman world and provided seating for more than 50,000 spectators. It was freestanding, with three storeys of around 80 arched entrances, supported by semicircular columns.

matches, and the main event of the day was the scheduled matches.

Gladiators specialized in different fighting styles and spectators enjoyed watching combat between well-matched opponents with complementary styles. Gladiators were expected to respect the rules of combat and submit to the interventions of a senior referee. A match was won when the gladiator overcame, or killed, his opponent. An outstanding fighter, even if he was a slave or a condemned criminal, might find that his bravery was rewarded with manumission or liberation. Gladiators who were unwilling to fight were 'persuaded' to do so by a whip-brandishing manager and slaves. A gladiator could acknowledge defeat by raising a finger; his fate might then lie in the hands of the crowd – a defeated gladiator who fought well might be granted remission. The final decision was ultimately made by the presiding magistrate (editor) who signalled his choice with his thumb.

Dying well was much admired, and meant that the deceased was given proper funeral rites, often paid for by a union (*collegia*), which would also provide a pension or compensation to wives and children. While many gladiators may have died in their first match, few survived more than ten contests, and a natural death was extremely unlikely.

Chariot races, which took place on special racetracks called circuses, provided a less bloodthirsty form of entertainment. Two- or four-horse chariots, driven with great skill and reckless bravery, raced for distances of 4.8–8 km (3–5 miles). Other equestrian events resembled today's thoroughbred horse racing.

Successive emperors appreciated that providing crowds with free entertainment was an effective means of controlling potential popular discontent. The frenzied excitement of gladiatorial games and horse racing bonded the people together, and their bloodlust was confined to the safety of the amphitheatre.

Gladiator Classes

The earliest gladiators were named after Rome's enemies: Samnites, Thracians and Gauls. The Samnite became the 'secutor' and the Gaul the 'murmillo' once these former enemies had been absorbed into the empire.

Secutor (Samnite): Named after the great Samnite warriors from whom the games may have originated, they were heavily armed with a sword or lance, a large square shield (*scutum*), and protective armour on the right arm and leg.

Thracian (Thraex): The Thracian had a short curved sword (*sica*) and a small round shield (*parma*).

Murmillo (Gaul): He had a fish-shaped crest on his helmet, carried a short double-edged sword, the *gladius*, and wielded a *scutum* like the Samnite, but had only padded armour on his arm and leg.

Retiarius: With no helmet or armour, apart from a padded shoulder, the 'net man' carried a weighted net in which he attempted to trap his opponent before stabbing him with a trident.

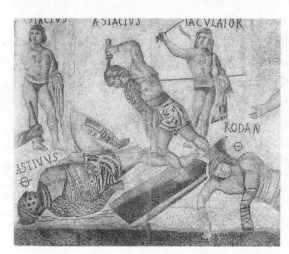

Gladiator mosaic from the Villa Borghese, c.320 CE. A retiarius, who fights with a weighted net, three-pointed trident and a dagger, attacks his prostrate opponent, a heavily armed secutor.

ROMAN PROVINCIAL LIFE

The Pax Romana created conditions in which the provinces of the Roman Empire could flourish: agriculture and commerce generated wealth locally and also provided huge tax revenues for the emperor. In the north and west, Rome introduced entirely new ways of life and made a lasting impact; in the east, Rome acquired wealthy territories with long histories of urban civilization.

GOVERNORS RULED PROVINCES; the governor was usually a senator who acted on detailed instructions from the emperor and was assisted by procurators, administrators who played an important role in the government of the provinces. His paramount duty was to preserve peace within the province, and he therefore spent a great deal of his time adjudicating local disputes, usually through an annual assize tour. Cities within the province retained their own courts in which they tried civil cases. Roman governors were also responsible for taking a regular census of their populations, an innovation introduced by Augustus. The censuses, which listed individuals and property, were the basis for taxation, and taxes were collected annually. Roman citizens in the provinces were expected to pay a tribute on land and a tribute on persons. Tax collectors were extremely assiduous in carrying out their duties, and many provinces regarded their taxes as burdensome, as evidenced by revolts against taxation in Gaul, Britain, North Africa and Judaea shortly after direct Roman rule was imposed.

Religious cults of Rome and the emperor were encouraged in the provinces, and everywhere local gods – as long as they did not challenge Rome's moral precepts, for example by demanding human sacrifice – were intertwined with Roman deities. Non-Roman polytheists could easily understand the basic precepts of Roman religion, which were concerned with ensuring prosperity and well-being, and were generally prepared to accommodate the new deities.

Initially, Roman citizenship was conferred on provincial subjects as a reward for service, for example as a magistrate or an army auxiliary. When subject towns were granted full 'municipal' status, the citizens of these municipia automatically received citizenship and the right to vote. Citizens in 'municipal' towns were expected to worship Roman cults, and were subject, as 'Latins', to Roman law, as it applied to family matters, slave-holding and the rights of the paterfamilias. The second order of municipia comprised important tribal centres, where citizens were liable to taxes and military service but did not receive the right to vote. By 212 CE, however, the Edict of Caracalla granted Roman citizenship to all free inhabitants of the Roman Empire.

WESTERN PROVINCES

From the wealthy and long-established provinces of south-west France and Spain, to the more recent acquisitions of Gaul, Britain and the

The Cupid Dolphin mosaic from the Roman palace at Fishbourne, West Sussex. The palace, which is the largest residential Roman building in Britain, dates to as early as 75 CE, although its sophisticated coloured mosaics were probably laid c.160 CE. It is thought that the palace was built for a pro-Roman local chieftain, who ruled a number of local territories during the first years of the conquest.

Germanies, Roman rule brought the benefits of widespread peace and commerce. Roman culture laid a strong and long-lasting imprint on these territories. Wherever they settled, the Romans founded new cities, with grid-plan street layouts, amphitheatres, temples and municipal baths. Elaborate aqueducts brought fresh drinking water to the cities, and well-engineered roads and bridges eased communication between them. Many of these Roman foundations, including London, Paris and Bonn, remain important cities to this day.

Subject peoples adopted many Roman luxuries with great enthusiasm. Bathers were enjoying the hot springs at Bath by as early as *c.*65 CE, and throughout the empire the new local upper class quickly adopted the luxury and display introduced by their Roman overlords. The Roman idyll of the country villa became widespread in Roman Gaul during the lifetime of Augustus, reaching Britain a century later. Even in this

Ruins of the ancient fortress of Masada, situated at the top of a rock plateau on the edge of the Judaean desert, Israel. Between 37 and 31 BCE, King Herod the Great, the Roman client king of Judaea, built two palaces on the mountain and fortified Masada. According to the Romano–Jewish historian Josephus, Masada was besieged by Roman troops from 73 to 74 CE at the end of the First Jewish–Roman War. The siege ended in the mass suicide of the 960 Jewish zealots who were hiding there.

barbaric, distant land, the wealthy could enjoy the amenities of elegant gardens, mosaic floors and hypocaust heating, and partake in pursuits such as banqueting and hunting.

EASTERN PROVINCES

Rome took control of Asia Minor, Egypt and the Levant in the 1st and 2nd centuries BCE, acquiring some of the wealthiest territories of the Mediterranean world, and some of the most sophisticated and urbanized cultures. The common language spoken in these regions was not Latin, but Greek, which was superimposed on myriad local languages, religions and cults. The Pax Romana allowed trade and agriculture to flourish, and the lavish buildings and monuments of the early centuries CE bear ample testimony to the prosperity of Rome's Eastern provinces. Roman occupation made little difference to the already vibrant cultural life of the region.

By the 2nd century BCE, the provinces had woven themselves into the heart of the Roman Empire, and the distinction between provincials and Romans had diminished; an increasing number of emperors, senators, citizens and soldiers came from provincial backgrounds.

TRIER

Trier, in the Moselle valley, is an eloquent monument to Rome's provincial might, a projection of Roman power, and an assertive statement of Roman values and the Roman way of life in a frontier district of north-west Europe.

TRIER (FORMERLY TREVES) was an ancient settlement of the Treveri, a Celtic-Germanic tribe who were subdued by Julius Caesar in the 1st century BCE. Their presence is testified by various religious sanctuaries near the city, including the temple of Lenus Mars, a Romanized native god. Trier, hitherto a remote outpost, began its rise to prominence when the Roman general Agrippa built the road from Lyon to Cologne in 30 BCE.

Following Augustus's visit to Gaul from 16 to 13 BCE, the newly founded city was named Augusta Treverorum, and was constructed with a typical Roman grid street plan. Around this time a bridge was built near the place where the River Saar empties itself into the Moselle and, substantially rebuilt in the 2nd century CE, its stone piers survive to the present day.

Positioned on the River Moselle, with easy access to the Rhine and the military encampments there, the town flourished. It rose to prominence in the 2nd century CE when it was the seat of the procurator of Gallia Belgica, Germania Superior and Germania Inferior. As a major administrative centre, the city is thought to have had as many as 50,000 inhabitants, with a large forum (measuring 275 x 135 m/900 x 443 ft), which was used for markets, and its size indicates that it was also an important commercial centre. It also had an amphitheatre for gladiatorial contests and a circus for horse racing. The Barbara Thermen (Barbara Baths) were the largest Roman bath complex north of the Alps, and were served by the aqueducts constructed around this time. The city lay at the centre of a rich territory, and was surrounded by luxurious villas and country estates. There was early vine culture in the Moselle valley and a thriving cloth trade.

However, the city's easily accessible location also made it vulnerable to attack from the Germanic tribes on the other side of the Rhine, and defensive precautions were taken in the late 2nd century CE when a 6.4 km (4 mile)-long wall was built, punctuated by fortress-like gates. The massive Porta Nigra, which was built entirely without mortar (only iron pegs hold the sandstone blocks together), is a dauntingly impressive symbol of the city. From 260–74 CE, Trier may have been the capital, or at least the second city after Cologne, of the independent Gallic Empire, under Postumus, which was a breakaway part of the empire that functioned as a de facto separate state from 260–74 CE.

At the end of the 3rd century CE, Trier was made capital of the prefecture of Gaul and became the main imperial residence in the west. In the 4th century CE, the city had between 60,000 and 80,000 inhabitants, and six emperors ruled the Western Empire from there. Under Constantine the Great (c.280–337 CE) it became a centre for the spread of Christianity

The Porta Nigra (Black Gate) in Trier, Germany, was built in grey sandstone after 170 CE. It was originally planned to include two four-storied towers, but was never completed. It was part of a system of four city gates, which stood at each side of the roughly rectangular city. The Porta Nigra guarded the northern entrance.

north of the Alps, and Constantine constructed a great brick cathedral there, begun in 326 CE. The Aula Palatina basilica, an administrative and legal building, was built as part of the imperial palace complex during the reign of Constantine, as well as the imperial baths, a grandiose vision that, after 30 years of expensive construction work, was never actually completed. Trier was the location of an important mint and its court became a centre of learning.

In the early 4th century CE, the capital of the prefecture was moved to Arles, reflecting a decline in the city's importance, and by 459 CE it had been seized by the Franks, a Germanic tribe. Trier's Roman era had ended, but the Romans had laid the foundations of a city that would re-emerge as an important Frankish centre. Like Trier, many of Europe's most important cities can trace their foundation to Rome.

WATER MANAGEMENT

Some of the most outstanding Roman remains that can be seen today are the magnificent arched aqueducts that span valleys and straddle rivers, and were originally built as part of Rome's ambitious scheme to bring fresh water to its settlements for baths, latrines, fountains and private households.

ROME'S WATER MANAGEMENT system had its roots in the methods developed in Ancient Greece to collect and distribute water. However, no previous system could match the sophistication of Rome's hydraulic engineering. Some towns and cities, such as Pompeii, had their own water sources, such as aquifers and springs, and the Romans simply had to construct cisterns for water storage. Other cities needed water to be piped in, and in Rome itself, with its booming population and passion for ornamental fountains and grandiose bath complexes, the demand for water was high.

The spectacular arched bridges, some of which still stand today, only account for a small proportion of Rome's aqueducts; most water was piped underground. Roman engineers simply applied the principle of gravity, creating a gentle downward slope from source to destination – the arched structures were necessary to maintain the downward momentum when crossing valleys or gullies, but because they were extremely ambitious structures, engineers kept their use to an absolute minimum, devising long detours if necessary. Aqueducts totalling 507 km (315 miles) in length supplied Rome itself; 433 km (269 miles) ran underground.

Subterranean tunnels were highly labour-intensive to create. Once the route of the aqueduct had been laid out, a series of shafts were dug, from which the tunnelling could begin. The shafts were also used for extracting rubble and sending down building materials. Cranes were deployed to lower stone blocks, probably quarried locally, which were used to line the tunnel walls. If no stone was locally available, bricks or concrete could also be used. The tunnel was lined with *opus signinum*, a mortar composed of crushed tiles and amphorae, which acted as a waterproof layer.

Arched overground aqueducts were built of stone, concrete, bricks, mortar and tiles, and were constructed on wooden scaffolding. They generally had two, occasionally three, tiers of narrow arches, optimal for weight bearing, and the conduit, which was roofed, ran along the top level of the aqueduct. Massive pillars supported the entire structure. Once the aqueducts had been constructed, a team of specialists had to maintain them and ensure that the water was clean, clearing the channels and removing blockages. Covered sedimentation tanks were incorporated along the routes of aqueducts to help reduce waterborne debris.

Rome's first aqueduct, the Aqua Appia, opened in 312 BCE. By the 3rd century CE, the city had 11 aqueducts, delivering an average of about 900

The Pont du Gard aqueduct was built in the 1st century CE to carry water more than 50 km (31 miles) to the Roman colony of Nemausus (Nîmes). The aqueduct only descends by 12.6 m (41.3 ft) over its entire length, a feat of precision engineering. The main construction work lasted for 10–15 years, and the aqueduct encompasses several hundred metres of tunnels, three basins and 20 bridges, of which the Pont du Gard is the most spectacular example.

litres (200 gallons) per person per day, mostly drawn from the springs and valleys of the River Anio, east of the Tiber. Water was piped into public distribution tanks; from here, the supply was subdivided and a network of lead pipes conveyed the water to licensed users. Constructing aqueducts and maintaining the water supply system was ruinously expensive, and was financed by a combination of public and private funds, with substantial contributions from the imperial coffers.

Copious water was piped in to Roman cities, but waste also had to be removed, and the Romans addressed this problem very early, constructing the Cloaca Maxima sewer, which flowed into the Tiber, in the 6th century BCE. Over time, the Romans built a network of sewers in Rome, most of which discharged into the Cloaca Maxima. By the 2nd century CE, many wealthy homes were connected directly to the sewers; poorer residents emptied pots into the sewers (or sometimes the streets) or visited public latrines. In smaller towns throughout the empire, which did not have public sewerage systems, sewage collectors were employed and human excrement was used as a fertilizer.

THE ROMAN VILLA

The idea of building a house away from the maelstrom of city life in the peace and quiet of the country compelled many wealthier Romans, who sought a domestic, contemplative retreat where clean air, beautiful views and freshly grown food would restore them. This rustic ideal has been perpetuated over the last two millennia, and contemporary owners of 'weekend homes' are following an ancient Roman tradition.

THE VILLA EVOLVED from a collection of rustic buildings, which probably originally served as a farmstead, into several different forms. The main factor they had in common was that the villa embodied a retreat from the city into the peace and quiet of the country. The *villa urbana* was a country home located within easy reach of the city; the *villa rustica* was a permanent country estate, connected with a self-supporting farm, with facilities for agricultural produce, such as a grape or olive press.

These two ideals – the idyllic retreat and the practical centre of agricultural activity – were often combined in the same villa. The more elegant ideals of a rustic retreat were represented in an open courtyard (atrium) surrounded by rooms for entertaining, dining and sleeping. The day-to-day business of the farm was kept out of sight and managed by slaves and a supervisor (*vilicus*). Sometimes, farm estates (*latifundia*) were very substantial businesses, and in these cases the villa was a practical farmhouse and centre of operations, lacking all luxuries.

In general, the *villa rustica* complex comprised three parts. The *pars urbana* was where the family lived. This consisted of a suite of rooms decorated with wall paintings and mosaics. There was often indoor plumbing and underfloor central heating, known as hypocaust. The *pars rustica* was the headquarters of the slaves, who worked on the surrounding farm, and the household servants. Living quarters for farm animals might also be located here. The *villa fructuaria* contained the all-important storerooms, where farm produce was held prior to transport and distribution.

The *villa urbana* allowed the rich and privileged to escape the frenzied pace of urban life for a night or two. Some were comparatively modest retreats, others were extremely lavish pleasure houses, such as Emperor Hadrian's magnificent villa at Tivoli. They were either situated in the cool serenity of Rome's surrounding hills or on the coast (*villa maritima*), where the villa-builders maximized the natural beauty of the setting by building on several storeys and following the contours of the land, with sweeping views of bays and cliffs.

Generally, the domestic part of a Roman villa opened on to the atrium, an open-roofed or partially roofed courtyard that was the centre of the household. Rainwater that entered through the roof was collected in a central pool. The *tablinum* was a reception area, which was generally separated from the atrium by columns, a doorway or curtains. Inside the

Hadrian's Villa at Tivoli was built by the Emperor Hadrian as a rural retreat from Rome between 117 and 138 CE. The complex constituted an elaborate ideal city, comprising residential buildings, recreational facilities, extensive gardens and reflective pools, all harmoniously blending to form a serene and contemplative oasis, away from the hurly-burly of the capital. The buildings that were specifically intended for the emperor and his court comprised the Maritime Theatre, the Imperial Palace, the Winter Palace, the Latin and Greek Libraries and the Golden Square – a vast peristyle surrounded by a two-aisled portico.

villa, ingenious wall paintings utilized bright colours and perspective, and occasionally deployed *tromp l'oeil* effects to create the optical illusion of size. Mosaic floors ranged from functional patterns to highly decorative designs, incorporating mythological scenes, wild beasts or flora and fauna.

Every wealthy residence had a peristyle, a colonnaded courtyard, which complemented the rooms around the atrium, and gave them access to daylight – window glass was a rarity and apertures were therefore very small. It was usually embellished with fountains and plants. Romans refined the Greek concept of ornamental gardens to create formal layouts, pruned trees, water displays and statuary.

During the imperial era, Rome's more privileged subject peoples embraced the classic villa as a symbol of the new Roman lifestyle, and elites were keen to demonstrate their sophistication by living in them. The Fishbourne Roman 'palace' near Chichester in southern England is a classic Roman villa, probably occupied by the Roman client-king Cogidubnus. In this, it was the precursor of the English country house – a seat of power of a local magnate.

Roman villas ranged from modest suburban retreats to substantial farmhouses and grandiose rural palaces. In every case, however, they offered Romans, and their subject peoples, the opportunity to enjoy the perceived pleasures and benefits of rural life.

ROMAN ROADS

Cutting as straight a line as possible through all kinds of territory, Roman roads built upon ancient routes and a huge number of new ones were constructed to create a transport network that was fit for an empire. The ambition of Roman engineers knew no bounds, creating more than 40,000 km (25,000 miles) of roads, supplemented by bridges and tunnels, which greatly assisted the movement of armies, people and goods.

ROME'S FIRST MAJOR ROAD was the Appian Way, constructed from 312 BCE, and covering 196 km (122 miles) from Rome to Capua. It was built with very little concession to geographical obstacles, and became a model for future constructions. At the peak of Rome's development, 29 great military highways radiated out from the city, and the Roman Empire's 113 provinces were connected by 372 great roads. There were three types of road: *via publica*, *via privata* and *via vicinale*. The *viae publicae* were the main roads, which were maintained at public expense. *Viae privatae* were secondary roads, which might be paved or gravelled, and were constructed by private individuals who could choose to allow members of the public to access them. *Viae vicinales* were country lanes that ran between villages, and were constructed by a mixture of private and public funding.

Before the building of major roads, extensive surveys of the terrain were undertaken, and various methods were utilized to clear as many natural obstructions as possible: marshes were drained, rivers diverted, land was cleared and forests were cut down. Major roads were a standard 4.2 m (13.8 ft) wide, which allowed the passage of two-wheeled vehicles. First, a trench was dug, and a foundation of rough gravel, crushed brick and clay was laid between kerbstones. A layer of finer gravel was added, mixed with lime-based concrete, and then the road was surfaced with blocks or slabs of dressed stone, cobbles or paving stones of basalt or limestone, or simply topped with a further layer of gravel. Roads were designed with a camber towards the edges so that rainwater would run off, and sometimes drains and drainage channels were added as well. Pedestrian pathways ran alongside the road, and kerbstones prevented wheeled traffic from straying on to the footpaths.

Bridges and tunnels were essential means of negotiating intractable natural features. Roman bridges were built to last, using massive stone piers, topped with stone blocks or concrete and brick. The bridge at Narni in Umbria, for example, is 180 m (590 ft) long, and spans four massive semicircular arches. Tunnels were important ways of negotiating mountains, and were constructed with great precision. The tunnel at Cumae near Naples, built in the 1st century BCE, is an impressive 1 km (0.62 miles) in length. Tunnels were generally constructed by excavating from both ends, with inspection shafts drilled down at regular intervals, which could also be used for excavating rubble.

A Roman road at Leptis Magna in Libya. Leptis's two main roads intersected under the massive four-way Arch of Septimius Severus, built in the 2nd century CE. Leptis stood at a major crossroads: one road ran east–west between Alexandria and Carthage, while the Cardo Maximus connected the city to its buffer zone of fortified farms to the south, a distance of some 72 km (45 miles).

Milestones were set at regular intervals. The modern word 'mile' derives from the Latin *milia passuum*, meaning 'one thousand paces', approximately 1,476 m (1,614 yards). Each milestone was inscribed with the number of the mile relative to the road on which it was placed, and the distance to the Roman Forum was also added. Non-military travellers could rest at government-maintained way stations (*mansiones*). Private houses near roads offered hospitality and became *tabernae* – hostels that provided food, drink and overnight accommodation.

Solidly built, well maintained and penetrating to the most remote outposts, Rome's roads were an essential tool in both the expansion and consolidation of the Roman Empire, facilitating the movement of troops, officials and merchants. They were, effectively, the arteries of empire.

ROMAN GLASSWARE

From the 1st century CE, with the advent of glass-blowing, the Romans became the master glassworkers of the ancient world. They not only became expert mass producers of glass vessels, which permeated Roman life, but they also experimented with refined techniques, such as gold leaf interlays and cameo-like decorations, to create exquisite objects d'art.

GLASS, WHICH RELIES ON HEAT to fuse soda, silica and lime, predates the Romans by more than 1,500 years. In the Republican period, glassworkers probably learned their techniques from Greek colonists in southern Italy. Glass was usually opaque because of the high number of bubbles within the glass that resulted from the firing process. It was made by casting, mainly using a Hellenistic technique known as 'sagging', whereby the molten glass was placed over a convex mould. These vessels were characterized by rich, dark colours, such as emerald green, peacock blue and dark cobalt blue.

Glass-blowing, a new technique whereby glass was blown while it was still hot through a long, hollow iron rod, appeared in the first half of the 1st century CE. It developed in the Syria–Palestine region, and is thought to have been brought to Rome by craftsmen and slaves. The blowing technique allowed the glassworker unrivalled creativity and versatility, totally liberating him from the technical restrictions of the glass casting process. A variety of extraordinarily intricate objects, such as delicately fashioned fruits and animals, could be made in glass. At around this time, the trend for strong colours died out altogether, and colourless glass began to dominate the more expensive end of the glass market. Since glass could now be blown into carved moulds, the mass production of certain designs was possible; glass ceased to be the preserve of the very wealthy and was increasingly widely used.

Side A (the reverse) of the Portland Vase, made in Italy c.15–25 CE, an amphora of translucent dark cobalt blue and opaque white cameo glass. The exact significance of the figures is not certain, but it is believed that the vase depicts a scene from Greek mythology – the wedding of the king of Aegina, Thetis, and the sea nymph Peleus.

Glass permeated every aspect of Roman daily life. Roman ladies used delicate glass bottles for cosmetics, perfumes and unguents. Merchants and traders used glass bottles and jars for storing and shipping food and drinks. Cheaper glass was made in pale shades of blue, green and yellow. Two-handled drinking cups, with carved handles and carved decorations, became widely used. More elaborate decorations included the use of gold leaf, which was sandwiched between two layers of glass and used to create delicate pictorial designs. Small purpose-made glass tiles, *tesserae*, usually in shades of yellow, blue and green, were made specifically for use in mosaics.

The Portland Vase

This finest known example of Roman cameo glass-cutting, a short-lived experiment in Roman glassware, was probably made around 15–25 CE. The vase, which is about 25 cm (10 in) high, has a very dark blue body, with a finely carved layer of white glass covering the entire lower half of the vase, beneath the handles. This outer layer was carved in fine detail to show, in white relief against the dark background, six human figures lounging on rocks and leaning against pillars, a cherubim and a large snake, all set within a landscape, indicated by trees. It is thought that this technique was achieved by blowing

an elongated bubble of blue glass, which was dipped while still glowing hot into a vat of molten white glass, and then blown together. The pictorial scene was then carved on the outer white layer. This stunning object has had an extremely chequered history. It was discovered in Italy, sold to the Duchess of Portland and loaned to the British Museum.
In 1854, a drunken Irish university student smashed the glass display case and Portland Vase to smithereens. It was painstakingly reassembled, but in 1948 it was discovered that 37 fragments had not been included in the Victorian repair effort. It was repaired again, but when it began to deteriorate, a further restoration project was undertaken in 1988.

THE JULIO-CLAUDIAN DYNASTY

Augustus was a highly effective emperor, but his four successors presided over some of Rome's most tumultuous history. Paranoid, jealous, egotistical and cruel, their reigns – some of which started promisingly with military conquests, administrative reforms and public building projects – invariably descended into chaos and cruelty. Their extravagance and licentiousness permeated Roman life, corrupting Rome's traditional ideals.

THE CLAUDIANS WERE one of the oldest families in Rome, while the Julians claimed descent from Aeneas who, according to the Roman poet Virgil, was the mythical ancestor of Romulus and Remus. When the Emperor Augustus married his third wife, Livia Drusilla, these two illustrious dynasties were brought together.

AUGUSTUS 27 BCE–14 CE

Following his victory in the civil war against Mark Antony and Cleopatra, Augustus became the first citizen of Rome, a city that was in turmoil. The Senate granted him almost total power, and he set about an ambitious programme of reform. After years of conflict and civic upheaval, Augustus believed that the city of Rome was in a state of moral decay and dissolution, and he reached back to an idealized vision of the Roman Republic, restoring the traditions of the old religions, reinstating the Secular Games, and cultivating a reverence for Roman history. He

Marble bust of Emperor Augustus, Capitoline Museum, Rome.

211

reformed the army and the bureaucracy, introducing tax reforms, and embarked on an ambitious programme of public works and building in Rome itself. By these means he established the Pax Romana, a period of relative peace throughout the empire.

TIBERIUS 14–37 CE

His reluctant heir was his stepson Tiberius, who was in his 50s. Tiberius had already proved his reputation as an effective military commander, but he was a severe disciplinarian who lacked the popular touch. Haughty and unyielding, he was not known for his generosity, giving few public shows and beginning public work projects that he did not complete. Increasingly paranoid, he initiated a growing number of treason trials. Beset by a dominant mother and grief-stricken following the death of his son, he withdrew from Rome altogether and retired to the island of Capri in 26 CE, leaving the day-to-day running of the empire to his advisor, the prefect of the Praetorian Guard, Sejanus. It was rumoured that his time on Capri was spent indulging in sexual orgies, and by the time of his death he was universally unpopular.

Bust of Tiberius, Romisch-Germanisches Museum, Cologne.

GAIUS ('CALIGULA') 37–41 CE

Tiberius's great-nephew Gaius was only 24 years old, with no military experience. However, he was the son of Germanicus, the nephew of Tiberius, who was universally popular. The first years of his reign were promising: he completed many of the building projects started by Tiberius and increased the number of games and festivals. He also awarded a long-overdue bonus to the Praetorian Guard. However, he became increasingly egocentric, paranoid and vicious. His erratic behaviour was frequently inexplicable and bizarre: he attempted to

Portrait of Caligula (Gaius Julius Caesar Augustus Germanicus) from Palazzo Massimo in Rome.

name his favourite horse Incitatus as a consul; and he ordered an army that was intended to invade Britain to pick up shells on a beach in Gaul and return home. He even exiled his own sister, Agrippina the Younger, and was rumoured to have had sex with his sister Julia Drusilla, enforcing an elaborate cult of her as a goddess after her death. He promoted the worship of himself as a god, with a 'shrine' on the Palatine Hill. After four years of torturing and terrorizing the citizens of Rome, he was murdered by a tribune of the Praetorian Guard.

CLAUDIUS 41–54 CE

An overlooked nephew of Tiberius, Claudius appeared to be an unpromising prospect. He was uncoordinated and stammered, and it has been theorized that he suffered from cerebral palsy. However, he confounded his critics, who thought he was simple-minded: he invaded Britain in 43 CE, annexed Lycia, Mauretania and Noricum, built a new harbour at Ostia and established a civil service. He was, however, conceited and pedantic, and much given t o buying the support of the people with over-lavish displays. Like his predecessors, he was also paranoid and intemperate. He was manipulated and betrayed by two successive wives, and it is very likely that it was Caligula's sister, Agrippina, who was responsible for his death by poisoning, thereby securing the succession for her son, Nero.

Marble portrait of Nero from the Augustan area on the Palatine Hill.

NERO 54–68 CE

Nearly 17 when he became emperor, and with no military experience whatsoever, Nero was both sadistic and vain. Held in check by advisers for the first five years of his reign, he restored much of the Senate's power, reduced taxes and laid on a series of extravagant gladiatorial tournaments, concerts, chariot races and displays – he performed himself at many of these events. Increasingly, these public shows deteriorated into debauched parties, in which sadism and sex were combined with staged extravaganzas. He had his mother murdered and kicked his wife Poppaea to death. When a Great Fire destroyed much of the city in 64 CE, he conceived a megalomaniac plan to build a 'Golden House'. Following two major conspiracies, culminating in a coup in 68 CE, Nero committed suicide, proclaiming, 'What an artist dies in me.'

Bust of the Emperor Claudius, Naples Archaeological Museum.

CONQUEST AND CONSOLIDATION

The early expansion of Imperial Rome saw a shift westwards in the political centre of gravity, as Italy acquired enormous wealth from Rome's conquests, achieving an unprecedented level of prosperity. After consolidating Roman rule in the west, the Emperor Trajan turned his attention eastwards, and the Roman Empire reached its maximum extent.

AUGUSTUS HAD INHERITED an empire that had been built up over two-and-a-half centuries of Republican government, starting with the acquisition of Sicily, Rome's first province, in the 3rd century BCE. Augustus's victory at Actium was followed by the conquest of Egypt, which became part of the emperor's imperial domain. In addition, he conquered the northern Balkans, bringing the frontier of Rome to the great natural barrier, the River Danube. In the east, the River Euphrates marked the boundary between Rome and Parthia. Another river was to prove decisive in Rome's imperial expansion. Julius Caesar had invaded Gaul and made the Rhine the frontier of his new province, but a slice of unconquered territory still lay between Gaul and Italy in the Alpine region, which Augustus now absorbed into the empire. However, in 9 CE, a rebellion in the Balkans led to the withdrawal of Roman troops, and thee years later there was a military disaster in the Teutoburg Forest in Germany when three legions, 10 per cent of the Roman army, were wiped out, curtailing further plans for conquest.

From this point on, military victories were about defending and consolidating the Roman Empire in the face of riots, rebellions and uprisings. However, there was some expansion under the Julio-Claudian successors of Augustus. In some cases, client kingdoms were smoothly absorbed into the empire; this happened in Mauretania in 44 CE and

Thrace in 46 CE. Claudius invaded Britain in 43 CE, an undertaking that was partly to prevent Britain from becoming a haven for rebellious tribes, but also a bid for power and prestige by the emperor.

Nero died in 68 CE, and the Julio-Claudian dynasty came to an end. 69 CE was a year of dynastic struggle that has been aptly named 'the year of the four Emperors'. The Flavian emperors emerged from the turmoil, led by Vespasian, a competent leader who was called to Rome while he was campaigning in Judaea during the Great Jewish Revolt (69 CE). He was in turn succeeded by his son Titus, who was famous for finishing his father's work and besieging and capturing Jerusalem in 70 CE. He was succeeded by his brother Domitian, who failed both to conquer Caledonia (Scotland) and to gain a decisive victory in Dacia (Transylvania).

Trajan (*r*. 97–117 CE) was a highly successful soldier-emperor who presided over Rome's greatest expansion. He annexed the Nabataean kingdom, creating the province of Arabia Petraea. He finally conquered Dacia, and conducted a war against the Parthian Empire, which led to the annexation of Armenia and Mesopotamia.

ROMAN EXPANSION

27 BCE	Roman Senate grants Octavian the title of Augustus.
19 BCE	Augustus ends the Cantabrian Wars in Spain.
12 BCE	Roman forces cross the Rhine into Germania.
9 BCE	Pannonia is annexed and incorporated into Illyricum.
4 CE	Augustus adopts his stepson Tiberius as his son.
9 CE	Battle of the Teutoburg Forest; three Roman legions are ambushed and destroyed.
14 CE	Death of Augustus; succession of Tiberius. Mutinies in Germania are suppressed.
17 CE	Tiberius annexes the client kingdom of Cappadocia.
26 CE	Tiberius retires to Capri; Sejanus, prefect of the Imperial bodyguard, rules from Rome.
37 CE	Death of Tiberius.
38 CE	Succession of Gaius (Caligula).

41 CE	Suppression of rebellion in Mauretania. Assassination of Caligula and succession of Claudius. Judaean monarchy is restored under the Herodian dynasty.
43 CE	Roman conquest of Britain. Claudius annexes Lycia as a province.
54 CE	Claudius dies and is succeeded by Nero.
58 CE	Start of the Roman Parthian War (58–63 CE), when Rome supports the Armenian choice of king.
64 CE	Great Fire of Rome causes massive destruction of property and loss of life.
66 CE	First Jewish-Roman War; Jewish population revolts against Roman rule.
68 CE	Death of Nero; Galba, governor of Hispania Tarraconensis, is ruler of Rome.
69 CE	Praetorian Guard assassinates Galba. Otho is acclaimed ruler of Rome; he is defeated by Vitellius on the lower Rhine and commits suicide. Vespasian, commander of Roman forces in Egypt and Judaea, is recognized as ruler.
70 CE	Vespasian's son Titus sacks the city of Jerusalem and destroys the Second Temple.
73–4 CE	Siege of Masada in Judaea.
79 CE	Vespasian dies and is succeeded by Titus. Eruption of Mount Vesuvius, destroying the cities of Pompeii, Herculaneum and Stabiae.
81 CE	Titus dies and is succeeded by his brother, Domitian.
86 CE	Domitian's Dacian War; the Dacian king invades Moesia. In 88 CE, he accepts his status as a Roman client.
89 CE	Revolt in Germania Superior against Domitian's rule.
96 CE	Domitian is assassinated and succeeded by Nerva.
97 CE	A revolt by the Praetorian Guard forces Nerva to adopt Trajan as his heir.
98 CE	Nerva dies of natural causes and is succeeded by Trajan.
101 CE	First Dacian War; Rome invades Dacia.

102 CE   Dacian king affirms his loyalty to Rome, ending the war.

105 CE   Second Dacian War; Trajan invades Dacia following raids on
          Roman Moesia.

106 CE   Following the death of its king, Nabataea is annexed to empire
          as the province Arabia Petraea. The Dacian Wars end with the
          suicide of the Dacian king.

113 CE   Roman-Parthian Wars; Trajan launches an expedition against
          Parthia.

114 CE   Trajan deposes the Armenian king and organizes the province of
          Armenia.

116 CE   The provinces of Mesopotamia and Assyria, conquered from
          Parthia, are organized. Trajan captures the Parthian capital of
          Ctesiphon.

117 CE   Death of Trajan; Hadrian is accepted as ruler.

Hadrian's Arch at Jerash, Jordan. This 11 m (36 ft)-high triple-arched gateway was built in honour of the Emperor Hadrian and his visit to the city in the winter of 129–30 CE. The Arch was built some distance from the city walls in anticipation of the city's further expansion; this never happened, and it now stands marooned.

THE ROMAN ARMY

*Rome's empire-building was entirely dependent on the skill, discipline
and professionalism of the Roman army, which was not only effective
in conquering new territory, but was also dedicated to defending
Rome's borders and suppressing uprisings and rebellions.*

ROME'S FIGHTING FORCE was originally modelled on Greek
lines, as a conscripted civilian militia, with the higher echelons of
Roman society, the *equites*, forming the cavalry. The first 'manipular'
legions (from the Latin for 'handfuls') were groups of 130–160 men,
who were able to outmanoeuvre the phalanxes of their enemies. By
the time of the imperial era, the backbone of the army was the legion:
infantry units of around 5,000 men. Each legion was divided into
centuries of 80 men, commanded by junior officers, or 'centurions'.
Six centuries made up a cohort, and there were ten cohorts to a legion.

The growth of the empire and the establishment of Roman provinces
overseas meant that the legions had to develop permanent bases on
the frontiers of empire, resulting in a shortage of manpower. Emperor
Augustus reorganized the army, reducing the number of legions to 28,
increasing the minimum length of service to 25 years and creating a
military treasury. In this way, he created a professional standing army,
with citizen conscription only necessary in times of emergency.

Auxiliaries fought alongside the legionaries. These were non-Roman
peoples who had been recruited from all over the empire. They operated
in cohorts of between 500 and 1,000 men under the command of a
Roman officer. They were less well paid than Roman soldiers, and were
expected to serve for longer periods, but on discharge they were granted
Roman citizenship. In the imperial era, the auxiliaries also supplied
Rome's cavalry needs, probably because there was a limited officer class
of *equites* in Rome, and the recruiting, training and equipping of cavalry
officers was seen as an unnecessary expense when excellent native cavalry

was available.

Soldiers fought mainly with a short sword and throwing javelin, and were protected by a rectangular wooden shield, covered by canvas or leather, and body-armour. They also wore an iron helmet with neck and cheek guards. A Roman soldier was expected to march 32 km (20 miles) a day, carrying all his armour and equipment (weighing about 27 kg/60 lb). Roman soldiers were well trained and highly disciplined, and therefore able to maintain their formations in the heat of battle.

The typical Roman formation was the three-line system, with the least seasoned men making up the front rank, and the veterans at the back. On the command of *'cuneum formate'*, legionaries would form a wedge and charge at the enemy, opening up their lines. They could also deploy their interlocking shields, held over their heads and in front of their bodies to form an impenetrable barrier, known as the *testudo*, or tortoise. This was used when approaching the walls of the enemy in siege warfare. Cavalry was typically deployed on the flanks of the infantry in battle, used to protect and screen the infantry in the early stages, and later to harry the flanks and rear of the enemy infantry. Horses were also used to mop up and clear retreating armies.

Roman soldiers were experts at siege warfare, and deployed many specialist weapons. *Onagri* (catapults) and *ballistae* were essentially stone-throwers, which were capable of wreaking terrible carnage. Smaller *scorpiones* fired bolts. Battering rams and siege towers were widely deployed, and sappers were expert at undermining defensive walls.

Under the early empire, legionaries were paid 900 sesterces a year, and signed up for 20 years, during which time they were forbidden to marry. Their pay was raised in the late 1st century CE and eventually they were allowed to marry and live with their families. This may have increased their loyalty to the army, or it may simply have been a measure to ensure that enough men were recruited to serve in the military. On discharge, they were given a generous bonus.

Most soldiers spent very little of their time on campaign. Most of it was taken up with military duties: training, patrolling and maintaining equipment. They also acted as a kind of police force for the military

A fragment of a 1st-century CE relief depicting the Praetorian Guard. In the imperial period, the Praetorian Guard was an elite force whose duty was to protect the emperor and Rome. At various times, the Praetorian Guard challenged imperial authority, and potential emperors were forced to gain its favour in order to retain power.

governors in the provinces, and played a crucial role in building the empire's infrastructure, constructing roads, bridges, walls and even entirely new cities. Up to the 3rd century CE, the army was spread thinly along the frontiers, with no reserve forces for emergencies, and was dominated by the cavalry. In the 3rd century CE, a mobile cavalry force was established; the army was eventually divided into fixed frontier troops and a more mobile field army that embraced cavalry and infantry.

Legionary Standard

Each legion was identified by a standard, which was a pennant, flag or banner attached to a pole, and carried by an aquilifer or standard-bearer. The most famous device on the legionary standard is the eagle (aquila), but others included the horse, Minotaur, wolf or boar. Legionaries took great pride in their standard, which was an important and highly visible rallying point in battle, often used to indicate tactics, or changes of formation or direction. When the general Germanicus led his troops into Germany in 16 CE to retrieve the standards lost in the Battle of the Teutoburg Forest in 9 CE, he was revenging a terrible humiliation, rallying his troops and restoring a sense of loyalty and purpose to the legions.

Roman Ranks

Praetor Military commander of a legion or grouping of legions; also a government official.

Legatus legionis Overall legion commander, usually a senator.

Tribune Second-in-command of the legion. Lesser tribunes served as junior officers.

Prefect Third-in-command of the legion. There were various types. The *praefectus equitarius* commanded a unit of cavalry.

Primus pilus Most senior centurion, acting as commanding centurion for the first cohort (the leading cohort).

Centurion Commander of the century. Prestige varied based on the cohort they supervised.

Decurio Commander of the cavalry unit.

Aquilifer Standard-bearer of each legion – a position of much prestige.

Signifer In charge of financial matters and decorations for each century.

Optio Equivalent to a sergeant, second-in-command of the centurion.

Decanus Equivalent to a corporal, commanded an eight-man tent party.

Munifex The lowest of the trained rank and file.

THE ROMAN FORT

A deterrent military presence was needed on Rome's vulnerable borders and in regions that were prone to uprisings. Accordingly, the Romans constructed both substantial permanent forts and temporary military camps, the latter being intended to house men and equipment rather than to withstand sustained military attack.

THE LATIN WORD *castrum* described any building or land that was used as a fortified military camp. These could range from permanent legionary forts to temporary encampments. When on campaign, the army was required to construct their own camps, and they had specialist engineers who were responsible for this duty, who requisitioned soldiers to undertake manual work. Choosing from a selection of standard plans, and paying close attention to the terrain, they were able to construct a temporary camp within a matter of hours.

More permanent forts were built within provinces, as a means of controlling conquered people and deterring rebellion, and on provincial frontiers to prevent incursions from 'barbarians'. Some provinces, such as Britain, required a permanent military presence to maintain control, and remains of more than 400 Roman forts have been found there. Even the very largest forts were not self-supporting, and as a result settlements sprang up in the vicinity to supply the soldiers' needs; forts and their associated settlements often formed the nucleus of medieval towns.

Permanent forts became more standardized during the reign of Augustus (*c.*27 BCE–14 CE). Standard forts, which could house a legion or a smaller unit, were typically rectangular, with rounded corners. First, a ditch was dug around the perimeter and the excavated material was used to construct a sloping earth rampart. The walls, initially a palisade of wooden stakes and later constructed of stone or brick, were set above the rampart, with at least three principal gates and watchtowers set at regular intervals. The excavated ditch also served as a moat to deter invaders.

Gates could be closed using wooden doors, possibly metal plated, which were secured by a crossbar on the inside.

Within the inner periphery of the fort there was an unobstructed space; this was where enemy missiles usually fell, doing little harm. Every camp included a main street, which ran north–south and was very wide. The heart of the fort was the *principia*, which lay at the junction of the main *via principalis* and the *via praetorian*, which ran at right angles. The *principia* complex had an open court at the front, behind which was a hall, shrine and offices. The precious legionary standards were located here and the fort's cash reserves were kept in a secure underground vault. The commanding officer addressed his troops from a raised platform (*tribunal*) outside the *principia*, and courts martial were held there. The commander's residence (*praetorium*) was located next to the *principia* or behind it. Other central buildings included accommodation for senior

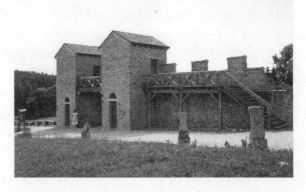

Reconstructed east gate of a Castrus Stativum, a permanent camp at Welzheim, Germany. The walls of permanent forts had three principal gates and watchtowers set at regular intervals. Gates had two arched entrances, which could be closed using heavy wooden doors, secured by a crossbar from inside. Gates were also protected by their own watchtowers and by a line of ditches projecting out from the walls.

officers (tribunes), workshops, equipment stores, a hospital and a water storage cistern. Some of the very largest forts also included the amenities of a small town, including shops, a marketplace and Roman baths.

Radiating out from the central plaza were barracks for the legionaries and cavalry. In permanent camps, these were constructed of wood or stone and heated with fireplaces. In less permanent camps, the men slept in tents. Water was essential for the life of the camp and the choice of location was dependent on water sources such as streams, springs and wells. The soldiers used public latrines, a row of seats placed over a channel of running water; the *praetorium* and high-ranking officers had their own latrines. Kitchens were set up near the walls to minimize the risk of fire. On the outermost periphery of the camp, closest to the gates, were the granaries, stores and workshops, and in some of the larger camps, bathhouses.

WOMEN IN THE ROMAN EMPIRE

Rome was a patriarchal society, and women were subordinate to the all-powerful paterfamilias. They were firmly consigned to the domestic sphere, but some educated upper-class women were able to reach their own accommodations with fathers and husbands, making a valuable contribution to society.

ROMAN SOCIETY revolved around the family and the role of women was generally perceived within the familial context, as wives and mothers. They lived a home-based existence, devoting their time to housekeeping, child-rearing and crafts such as weaving and spinning – although educated upper-class women were able to explore their interest in literature and philosophy. Many girls went to elementary schools and learned to read and write, and elite families ensured their daughters were well educated in order to increase their appeal on the marriage market. Lower-class women, on the other hand, moved freely in the public sphere as they had to work for a living: usually as servants, shopkeepers, wet nurses (upper-class women never breastfed their children) or craftspeople.

Legally, a woman was obliged to have a male relation, usually her father, who acted on her behalf, and the purpose of this law was to keep all financial matters under male control, and to ensure that any inherited property was kept within the family. In reality, there were women who exercised some control over their own finances, and each family evolved its own way of dealing with these issues. The fact that husbands effectively had no legal jurisdiction over wives gave some women a measure of independence.

The law decreed that girls could be married as young as 12, capitalizing on their most fertile years and ensuring that they fulfilled their primary duty: to have children. The paterfamilias usually arranged his daughters' marriages. Divorces were easily obtained – there was no legal procedure, simply a statement of intent to divorce by either party – but male members of the family always retained custody of the children. Since fathers retained legal guardianship over their daughters even after marriage, they were able to reclaim her property after a divorce, keeping family fortunes intact. Second marriages were extremely common.

Roman history is full of tales of powerful, ruthless women who were able to manipulate their husbands in order to influence public affairs and shape their own destiny. The wives of Roman emperors were treated as 'first ladies', memorialized on coins and in sculptural portraits, and female relations were expected to project an image of a harmonious, loving family, even if that was very far from the truth – in 2 BCE, Augustus was forced to adhere to his own stringent legislation on adultery and exile his unfaithful daughter, Julia. The fact that women presided over imperial households brought them into the heart of power and government, which had not been the case in the Republican era. While some emperors' wives were certainly ambitious, ruthless and murderous, many of the scurrilous tales may simply have reflected discomfort at the unprecedented power these women possessed.

Roman men were frequently hypocritical about sex, upholding the ideal of the chaste Roman matron, and severely restricting the freedom of their own wives and daughters, while seeking out prostitutes, easily identifiable because they wore a toga. Most prostitutes were slaves or freedwomen, and while prostitution was legal, it was closely regulated and prostitutes were denied many civic rights. Many brothels were extremely squalid, but some prostitutes became celebrated and wealthy courtesans who cultivated elite patrons. Romans also assumed that actors and dancers would provide paid sexual services.

COSMETICS

The Romans revered the natural look as a sign of chastity, and many Roman men mocked women who were excessively made up. On the other hand, women in Ancient Rome were expected to look good, partly because their appearance was seen as a reflection of their husbands' status, and there was a thriving cosmetics industry. Some of the ingredients used in skin creams, such as crushed rose petals and honey, are uncontroversial, but less fragrant ingredients, such as vinegar, bile, animal urine and sulphur, were also used. A typical Roman remedy for spots was chicken fat and onion, while ground oyster shells were used as an exfoliant. A pale face was sought after, so women used chalk powder or white lead. Rouge was made using rose and poppy petals, red ochre or even crocodile dung. The Romans admired large eyes and long eyelashes, and kohl was the main eye make-up ingredient, which was applied using a rounded stick of glass, bone or wood. Eye shadows were made using malachite and azurite. Not surprisingly, since many cosmetics were extremely noisome, perfume was universally popular, and was made by macerating flowers and herbs in oil.

A Faiyum mummy portrait of a woman from Roman Egypt, with a ringlet hairstyle. Roman women wore their hair in increasingly complex styles in the late 1st century CE, including ringlets and nested plaits.

ROMAN BATHS

Bath complexes offered to soothe the body and stimulate the mind, as many bath complexes also incorporated lecture halls and libraries. Bathing was a social activity, and because they were so cheap, bathhouses provided a classless environment where the wealthy and powerful rubbed shoulders with common citizens. A daily necessity was elevated into a rejuvenating, social and stimulating ritual.

THE ROMANS INHERITED the custom of bathing from the Greeks, and bath complexes began to appear in Roman cities in the 2nd century BCE, and were soon found throughout the empire. The Romans departed from the more austere Greek model, elaborating the idea of baths to include total submersion, ranges of water temperature, swimming pools, and dry- and wet-sweating rooms. The *palaestra* was a colonnaded open courtyard where bathers could lounge or exercise, perhaps running, weightlifting, wrestling, boxing or playing ball games. In more elaborate complexes, visitors could also use the libraries, lecture halls and gardens leading off the *palaestra*. Baths were available to all, and charged the absolute minimum: 2 denarii (the smallest-value bronze coin).

A typical Roman bath complex incorporated an array of facilities: changing rooms; exercise rooms; a superheated dry-sweating room (*laconium*); a *caldarium* (hot room), heated but with a small waist-high basin of cold water with which the bathers could splash themselves; a *tepidarium* with a pool of tepid water; and a *frigidarium* (cool room), unheated and with a cold-water basin. The *frigidarium* was often large and imposing, with high ceilings, forming the heart of the bath complex.

The range of temperatures available in a Roman baths required an elaborate heating system. Underfloor (hypocaust) heating was fuelled by wood-burning furnaces, that sent warm air billowing under the floor, which was raised up to 6 m (19.7 ft) on hollow cylinders or bricks. Hollow rectangular tubes could also be placed in the wall, which carried the hot air that was circulated from the furnaces. From the 1st century CE, glass was available for windows, which aided a more refined regulation of the temperature.

Purpose-built aqueducts carried vast quantities of water to bath complexes, which was stored in huge reservoirs and cisterns. Large boilers fitted over the heaters were used to heat water, which was fed to the pools through lead pipes.

The local bathhouse was a meeting point which served a useful social function. People used the baths to relax and gossip, or catch up on the latest news. Visitors to the bathhouse usually arrived at about 2 pm, at the end of the Roman workday, stripped naked or donned special bathing attire, perhaps exercised to work up a sweat, then moved to the

The Stabian Baths in Pompeii date back as early as the 4th century BCE, though most of the remains that can be seen today are from the 1st century BCE. The establishment covers a total area of 3,500 sq m (37,675 sq ft), and was divided into two adjacent sections, reserved for men and women, and a colonnaded courtyard, the palaestra. *Bathers undressed in the* apodyterium *(changing room), then enjoyed a* tepidarium *(warm bath),* caldarium *(hot bath), finishing in the* frigidarium *(cold bath), which was richly decorated with frescoes of garden scenes and a domed ceiling. Men's facilities were on the west of the* palaestra, *women's on the east. Both sides shared a heating plant, with furnaces and three large cylindrical boilers. On the west side of the* palaestra *was a substantial swimming pool, which was 1.5 m (4.9 ft) deep. The* destrictarium, *the dressing room for the pool complex, was where athletes undressed and massaged themselves with oil before exercising in the courtyard. They would scrape off the oil before washing and plunging into the pool.*

tepidarium, and from there to the *caldarium*, or vice versa; the idea was they would sweat out dirt, and slaves would then rub olive oil into their skin, using a *strigil*, a curved metal instrument to scrape off the dirt. At some point, they might visit the *laconium*, which was similar to a sauna. The *frigidarium* was a welcome way of cooling down, and visitors could also then use the swimming pool, or perhaps avail themselves of the services of a professional masseuse.

Roman grandees sponsored bath buildings, and strove to outdo each other in expenditure and deluxe innovation, even waiving entrance fees on certain days. Some baths were much more luxurious than others, and different bath complexes went in and out of fashion. Some bathhouses had reputations as less respectable establishments where prostitutes solicited men. In some baths, men and women bathed together naked, but as that was not invariably the case, it was probably a matter of personal choice.

A ROMAN CHILDHOOD

With high rates of infant mortality, many Roman parents must have regarded the early years of their children's lives as precarious. However, parents' attitudes to their children's upbringing was rigorous and socially cohesive, managing the transition from home-bound infancy to young adulthood in a series of preordained stages.

TWENTY-EIGHT PER CENT of all Roman children died before they reached their first birthday. The first nine days of a child's life were considered the most dangerous, and passing the nine-day threshold was celebrated with a *dies lustricus*, when the child was given its name and showered with gifts called *crepundia*, a selection of trinkets that included rattles, miniature tools and instruments. The auspicious day was celebrated with offerings of wine, incense and cakes, and boys received a *bulla*, two concave pieces of gold, fastened together and containing an amulet as protection against evil forces, which was hung around the child's neck. For the less wealthy, *bullae* were made of tin or leather. Girls wore a crescent moon-shaped amulet called a *lunula* until the eve of their marriage.

Roman parents did not indulge the vulnerability of childhood. They believed that their children needed to be moulded into young adults, sometimes by harsh means such as cold baths and corporal punishment, and since the power of the father was absolute, there was no challenge to disciplinarian treatment. It was essential that an absolute respect for authority, as well as a reverence for the gods and the paterfamilias, was instilled into the child.

Children of wealthy parents were looked after by wet nurses, and were taught by private tutors, called 'pedagogues'. Many children formed lasting bonds of affection with their nurses, who became their advisers and confidantes, and some wives even took their nurses into their households when they married.

An ivory doll, found in a sarcophagus at Tivoli, late 2nd century CE. Dolls had jointed arms and legs, and even had their own clothes and ornaments, much like modern Barbie dolls.

Children played with dolls made of clay or wax, and miniature carriages have also been found. There are many depictions of children playing with spinning tops, stilts, balls, and hoops and sticks. Board games, using dice, knucklebones and stone pieces, were popular with young and old alike. In upper-class homes, the mother taught her children the fundamentals of reading and writing until they reached the age of seven.

At this point, boys passed into the hands of teachers, but girls remained with their mothers, and were taught womanly skills such as spinning, weaving, sewing and household management.

Outside school hours, boys spent more time with their fathers. If they were plebeians, they learned about their father's work, and farmers' sons helped their fathers in the fields. In more upper-class families, the son stood by when their father entertained guests, learned their guests' names, and listened to their conversation. In this way, he acquired a practical knowledge of politics, and when he was old enough, he was sent to the Senate to hear the great orators debate. In pursuance of Rome's rugged notions of masculinity, he was trained in the use of arms and military exercises, and encouraged to take part in manly sports, such as swimming, riding, wrestling and boxing.

Girls passed seamlessly into marriage and adulthood after they reached the age of 12. For boys, however, the transition was marked by a special ceremony some time between the ages of 14 and 17, when a boy discarded his *bulla* and childhood tunic, made sacrifices and then clothed himself in a white man's tunic and a *toga virile* (man's toga). The boy was then taken to the Forum, where his name was registered and he became a fully fledged Roman citizen.

Schooling

The availability of education was dependent on parents' wealth, and approximately only 20 per cent of Roman citizens were literate. Whereas earlier Republican notions of education had been loose and informal, by the time of the conquest of Greece in 146 BCE, Romans were appropriating the Greek education system, and many Greek slaves came to Rome as tutors. Typically, boys did not go to school until they were seven. Here, they were taught by a *litterarius*. The syllabus included reading, writing using a wax tablet and stylus, and basic arithmetic using an abacus. At the age of 12 or 13 they went to a grammar school, where a *grammaticus* taught arts and poetry, Greek, and ultimately rhetoric and philosophy, although very few boys studied these latter subjects. Education was by rote, and corporal punishment was frequently deployed. Schools rented out space wherever they could, and classrooms might be located behind shops, in the colonnades of bathhouses, or other public spaces. Schools were open seven days a week, although frequent religious holidays must have offered some relief.

ROMAN DINING

Food was a status symbol in Ancient Rome and dining with friends was the main social event on every Roman's calendar. Only the upper classes had kitchens at home, so most Romans purchased food from vendors. A wide range of ingredients, skilfully cooked by slaves in a domestic kitchen and served to guests who reclined on couches in an elegant dining room, was a sure sign of wealth and status.

THE ROMAN STAPLE was bread, made from spelt, wheat or corn (which was sometimes distributed as a state dole for citizens). There were many bakers throughout the city of Rome, turning out a variety of breads that ranged from flat, round loaves to honey- and wine-soaked breads, and loaves that were cooked with nuts and honey in clay moulds.

There were usually three daily meals: breakfast (*ientaculum*); an early luncheon (*prandium*); and dinner (*cena*), which was eaten in the late afternoon. Poorer people ate bread sprinkled with salt for breakfast, while the rich ate bread, wheat pancakes, dates and honey. Lunch was a simple meal of bread, salad, olives and cheese. This was followed by a midday siesta, and the streets of the capital emptied out. The main dining event of the day was dinner, which might take as long as four hours if guests were attending.

For poorer people, dinner probably consisted of a kind of barley porridge mixed with vegetables, and legumes – peas, beans and lentils. This was a marked contrast to the wealthier Roman citizens, whose simplest dinners were divided into at least three parts: the *gustatio* (appetizer), the *mensae primae* (main course) and the *mensae secundae* (dessert). Appetizers comprised oysters and shellfish, pickled vegetables, lettuce, eggs and piquant sauces. Meat, which was expensive and only regularly enjoyed by the upper classes, was mainly poultry and wild game, such as rabbit, hare and boar, supplemented by birds like geese and ducks, and even small birds such as blackbirds, thrushes, doves and magpies.

In addition, more affluent Romans enjoyed a wide range of vegetables, including asparagus, turnips, carrots, onions, leeks and cucumber. Desserts comprised fruits, including apples, figs, plums, dates, cherries, grapes and peaches. The addition of whole carob pods to desserts was very popular, as they added a chocolate-like flavour to dishes.

Food was boiled, grilled, stewed or roasted on a spit and was preserved by smoking, pickling or salting. The Roman palate obviously craved piquant flavours, as dinner ingredients were all enhanced by a wide range of spices and flavourings, including mint, coriander, honey, vinegar, celery, parsley, capers and pine kernels. The popular fermented fish sauce, garum, was a universal addition. Garum was made of fish intestines, which were fermented with salt to create a liquor that was evaporated down to a thick paste. It was exported all over the Roman world, and was considered to be an essential flavouring in much Roman cuisine.

Romans ate with their hands, sometimes supplemented with spoons and knives; they did not have forks. They held the plate in their left hand, using the right hand to take food. Upper-class Romans ate reclining, on low couches, which were angled upwards towards the dining table. Each couch was divided by cushions into three parts, which could accommodate three diners, and dining rooms were designed to hold three couches around a table, with the fourth side left empty, hence the name for a dining room, *triclinium*. A diner would recline on his left side, supported by his left elbow, which rested on the couch. The middle couch in the arrangement (*lectus medius*) was considered the most prestigious, and it was here that the most honoured guests would be seated. Women joined in these dinner parties, and dined on couches; children were expected to sit on stools.

Copious amounts of wine accompanied Roman dinners. Wine was always drunk diluted with water, and was often served spiced or sweetened with honey. The wine was mixed in a large bowl (*crater*) and then ladled into goblets. Toasts were frequently drunk and diners were expected to drain their glasses, which must have led to very heavy wine consumption – it was quite common for Romans to eat and drink to excess, vomit, then start again. At more elaborate dinner parties, musicians would provide entertainment.

Silver tableware from the Tivoli Hoard, mid-1st century BCE. *The hoard comprised 30 elegant utensils, including wine cups, a pitcher, a wine ladle and several spoons. Inscriptions on the drinking cups and ladle give the owner's name, 'Sattia, daughter of Lucius'. The hoard was probably buried as a result of the civil wars at the end of the Roman Republic.*

A Roman recipe for ostrich ragout with garum

This recipe is taken from *Apicius*, a collection of Roman recipes thought to have been compiled in the 1st century CE.

For boiled ostrich: pepper, mint, roast cumin, celery seed, dates or Jericho dates, honey, vinegar, passum, *garum, a little oil. Put these in the pot and bring to the boil. Bind with* amulum, *pour over the pieces of ostrich in a serving dish and sprinkle with pepper. If you wish to cook the ostrich in the sauce, add* alica.

You may prefer to roast or fry your ostrich, rather than boil it. Whichever method you choose, this sauce goes with it well. For 500g ostrich pieces, fried or boiled, you will need:

2 teaspoons flour
2 tablespoons olive oil
300ml *passum* [dessert wine]
1 tablespoon roast cumin seeds
1 teaspoon celery seeds
3 pitted candied dates
3 tablespoons garum or a 50g tin of anchovies
1 teaspoon peppercorns
2 tablespoons fresh chopped mint
1 teaspoon honey
3 tablespoons strong vinegar

Make a roux with the flour and 1 tablespoon of the olive oil, add the *passum*, and continue to stir until the sauce is smooth. Pound together in the following order: the cumin, celery seeds, dates, garum or anchovies, peppercorns, chopped mint, the remaining olive oil, the honey and vinegar. Add this to the thickened wine sauce. Then stir in the ostrich pieces and let them heat through in the sauce.

POMPEII: FROZEN IN TIME

The eruption of Mount Vesuvius that took place on 24 August 79 CE completely devastated three Roman towns in the Bay of Naples: Pompeii, Herculaneum and Stabiae. The deluge of volcanic material that engulfed the towns and killed many thousands of inhabitants also preserved an intact, and remarkable, record of the towns, their residents and their everyday lives.

POMPEII WAS A RELATIVELY PROSPEROUS Italian town, and probably typical of many other minor towns in the Roman Empire. Its wealth came from its port and agricultural hinterland, and during the late Republican era its residential areas expanded and important public buildings, such as the Stabian Baths, the *basilica* (stock exchange and law court) and the Temple of Jupiter, advertised its growing prosperity.

It was a medium-sized town of about 15,000–20,000 inhabitants, dominated by volcanic Mount Vesuvius, which rose about 10 km (6.2 miles) to the north. It was positioned on the coast and at the mouth of the River Sarno, making it a natural centre for trade and communications (subsequent post-volcanic changes to the coastline mean that it is now located nearly 2 km/1.25 miles away from the sea). Pompeii had already experienced an earthquake in 63 CE, probably one in a series of shocks that presaged the final eruption, and when Vesuvius wiped the town off the map it was, in effect, a giant building site, with a great deal of reconstruction work taking place on public and private buildings.

Seismic activity was common in the area, and it is probable that most of the residents ignored the minor quakes that preceded the eruption. But shortly after noon on 24 August, there was a deafening explosion and a mass of volcanic material was hurled violently upwards in a mushroom-shaped cloud, which rose more than 13 km (8 miles) into the atmosphere, instantly darkening the sky and blotting out the sun. Pliny the Younger (61–*c.*113 CE), the eyewitness who observed the eruption from across the Bay of Naples in Misenum and left an incomparably detailed account of the three fatal days, described it as being 'like an umbrella pine tree'. The volcanic debris was then carried south-eastwards directly over Pompeii and Stabiae, a nearby villa resort. The initial fallout was in the form of lapilli, small pumice stones that quickly accumulated to a depth of 3 m (9.8 ft) in the houses and gardens of Pompeii. The violent rain of debris caused many roofs to collapse, suffocating people left inside. During this first day, many residents were able to escape, being taken off the coast by boat.

At this stage, nearby Herculaneum was spared the fallout because of the direction of the prevailing wind. However, shortly after midnight, a cataclysmic volcanic mudslide submerged Herculaneum. At 6.30 am the following morning, a violent pyroclastic flow, a mixture of ash, lava and poisonous gases, rolled down the slopes of Vesuvius and engulfed Pompeii. Five times hotter than boiling water, it quickly asphyxiated all those who had been left behind. Most people died instantly, as superheated air burned their lungs and contracted their muscles, leaving their bodies in foetal positions. Earthquake shocks accompanied the eruption, destroying many buildings. The eruption finally ceased on the third day, and by this stage the town was buried by up to 4 m (13.2 ft) of debris.

When the amphitheatre at Pompeii was first excavated in 1815, it was found to be decorated with a remarkable series of colourful frescoes depicting wild animals and gladiators; within a few months of their discovery, the frescoes were destroyed by frost, although fortunately accurate drawings had been made. Other fragments of frescoes have been found all over the city, most notably in the house of Julia Felix, which leave an extraordinary record of everyday life; scenes depicted include a beggar, a boy being whipped, a man cleaning another man's shoes and merchants displaying their wares. Pompeii's famous erotic wall paintings do not necessarily indicate the presence of brothels; in fact, they are a ubiquitous decoration. Copious graffiti in the Forum bring back the lost voices of Pompeii; scurrilous, gossipy, malicious ('Chios, I hope your piles irritate you so they burn like they've never burned before'; 'Lucilla was making money from her body').

*'You could hear the shrieks of women, the wailing of infants,
and the shouting of men; some were calling their parents,
others their children or their wives, trying to recognize them
by their voices. People bewailed their own fate or that of
their relatives, and there were some who prayed for death
in their terror of dying. Many besought the aid of the gods,
but still more imagined there were no gods left, and that the
universe was plunged into eternal darkness for evermore.'*

PLINY THE YOUNGER

The most famous, and eloquent, remains from Pompeii are the plaster casts of the bodies of men, women and children, and animals. As excavators began to uncover human remains during the mid-19th century, they noticed that the skeletons were surrounded by voids in the compacted ash. By carefully pouring plaster of Paris into the spaces, the final contorted, agonized poses, clothing and terrified faces of the last residents of Pompeii came to life.

A fresco depicting a banqueting scene from the Casa dei Casti Amanti (House of the Chaste Lovers), Pompeii. The house forms part of a large insula, *which contains several small shops, and gets its name from the fresco depicting two couples reclining on couches during a banquet. This decorous image is in marked contrast to many frescoes in Pompeii, which are explicitly sexual.*

SHADES OF THE DEPARTED

The funeral monuments of Ancient Rome are eloquent testaments to both the Roman belief in the afterlife and the social status of the deceased, and their inscriptions articulate feelings of love, loss and grief. Roman funerary art, commissioned to memorialize the dead, remains one of the largest surviving bodies of evidence of Roman art.

THE ROMANS BELIEVED that the spirits of the dead were called the 'Manes'. It was thought that the Manes needed to be nourished with offerings of food and drink, and some graves even had tubes leading to the surface, through which these offerings could be conveyed. There was disagreement about where the dead actually lived: some thought they were taken deep into the underworld; others believed that they ascended to the heavens.

Wealthy Romans erected funerary monuments over their burials, and graves were located, by law, outside the city limits, where they lined the main arterial roads. In Rome itself, cemeteries grew up alongside the Via Appia. Communities of Jews and Christians were buried in catacombs, underground complexes of rock-cut graves.

Traditional burial rites were clearly ordained: the body was washed, anointed and laid out for burial. A coin was placed in the mouth of the corpse to pay for Charon the ferryman to transport the deceased over the River Styx, the river that carries the dead from the land of the living to the land of the dead. On the day of the funeral, the body would be conveyed, in a procession, on a funeral couch or a simple bier to the cemetery, where it would either be buried or cremated. The procession to the grave was an occasion for a public display of grief, and professional mourners and musicians might be employed to join the family. Sometimes, the procession took on a carnivalesque atmosphere, with professional actors dressing up as the ancestors of the deceased, or even impersonating the deceased. The funeral ended with a eulogy and a ritual feast.

'This memorial was made for Marcus Caecilius.
Thank you, my dear guest, for stopping at my abode.
Good luck and good health to you. Sleep without a care.'

FUNERARY INSCRIPTION
APPIAN WAY, <i>c.</i>140 BCE

Cremation was the dominant rite in Republican Rome, but by the 2nd century CE inhumation had become much more widespread. As inhumation became the predominant practice, increasingly elaborate sarcophagi (stone coffins), beautifully carved with mythological figures, were adopted by the very wealthy.

Commemoration was important to the Ancient Romans, and the feast of Parentalia, from 13 to 21 February, was set aside for remembering loved ones. Funerary monuments are extremely varied. At the grander end of the scale, emperors and rulers were memorialized with mausolea, frequently substantial buildings in their own right, such as the Mausoleum of Augustus built in 28 BCE in preparation for his death. Funerary altars were originally made to house cremation ashes, but subsequently made to memorialize the dead. Epitaphs on funerary altars listed the name of the deceased, sometimes their age and profession, and a few words of tribute. Epitaphs also normally mentioned the name of the person who had built the altar, emphasizing their relationship to the deceased, and the grief they had suffered (especially true of children's altars).

Tombstones were widespread throughout the empire, and epitaphs were used to highlight wealth, honour and status. They were frequently inscribed with the name of the deceased, a portrait, an inscription to 'Diis Manibus', the spirits of the dead, and sometimes an epitaph to the deceased, or a brief summary of their life. Soldiers who had died while serving the empire were honoured with a simple funerary stele, a rectangular slab of stone inscribed with the name, rank and unit of the dead soldier, as well as his age and years of service in the army. In some cases, when a soldier died in battle and his body had not been recovered, families erected cenotaphs to commemorate him, but the vast majority of soldiers killed in battle would have been buried in unmarked graves.

An Asiatic garlanded sarcophagus, probably sculpted from Phrygia, then shipped to Rome, c.150–80 CE. Garlands are held by Cupids and by winged goddesses on the corners, which wreathe busts of a crowned deity (left) and a young girl (right), for whom the sarcophagus is probably intended. There are masks of Tragedy and Comedy on each side in the centre, while Medusa (gorgon) faces decorate the ends. The garlands evoke the actual swathes of flowers and leaves frequently used to decorate tombs and altars.

ROMAN TRADE

*Rome's sophisticated trade network, which centred on the
Mediterranean basin but extended via the Silk Road to the Far East,
was dependent on efficient road and sea communications, a stable
coinage and state-operated quality controls.*

TRANSPORT WITHIN ROME was based on roads, navigable rivers
and sea routes. Bulky goods invariably travelled by water; in the Edict of
Prices laid down by the Emperor Diocletian in 301 CE it was stated that it
was cheaper to ship grain from Spain to Syria than to move it 120 km (75
miles) inland by road, and it was estimated that the cost of sea transport
was 60 times lower than by land. North Africa was the breadbasket of
Rome, and grain was shipped from Egypt and Africa (modern Tunisia)
to Rome to provide a monthly corn dole for the Roman citizenry – the
population of Rome reached 1 million during the imperial period.

The Mediterranean was Rome's trading nexus and the empire drew
on the resources of North Africa, Spain, France and the Middle East
to supply the capital and its Italian hinterland. Apart from grain, other
major imports included everyday commodities such as olive oil, wine,
cattle, wood, iron, marble and leather. As the empire expanded, certain
regions began to develop specializations and the ability to produce huge
tradable surpluses: corn from Egypt; olive oil from Spain; and wine from
southern France. Some regions were richly endowed with sought-after
commodities: salt from the Balkans; tin from the western British Isles;
and horses from Thrace.

While most inhabitants of the empire survived, as they always had
done, on local produce, the wealthy increasingly spent money on exotic
luxuries, which proclaimed their status. The further the goods had
travelled, the greater the value. Some products, such as silk from China
and spices from Southeast Asia, were transported by camel caravan along
the so-called Silk Road, which passed through Central Asia. Roman

merchants traded glassware, gold and other manufactured goods with the East, and Roman artefacts have been found as far afield as Malaysia and Vietnam. Other luxury products included ivory, papyrus, semi-precious metals and Arabian incense.

The majority of merchant ships were sailing vessels, with one, two or three masts. While shipping was the most economical form of transport, it was also the most dangerous, as the huge number of Roman shipwrecks testify. As well as storms at sea, Roman shipping was vulnerable to raids by pirates. Numerous lighthouses, docks and harbours facilitated the safe passage of trading ships around the Mediterranean. The port of Rome was located at Ostia, at the mouth of the Tiber, and commodities were offloaded there and shuttled in smaller boats up the river to Rome. An artificial harbour was constructed under Claudius, and enlarged by Trajan, to handle the sheer volume of goods.

During the Republican era, individual merchants, who owned their own fleets, grew extremely wealthy on trade. During the imperial era, the state increasingly took control, replacing private shipowners with a state-owned merchant fleet. The state taxed the movement of goods between provinces and controlled markets. There was also a system of stamping or sealing goods, with information about their origin, purity, weight and so on, and this practice guaranteed quality and prevented fraud. A standardized stable currency and a reliable system of weights and measures were vital in the control of empire-wide trade.

Roman Amphorae

These ceramic jars were used for transporting a wide range of goods, in particular olive oil, wine, garum and preserved fruits. They were vital in long-distance transport, especially by ship. They are generally plain and unglazed, with a narrow mouth and two handles, thick walls for strength and a tapering base to facilitate pouring and stacking in ships. A full amphora would have been very heavy, and the two handles allowed it to be carried by two men. Amphorae were sealed using clay stoppers, and some had a ceramic lid, when used to transport dried goods. Many amphorae were stamped before firing on the neck, rim or handles, with information about origin, quantities and even 'use by' information. Monte Testaccio in Rome is an artificial mound of pottery shards from some 53 million discarded amphorae, an indication of the vast numbers in use. In addition, very large quantities of amphorae have been found in Roman shipwrecks, and they have provided a great deal of information about the nature, scale and range of Roman trade.

There were many different types of amphorae, which were adapted according to the goods that were to be transported and the means of transportation used. Many were produced with pointed bases to facilitate upright storage, probably roped together, on ships. The largest known wreck of a ship containing amphorae was off the coast of Kefalonia in the Ionian Sea; it was carrying 6,000 pots.

TRIUMPH

The Romans exploited the propaganda potential of their military victories, granting conquerors spectacular triumphs in the form of victory celebration parades that glorified Roman might and superiority. During the imperial period, Rome turned to more permanent commemorations, honouring their military heroes in stone and marble.

TRIUMPHS PROBABLY ORIGINATED with the Punic Wars (3rd–2nd centuries BCE), and the general procedure dated to this point. Once the Senate had confirmed a commander's victory, he was granted the honorary title of Imperator until the end of his public triumph or until he crossed the pomerium, the sacred boundary of Rome. He then proceeded to the outskirts of Rome, where members of the Senate came to meet him, convening in the Temple of Bellona to hear him speak. After prayers of thanks had been offered to the gods, he would praise his legions, singling out certain individuals for their valour and distributing bonuses to his troops. He then put on special purple-coloured robes and processed into the city through the Porta Triumphalis, only used for this purpose, led by the consuls and politicians and accompanied by captives from the battlefield, often extravagantly chained. Paintings of famous scenes from the battle were carried in the procession and were sometimes re-enacted. Musicians, torch-bearers and flag-wavers added noise and colour to the scene, and cheering crowds lined the streets. War-booty was proudly displayed and the general followed behind, drawn in a tall-sided chariot pulled by four horses. His children and officers followed on horseback. At the temple of Jupiter Optimus Maximus, the commander generally freed a prisoner or two, then sacrificed a bull to Jupiter, making offerings of war-booty to the god. The events of the day were rounded up with a huge banquet.

The last non-royal triumph was in 19 BCE, and from this point on, the grand spectacle was reserved for imperial candidates only. The triumphs for Vespasian and his son Titus in 71 CE, following their victories in Judaea, were flamboyant affairs, and triumphs became progressively more lavish as unpopular emperors sought to curry favour with the Roman people. Triumphs became increasingly rare and there were probably no more than 20 over the next 200 years. From this point on, the Romans were inclined to choose a more permanent memorial to their great military heroes: the triumphal arch and the column.

Most triumphal arches were built between 27 BCE and 476 CE. Arches commemorated military victories, but also marked significant events, such as the accession of a new emperor. They were built all over the empire and served a symbolic function, unrelated to any existing network of city walls and gates. The basic form consisted of two piers, connected by an arch and crowned by a superstructure that served as a base for statues and bore commemorative inscriptions. There were 36 triumphal arches in Rome, though few survive. The Arch of Titus (c.81 CE) displayed Titus riding a bronze four-horse chariot (*quadriga*) and stood in the Forum Romanum. The Arch of Septimius Severus (203 CE) commemorated his victories in the Parthian campaigns of 194–5 and 197–9 CE. The central arch has two side arches and is crowned by a statue of the emperor and his two sons in a four-horse chariot, accompanied by soldiers. The dedicatory inscription refers to him as 'the best and bravest of emperors'.

The Romans also devised a monument in the form of a towering column, erected in honour of triumphant emperors and ornately decorated with scenes from their defining military campaigns. The most famous is Trajan's Column (c.107–113 CE), which towers 35 m (115 ft) high, commemorates, in an elaborate spiralling frieze, Rome's successful wars in Dacia (101–2 and 105–6 CE) and also serves as the emperor's tomb. Trajan's frieze provides an unparalleled resource for the study of the Roman military, as well as their arms, equipment and tactics. It also clearly displays the Roman belief that their orderly civilization triumphed over the unkempt Dacian 'barbarians'.

The Roman people also erected the Column of Marcus Aurelius (c.180 CE) to commemorate his victories over the Germanic tribes in

176 CE. It is also decorated with a spiral narrative relief that – unlike the cool objectivity of Trajan's column – conveys great drama and empathy, prefiguring the artistic style of late antiquity.

The triple Triumphal Arch of Orange, south-east France, dates to the reign of the Emperor Augustus (c.27 BCE–14 CE). Originally built to honour the heroes of the Gallic Wars, it was remodelled by the Emperor Tiberius to celebrate the victories of Germanicus over the German tribes in the Rhineland. It contains an inscription dedicated to the Emperor Tiberius, dated 27 CE.

LIFE ON THE FRONTIER

Roman soldiers were sent to the very periphery of the empire to man Rome's fortified frontiers, which marked the outermost viable limits of imperial expansion. They utilized natural features, such as rivers, and man-made structures, such as walls and palisades, to separate the lands of the empire from the 'barbarian' lands beyond.

MUCH OF THE CONSOLIDATION of Rome's borders took place under the rule of Hadrian (r. 117–38 CE), a pragmatic emperor who prioritized maintaining Rome's existing territories rather than endlessly expanding them. In the words of the Greek author, Appian (c.95–165 CE), the Romans 'aimed to preserve their empire by the exercise of prudence, rather than to extend their sway indefinitely over poverty-stricken and profitless tribes of barbarians'. Hadrian's restless journeys throughout his imperial territories left a network of forts, roads and walls, ringing the entire 'civilized' world with fortified frontiers.

The wall that takes his name in Britain is one of the best-preserved Roman frontiers, built to defend Roman Britain against the Caledonians and Picts to the north. It ran for some 127 km (79 miles) from east to west, and for the most part stood an intimidating 5.5 m (18 ft) high. Small fortified outposts with gates were situated at roughly mile-long intervals, with some 17 forts placed at more important sites. Each housed between 500 and 1,000 men. A deep ditch fronted the wall on the northern side, with small forts constructed a few miles to the north of the wall to act as scouting posts.

It is clear that the soldiers on duty here experienced a far higher standard of living than the natives, with excellent food, and imports such as Spanish olive oil and Portuguese garum from distant parts of the empire. They could use their pay to acquire creature comforts from neighbouring villages, and were able to receive care packages from home, conveyed northwards by the efficient Roman transport system. Forts included facilities such as baths and hospitals, which were unknown to the *Brittunculi* ('wretched little Brits'). The officers probably enjoyed dinner parties and hunting expeditions and, joined by their wives, children and slaves, were able to live a full family life. Inevitably, there were complaints about British weather.

In Germania, 900 km (560 miles) from the Roman heartland, much of the border followed the Rhine and Danube rivers. Between *c*.70 CE and 260 CE, the Romans created a land frontier, the Upper German-Raetian Limes, that was more than 500 km (310 miles) long, with some 900 watchtowers and 120 forts, to connect the two rivers. The border must have been a startling sight in an otherwise desolate wilderness. It was marked by a stout timber palisade, or in some areas a stone wall, with forts, fortlets and watchtowers set back from it, creating a broad boundary. Forts and watchtowers did not punctuate the border with

The construction of Hadrian's Wall began c.122 CE. It symbolized the northernmost limit of Roman power in Europe, and may have acted as a customs border, rather than an actual barrier to invasion. It has some 17 larger forts placed along it at important sites. The wall traces the topography of the landscape, accommodating natural features such as the rocky outcrop of Whin Sill. Milecastles are fortlets attached to the main wall, and it is assumed that these served as outposts for troops sent from the larger fortresses. Castle Nick Milecastle (39) was used as a milking parlour in the Middle Ages, like many other milecastles, which were reused for agricultural purposes.

the regularity that was seen on Hadrian's Wall – they could be built, enlarged, relocated or abandoned as circumstances required.

Manned by remarkably few soldiers, this border would have been useless against invading armies, but was a highly effective way of policing small-scale bandits and smugglers, and collecting customs dues. The frontier was less about repelling invaders and more about controlling the movement of people. The tribes outside the frontier were held off through diplomacy, trade and military assistance, and friendly barbarians frequently served in the Roman army.

Ultimately, Roman fortifications – even the exceptionally well-engineered and permanent Hadrian's Wall – may well have been border markers and displays of Roman power rather than physical barriers to invasion. When the Germanic tribes breached the borders, the concentration of forces along the frontier greatly disadvantaged the Roman defenders, leaving the interior regions exposed. In Britain, the threats ultimately came by sea, and the late Roman military command of the Saxon Shore, on both sides of the English Channel, concentrated on maritime, rather than land, defences.

The Vindolanda Letters

In 1973, excavators at Vindolanda, one of the forts on Hadrian's Wall, uncovered piles of Roman rubbish, preserved in oxygen-free conditions under a thick layer of clay. They discovered hundreds of thin wooden tablets covered in writing, which evoke a detailed picture of life on Hadrian's Wall.

Some of the remnants were administrative, recording work assignments, lists of supplies and duty rosters. It is clear that the wall's guardians ate well: bacon, ham, venison, chicken, honey, eggs and apples were all listed, as well as Celtic beer, wine and the universal fermented fish sauce, garum. Clearly, many soldiers lived on the fort with their families – dozens of children's shoes and babies' booties have been discovered. One of the letters was an invitation to a birthday party from one officer's wife to another. Many of the personal letters were written from home, and conveyed concern about the uncomfortable conditions in northern England: 'I have sent you ... socks ... two pairs of sandals and two pairs of underpants' wrote one caring correspondent. The soldiers were clearly well looked after: a cavalry Decurion, Mausculus, wrote to his commander, 'Please, my lord, give instructions on what you want us to do tomorrow. Are we all to return with the standard or just half of us? ... My fellow soldiers have no beer. Please order some to be sent.'

'Sollemnis to Paris his brother, very many greetings.
I want you to know that I am in very good health, as I
hope you are in turn, you neglectful man, who have sent
me not even one letter. But I think that I am behaving
in a more considerate fashion in writing to you ...'

VINDOLANDA TABLET 311

ROME IN THE EAST

In the East, the Romans were grafting their civilization on to already well-established and thriving cultures. Loyalty was secured by supporting the existing elites or upper classes, and no further grant of privileges were required. Rome's most characteristic new cities in the East were foundations in which transplanted Roman citizens, for example army veterans, were expected to put down roots.

THE EMPEROR HADRIAN (r. 117–38 CE), in particular, was a dedicated lover of Greek culture who craved acceptance and admiration from his Greek subjects. He was a liberal benefactor, particularly to Athens, and founded cities in Greece and Asia Minor. Rome's expansion in Asia Minor began with the acceptance of the legacy of Attalus of Pergamon in 133 BCE. The cities of western Asia Minor were substantial and exuberant, supported by a rich agricultural hinterland. The upper classes took readily to the new luxuries and display introduced by the Romans, and were happy to parade the titles and privileges they introduced.

Ephesus was home to the Temple of Artemis, a masterpiece of Hellenistic architecture in a largely Roman city. The splendid Temple, just outside the city walls, was a huge tourist attraction, bringing pilgrims to the city. Ephesus competed with Smyrna for the title of 'first city' of Asia Minor. In the early centuries CE, the city was rebuilt on a magnificent scale, with colonnaded streets, a large bathing complex, an amphitheatre that could seat 24,000 people and the great library of Celsus, which housed up to 12,000 scrolls. Mural paintings in houses in the central area near the agora demonstrate the great wealth of the city's residents. The port, source of much of the city's wealth, was linked to the sea by a narrow channel, which was reached by a grand colonnaded street, oil-lit at night-time.

Further east, Roman control was built on the ruins of the Seleucid kingdom, which was first conquered by Pompey and annexed to the Roman Republic as the province of Syria in 64 BCE, and then gradually extended by the progressive absorption of 'client kingdoms', culminating in the annexation of Arabia and Mesopotamia in the early 2nd century CE. With an urban history that dated back 4,000 years, the Roman presence in the 'Fertile Crescent' made little difference to the cultural life of the region. Greek and Syriac were still the predominant languages, although Latin was spoken in the Roman administrative capital of Antioch. However, the people of the East certainly had an impact on the Roman Empire, and travelled widely, spreading innovative religious and philosophical ideas.

Located on the Orontes River, Antioch was the capital of the province of Syria, which grew wealthy on its agricultural hinterland and trade in olive oil and wine. Located some 25 km (15 miles) inland, it was

A colonnaded street in Jerash, northern Jordan. This area was annexed to the Roman province of Syria after the Roman conquest in 64 BCE, and Jerash became one of the Decapolis, a series of ten semi-autonomous cities located in Syria. In 106 CE, Emperor Trajan absorbed Jerash into the Roman province of Arabia. Situated at the axis of several major trade routes, Jerash flourished. Several new roads were built, including the Via Nova Traiana. An extensive programme of public works included the construction of a new Temple of Artemis and a triumphal arch, 'Hadrian's Arch', built to commemorate the visit of the Roman emperor to the city in 129 CE.

connected by a good road with the local port of Seleucia. The city had substantial fortifications because, from the 3rd century CE, it was subject to Persian attacks. The beautiful mosaics and friezes found in the villas located in the suburb of Daphne, to the south of the city, are a testament to the luxurious lifestyle enjoyed by the Roman elite.

Octavian (later Augustus) acquired Egypt after the capture of Alexandria in 30 BCE. He and his successors treated Egypt as an imperial domain, asserting rule over a region that had been controlled for 3,000 years by pharaohs and subsequently by the Hellenistic Ptolemaic dynasty. This region, held together by the River Nile and its annual cycle of flooding and fertilization, had always been highly centralized and subject to government control. The cities of the Nile delta were Hellenized, but farmers and country folk populated the smaller towns and villages along the banks of the Nile and retained their Egyptian customs, language and religion under Roman rule.

Founded by Alexander the Great in 331 BCE and laid out by the Ptolemies, Alexandria remained primarily a Hellenistic foundation, the second city of the Roman Empire, with a population of half a million people. It was from here that the corn ships were dispatched to Rome, carrying grain from Africa and Egypt, and cosmopolitan Alexandria acted as a clearing house for trade from the East, en route to Rome.

ROMAN PORTRAITURE

Roman portraits, whether in marble, bronze or mosaic, or painted on wood, eschewed the standardized heroic or mythical iconography of Greek art. They sought to convey respect through an exaggerated naturalism ('verism'), or to communicate imperial propaganda about authority and control, or simply to commemorate a relation in loving and naturalistic detail.

FOR ROMANS, the main essence of a portrait was the head, and many sculpted heads were closely rendered and then placed on generic nude or draped bodies. Portrait busts, which could be exhibited in niches or architectural frameworks, were the most popular form of portrait.

Private portraits in Ancient Rome were associated with funerary art, either as portrait reliefs or portrait busts, which were placed with urns in niches, called columbaria. In the early Republican era, these portraits were startlingly realistic, opting for character over beauty, but by the 1st century BCE funerary portraits were widespread through all strata of society, and had become standardized and much more stereotypical.

In the Republican era, honorary public sculptures depicted prominent politicians and military commanders, and were often ordered by the Senate to commemorate notable military victories or political achievements, such as conquests or the drafting of treaties.

Since the Republic revered public service and military prowess, portraits from that era endorsed that ideal. As a result, every wrinkle and imperfection was lovingly represented, because it was thought that realism displayed strength, individuality and confidence, rather than relying on superficial ideals of beauty. Power and character were at a premium. As the great Roman families intermarried and expanded, these honorary statues proliferated, playing an important role in 'ancestor galleries', which accumulated portraits to reinforce notions of pedigree and heritage.

Faiyum mummy portrait of a man, 1st century CE. The Faiyum mummy portraits are among the best-preserved paintings of the Roman era, and are renowned for their realism. However, they may not depict the subjects as they really were; it appears that painters worked from a number of standard types, and did not make detailed observations of facial characteristics. The frontal perspective and concentration of facial features clearly prefigures later icon painting.

With the establishment of the empire, the imperial family monopolized official public statuary. These portraits were propaganda tools that served to promote the imperial cult by projecting ideals of youth, beauty and benevolence. Visual links to predecessors helped to validate dynasties and added legitimacy to their authority. However, the turbulence of the years 68/9 CE, when three emperors acceded in rapid succession, led to a change in imperial portraiture, with a return to a more realistic, less idealized mode, which emphasized rugged, battle-hardened virility. During this period, portraits of the women of the imperial household became increasingly popular, as they represented the height of fashion, with their lovingly rendered corkscrew curls and elegant draperies.

The Emperor Hadrian, who revered all things Greek, was the first emperor to be portrayed with a Greek-style beard and a full head of curly hair. His successors Marcus Aurelius (r. 161–80 CE) and Commodus (r. 177–92 CE) also opted for ultra-realism, emphasizing not only their physical strength but also their intelligence. Caracalla (r. 198–217 CE) is portrayed with a short, military-style haircut and trimmed beard and a fierce, brooding expression. He appears to be supremely authoritative.

Ultimately, the intense, barely concealed aggression and machismo of the soldier-emperors would be supplanted in the 4th century CE by portraits of Constantine the Great. He was portrayed as a 'good' emperor, and is depicted as clean-shaven, with a serene, youthful face that recalls the classicizing idealism of Augustus and his Julio-Claudian descendants.

Faiyum Mummy Portraits

The Romans privately commissioned painted portraits, but far fewer of these survive than sculptures in marble and stone. The hauntingly lifelike portraits on wooden panels, which were placed over mummies in Faiyum in Roman Egypt, provide a rare insight into Roman painted portraiture. It has been suggested that these paintings were made from life and hung in frames in homes until they were eventually placed over the mummy, although it is also possible that they were made shortly after death, as on close scrutiny the pose and faces appear to be formulaic. The painstaking detail of hairstyles, clothes and jewellery has allowed scholars to date the paintings very precisely. Most of the people portrayed are in the prime of life, reflecting the low life expectancy of the ancient world. The forward-facing pose and concentration on facial features, with the eyes being rendered with particular intensity, seem to prefigure a later tradition of icon painting.

THE TROUBLED CENTURY

The 3rd century CE was characterized by a gradual decline in central authority, which was further destabilized by the powerful enemies that appeared beyond the Roman frontiers. The chaos culminated in the break-up of the empire into regional powers, but increasingly effective military emperors restored authority and prepared the ground for a more radical reorganization.

IN THE LAST DECADE of the 2nd century CE, the Praetorian Guard was at the peak of its powers and influence. Its members saw themselves as king-makers, but their choice of the ineffectual Didius Julianus as imperial successor in 193 CE sparked off a series of revolts in the provinces, as the frontier legions began to proclaim their own candidates. Septimius Severus from the Danube province was ultimately successful and vanquished his fellow contenders. He originated from Cyrenaica (modern Libya), and his accession marked the growing importance of provincials in the life of the empire. He was married to Julia Domna, a high-ranking Syrian, and the African-Syrian Severan dynasty he founded survived for three generations.

The army had made Septimius Severus's fortune and he relied on the military to maintain it. He instituted a number of army reforms, raised new legions and embarked on wars in Britain, North Africa and the East. While his military adventures were successful, the Italian heartland was in economic decline. When Severus stationed a newly formed legion in Italy, it seemed that the transformation was complete; Italy was just another Roman province and the provincials were in control. Severus's son Caracalla came to power in 198 CE by murdering his brother, and his notoriety was only confirmed when he ordered the massacre of young men in Alexandria in 215 CE. He was also dependent on the goodwill of the army, which he placated with pay rises.

After Caracalla was murdered in 217 CE, there was a brief interlude before the Severan dynasty was restored, with the ascent of Elagabalus, a 14-year-old who relied on the authority of his Syrian mother and grandmother. A hereditary High Priest of the Syrian sun god of Emesa, Elagabalus soon became entangled in dubious sexual practices and exotic rituals, and was murdered. He was succeeded by his cousin Severus Alexander (r. 222–35 CE) who immediately clashed with a renascent Parthian Empire under the aggressive new ruler, Ardashir. In 235 CE, Severus Alexander was assassinated by his own troops because of his perceived unwillingness to engage in battle against the Germanic tribes.

The army now rose to prominence as the power broker in imperial politics, especially at a time when the empire was beleaguered, surrounded by aggressive foreign powers and on the defensive. Increasingly, the important events were taking place on Rome's frontiers and not in Rome itself, and successive short-lived emperors, raised to power by

Rock face relief at Naqsh-e Rustam, showing the Persian Emperor Shapur I taking the Emperor Valerian captive. After Valerian had been soundly defeated at the Battle of Edessa in 260 CE, he was forced to meet Shapur and negotiate a peace settlement. Shapur broke the truce and captured Valerian, holding him prisoner for the rest of his life. Valerian's capture was a huge blow to Roman morale.

the army and therefore known as 'barracks emperors', presided over a galloping crisis as Germanic tribes, Goths and Persians threatened. There were more than 20 emperors in the period between 235–84 CE, many of whom were killed by their own soldiers or the Praetorian Guard. The rulers of Palmyra established a semi-independent state under Queen Zenobia (240–70 CE) and the Western provinces broke away to establish a separate Gallic Empire under Postumus. Everywhere there was economic hardship and social turmoil.

From 268 CE, a new series of soldier-emperors, who originated in the Balkans, began to restore imperial authority. The ruthless Aurelian (r. 270–5 CE) defeated Zenobia, and the Palmyrene kingdom was dismantled. Aurelian then marched west, where he nearly annihilated the armies of the Gallic Empire at the Battle of Châlons (274 CE). Carus (r. 282–3 CE) invaded Mesopotamia, sacked the city of Ctesiphon and turned back the Persian tide.

Diocletian (r. 284–305 CE) built on Aurelian's initiatives and secured the empire's borders. He also elevated the position of the emperor, creating an aura of divinity around himself, which ensured that he was no longer reliant on military support. Mobile armies within the empire were able to move quickly to trouble spots, reducing the power of the standing frontier armies. Diocletian also countered inflation by introducing a stable currency. Diocletian's most significant reform was his radical restructuring of the Roman government. He established the Tetrarchy, a system of rule in which four men shared rule over the empire, which was effectively divided in two, with an Augustus and a subordinate Caesar in each half.

MAJOR 'BARRACKS EMPERORS' (CE)

235   Alexander Severus is assassinated; Thracian soldier Maximinus Thrax takes control (killed by troops in 238 CE).

238   Gordian I and Gordian II, father and son, are made emperors. Gordian II is killed in battle fighting pro-Maximinus forces; Gordian I commits suicide. Succeeded by Gordian III.

244   Philip the Arab probably assassinates Gordian III.

249   Philip the Arab is killed in battle by his successor Decius, and his

12-year-old son (his co-emperor), is murdered by the Praetorian Guard.

251   Decius and his son, the co-emperor, are killed in battle fighting a Goth coalition. After ruling for five months, Hostilian, the younger son of Decius, dies of plague. He is succeeded by a commander under Decius, Gallus.

253   Gallus is assassinated by his own troops and Amelianus is elevated. Amelianus rules for two months and is also assassinated in favour of Valerian, who makes his son Gallienus co-emperor.

260   Valerian is captured by the Persians under Shapur I, and dies as their prisoner. He is succeeded by his son, Gallienus.

268   Gallienus is assassinated by his own troops when on campaign in a conspiracy involving the future emperor, Aurelian. He is succeeded by Claudius Gothicus.

270   Claudius Gothicus, following victories over the Goths, dies of plague. He is succeeded by his brother Quintillus, who dies shortly after his accession, probably murdered by Aurelian, who succeeds him.

275   Aurelian is assassinated by his commanders following successful campaigns against the Gallic and Palmyrene empires.

MYSTERY CULTS

'Mysteries' were sacred truths revealed only to the initiated. In the late Republican period, mystery cults of Oriental origin began to be introduced throughout the empire by traders, merchants and slaves, reflecting Rome's expanding frontiers and increasing assimilation of new ideas and practices.

EACH OF THE MYSTERY CULTS evolved its own elaborate rituals, liturgies and doctrines of immortality, death and rebirth, and was able to satisfy the aesthetic, intellectual and spiritual aspirations of a wide variety of people. Part of the attraction of the mystery cults was that the initiate attained an equality of status with his fellow initiates which transcended social and ethnic barriers. The community that was established by cult members was something akin to the fellowship of freemasons, drawing people together in ways that could be materially, as well as spiritually, beneficial.

The cult of Cybele, or Magna Mater ('Great Mother'), is the earliest of these introductions, which occurred during the Second Punic War, when the black stone of Cybele was brought from her sanctuary at Pessinus in Anatolia and installed on the Palatine Hill in 204 BCE, because it was believed that she would help the Romans against Hannibal. The mother goddess Cybele is often portrayed riding a chariot drawn by lions, symbolizing her role as the mistress of wild beasts. She is joined by her consort, the vegetation god Attis, whose death and resurrection is reflected in the cycle of the seasons. The worship of Cybele was famous for the purification ritual of taurobolium, in which an individual stepped into a pit and was bathed in the blood of a sacrificed bull. The rites of the goddess were ecstatic, and involved dancing, flagellation and self-mutilation.

The cult of Isis, the consort of Serapis, was an Egyptian import that was brought to Rome through commercial contacts. During the Hellenistic period, Isis was identified with Hellenistic deities such as Demeter and Aphrodite, and Serapis was identified with Zeus and Dionysus. Greek and Egyptian emigrants honoured Isis as the protector of the family (especially women) and newborns, and the goddess who could cheat Fate and Death. When sailors and slaves introduced the cult to Rome, it proved enduringly popular among women and the lower classes – unusually, women were permitted to become priestesses of Isis. Augustus viewed the cult with suspicion, partly because it was associated with his old enemy Egypt, and there were accusations of scandal involving the cult, including rumours of sexual promiscuity. Caligula legitimized the cult of Isis, and many subsequent emperors were equally tolerant. Isis

Double-faced Mithraic altarpiece, found near Fiano Romano, near Rome, 2nd–3rd century CE. On the obverse, it depicts a tauroctony scene, and on the reverse, a banquet.

was worshipped in the Iseum, which was a walled-off sanctuary where rituals involving fire, water and incense were conducted in front of sacred statues. Caracalla (*r.* 198–217 CE) revered Serapis, who up to this point had been eclipsed in popularity by his consort, Isis. He was worshipped as the god of healing, and a gigantic temple to Serapis was erected in Rome.

The god Mithras was of Persian origin, and became particularly popular in the Roman army from the 1st century CE. Mithras was a god of light, who was engaged in a permanent struggle with Ahriman, the evil prince of darkness. Mithras was depicted in his shrines wearing a Persian (Phrygian) cap, slaying the mystic bull whose blood was the source of life. The slaying took place in a cave, reflected in the underground location of Mithraic temples. Mithraic believers sought moral purification through self-denial and physical ordeals, and initiates had to take part in tests of courage. This strictly male cult was spread through the frontier provinces of the Roman Empire by the army, where its rigid hierarchy of initiation and priesthoods, which emphasized loyalty and discipline, was enthusiastically adopted.

THE MOSAICS OF
NORTH AFRICA

The best-preserved and most vividly naturalistic mosaics of the Roman Empire can be found in the province of Africa Consularis (Tunisia, north-east Algeria, western Libya), a region that came under Roman control at the end of the Punic Wars in 146 BCE.

THE PLETHORA OF MOSAICS that began to appear in North Africa in the 2nd century CE are the result of the region's accelerating wealth, much of it derived from its rich agricultural hinterland, which was supplying grain to Italy. North Africa also supplied olive oil, gold and even wild animals – destined for the entertainment of crowds in amphitheatres – to Italy. As the cities of North Africa became more Romanized, monuments and mosaics were commissioned by wealthy families seeking to assert their status. Mosaics were used to adorn reception and dining areas in luxurious Roman villas, and could also be found in a variety of public buildings, including baths, temples and churches.

The earliest mosaics of North Africa, probably introduced by itinerant Italian craftsmen, used black and white tiles and complex geometric designs. But gradually, stylized vegetation designs began to embellish the strict geometry, and discoveries of plentiful local supplies of colourful limestone and marble transformed the pavements into vibrant polychrome.

At about the same time, mosaics began to depict figurative subjects, with human figures and individual scenes set in picture panels (*emblemata*) within the decorated floors. Frequently, these panels surrounded a dominant main scene, which depicted favoured Roman subjects such as hunting, gladiatorial conquest and mythology.

By the 3rd and 4th centuries CE, large-scale pictorial compositions had become dominant, and these complex, intricate scenes are found in great abundance. A huge variety of subjects were depicted: hunting, wild game and gladiatorial combat were favoured ones, but scenes of everyday life – farming, fishing, loading grain and animals on to ships at anchor – were also popular. North Africa is also the source of the only known mosaic of the Roman poet Virgil, who is depicted writing his famous epic, the *Aeneid*, flanked by the muses of tragedy and history. The enduring power of Homer is reflected in a depiction of Ulysses, resisting the lures of the Sirens. Mythological scenes abound, including a unique portrayal of Diana the Huntress shooting a gazelle, while *The Triumph of Neptune*, which measures more than 100 sq m (1,076 sq ft), depicts the god of the sea surrounded by the four seasons.

The accomplished composition and imagery of these innovative North African mosaics influenced other regions of the Roman Empire, especially Italy and Sicily, and large-scale North African-style mosaics are also found in the Eastern Roman Empire.

A mythological mosaic from Dougga, northern Tunisia depicting Ulysses (Odysseus) and his crew sailing past the Sirens, 3rd century CE. The sorceress Circe has instructed Ulysses to seal his sailors' ears with beeswax, so they will not be seduced by the Sirens' song. Ulysses himself is tied to the mast, and therefore physically restrained. The Sirens are represented with wings and birds' feet; one of them is shown at far right.

A CHRISTIAN EMPIRE

The punishments meted out to Christians in Ancient Rome, especially the practice of throwing them to the lions in the Colosseum, have been described in lurid detail, although they may have been the exception rather than the rule. Persecution was fitful and localized until Emperor Decius initiated a campaign of persecution throughout the empire in 250 CE. Just over 60 years later, Rome became a Christian empire under Constantine.

FOR MANY YEARS, the Romans perceived Christianity as yet another Oriental religion, which gained a number of adherents in the cities of the empire. When Nero made Christians the scapegoats for the Great Fire of Rome in 64 CE, a pattern of alternating periods of persecution and toleration was established. Domitian (*r.* 81–96 CE) persecuted Christians; Trajan (*r.* 97–117 CE) ignored them. In reality, persecution was always piecemeal, and on the orders of provincial governors. A hysterical outbreak of anti-Christian feeling in Lyons in 177 CE, when Christians were accused of cannibalism and incest, led to the torture and execution of the Bishop of Lyons with many of his flock, on the orders of the governor. The Christian theologian Tertullian (*c.*155–240 CE) lamented that 'Away to the lions with the Christians!' was the stock response to any calamity.

It was only during the 3rd-century political crisis, when Rome was ruled by a rapid succession of contending soldier-emperors, that Christianity really became a live issue. By this time there were perhaps 150,000–200,000 Christians in the empire, with many concentrated in the east and around the Mediterranean basin. Although Christianity was a minority religion, it was seen as yet another force that was ripping the empire apart. As a result, Christians became the scapegoats for all kinds of misfortune, including natural disasters, failed harvests, plagues and political turmoil.

Emperor Decius ordered the first great Christian persecution in 250 CE, following Christians' refusal to offer the traditional pagan sacrifices for the welfare of the empire. A second imperial edict in 257 CE forbade public worship, and a year later new laws were turned against the Church and Church property. During this period, many Christians escaped persecution by going underground.

The enforcement of these edicts varied from province to province, and conversions to Christianity continued to rise. The heroic suffering of the Christian martyrs presumably added lustre to the new faith. In 260 CE, the authorities admitted that their persecutions had failed to prevent the spread of Christianity, and for the next 40 years Christians were left alone.

The suspension of persecutions was not destined to last. In 303 CE, the Eastern Emperors Diocletian and Galerius issued an edict ordering the destruction of churches and scriptures. When a spate of further edicts culminated in an order that everyone must sacrifice to the pagan gods, the Christians refused to comply and retribution was savage. Many thousands were exiled, condemned to hard labour in the mines, mutilation or death. The compromises and evasions made by clergy and individuals during this period led to many rancorous doctrinal disputes and schisms in the 4th century CE.

Constantine (r. 306–37 CE) became emperor after a series of civil wars and political settlements, which culminated in the victory over his rival, Maxentius, at Milvian Bridge, just north of Rome, in 312 CE. He claimed to have seen a vision of a cross in the sky shortly before the battle, with the command 'Conquer by this'. From this point on, Constantine became a committed Christian and, alongside his Eastern counterpart Licinius, granted legal status and official tolerance to the Christian religion in the Edict of Milan (313 CE). Constantine eventually defeated Licinius in 324 CE, and devoted his considerable energies to Church doctrine and the restoration of confiscated privileges to the clergy and Christian congregations. An effective autocrat, he supported the central authority of the Church, convened the First Council of Nicaea in 325 CE and was eager to uphold Church dogma and eradicate perceived heresies. He confiscated the treasuries of the pagan temples, using the money to dedicate new churches, including the first St Peter's in Rome and the Church of the Holy Sepulchre in Jerusalem. Constantine was baptized on his deathbed in 337 CE.

Many of Constantine's high-ranking supporters at the imperial court were Christians, whose beliefs and behaviour permeated the upper strata of the ruling class. In addition, the ranks of the bureaucracy were filled by the urban middle classes, many of whom had been early converts to Christianity. The link between the Church and the apparatus of state was to remain a powerful force for centuries to come.

CITY OF CONSTANTINE

Constantine was unwilling to share power, and defeated his rival to become the sole ruler of a resurgent empire. When he dedicated a new Christian capital at Byzantium on the Bosporus, he abandoned Rome's legacy of pagan temples and institutions. The new capital was renamed Constantinople and its site reflected the increasing importance of the Eastern provinces as the Western ones slipped into decline.

DIOCLETIAN HAD DIVIDED the empire into a tetrarchy, with an emperor (Augustus) and co-emperor (Caesar) in east and west. This system of divided rule did not long outlast his retirement in 305 CE. In the Western Roman Empire, there was a struggle between Maxentius, who had seized Italy and North Africa, and Constantine, who had succeeded his father Constantius as Western emperor in 305 CE. Constantine's victory over Maxentius at Milvian Bridge in 312 CE left him in sole charge of the Western Roman Empire. He agreed to divide power with Licinius, the ruler in the east, but in 316 CE he attacked his rival and seized Greece and the Balkans. Constantine finally defeated Licinius in 324 CE, reuniting the Roman Empire under a single ruler.

The city of Rome was in decline; its economy was stagnating and its infrastructure was deteriorating. Thus, Constantine chose to relocate his capital to the ancient Greek city of Byzantium, which had first been established in the 7th century BCE. Located on the European side of the Strait of Bosporus, the city faced Asia. Constantine recognized that this location symbolized the reunion of east and west and heralded a new era in Roman history. The city, situated at the very epicentre of the Roman world, was surrounded by water and therefore easily defensible. It also controlled access to the Black Sea and trade with the east.

Constantine embarked on an ambitious building project to create his city of New Rome in 328 CE. Situated, like Rome, on seven hills,

Constantine demarcated a city that was to be many times larger than its Greek predecessor. He selected the rising ground just outside the walls of the old city as a magnificent new forum, endowed with a large meeting hall that served as a market, stock exchange and court of law. The city focused on two main colonnaded streets, lined with statues of Roman gods and emperors, which intersected at a four-way arch, the tetrapylon.

To the south-east, overlooking the Bosporus, Constantine constructed an imposing new palace. The Great Baths, or Baths of Zeuxippus, were built on a magnificent scale, and adorned with statues that had been taken from the prominent towns of Greece and Asia Minor. A grand new Senate House was also constructed, and many of Rome's old senatorial families were persuaded to relocate to the new city. The original Greek amphitheatre, scene of gladiatorial contests, was abandoned. Instead, the hippodrome was enlarged for horse and chariot races, which played a very prominent role in the life of the new city, which was renamed Constantinople.

The city was a Christian capital, reflecting Constantine's acceptance of Christianity (although he was only baptized on his deathbed); the great churches of Hagia Sophia, which burned down and was subsequently rebuilt, and Hagia Eirene were first built during Constantine's reign, and the Church of the Holy Apostles was destined to be the burial place of Constantine's family.

The water supply to the new city was an urgent priority. As well as a network of aqueducts, pipes and conduits, the city needed

The head from the Colossus of Constantine, a huge c. 12 m (39.4 ft)-high enthroned statue of the Emperor Constantine (c.280–337 CE) that once occupied the west apse of the Basilica of Maxentius near the Forum Romanum. The emperor's face is treated symbolically, with its aquiline nose, deep jaw and larger-than-life eyes. It is more like an effigy of a god than a portrait statue, designed to fill the viewer with a sense of the emperor's grandeur rather than his humanity.

a water storage facility and the Binbirdirek Cistern, built to solve the problem in 330 CE, still survives. Defence was also crucial, and the city walls extended *c*.20 km (12.4 miles) in length.

Senators, bureaucrats, imperial officials and functionaries were all induced to move to the new city, with offers of land for new housing. Artisans and craftsmen were enticed by offers of special privileges and the old Roman tradition of distributing free corn to the population was revived. Merchants and seamen flocked to Constantinople, scenting commercial opportunities. In 330 CE, a festival was held in which Christian bishops consecrated the partially completed palace and held a service in Hagia Sophia, marking the beginning of a new era; Rome's centre of gravity – both spiritual and temporal – had shifted.

DIVIDED EMPIRE

*Throughout the 4th century CE, the barbarian threat on the Rhine–
Danube frontier remained constant, and much of the government's
revenue was used to support the army that was guarding the frontier.
As emperors vied for power, seeking to unite the empire under
Christianity or paganism, the Roman economy was fatally weakened
and the barbarian threat was barely contained. In 395 CE, on
Theodosius' death, the empire permanently split into two halves.*

THE DEATH OF CONSTANTINE (*r.* 337 CE) was followed by a
spate of murders in his extended family, presumably in an attempt to
ensure a clear dynastic succession for his own sons, Constantine II,
Constantius and Constans. It was becoming increasingly evident that
the continual pressure from the Germanic tribes on the Rhine–Danube
frontier could only be effectively countered by a separate government in
the west, and an emperor with local authority.

In 355 CE, Julian, a nephew of Constantius, was appointed Caesar
in Gaul. It was intended that Julian would devote all his energies to
the military threat on his frontier, and he was very effective in that
role, winning a great victory over the Alamanni near Strasbourg in 357
CE. However, he became increasingly ambitious, proclaimed himself
as Augustus, and set himself the task of restoring the worship of the
ancient pagan gods before he was killed on an ill-advised campaign in
Persia in 363 CE.

The second half of the 4th century CE saw a number of serious
setbacks. The Goths from beyond the Rhine–Danube frontier had been
displaced by invading Huns, and had sought permission to settle within
the Eastern Roman Empire. However, the newcomers were severely ill-
treated by provincial commanders, and eventually this led to a revolt.
The worst setback in this conflict was the Battle of Adrianople (378

CE), when the Visigoths overwhelmingly defeated Emperor Valens (*r.* 364–78 CE), who died in battle. Adrianople is considered to be a major turning point in Rome's fortunes; the barbarians had become powerful adversaries, leaving the empire severely weakened.

Emperor Theodosius I (*r.* 379–95 CE) was the last emperor to rule over both the Eastern and Western halves of the Roman Empire. Following his elevation to emperor, he campaigned against the Goths and other barbarians. Unable to drive them out of the empire, he accepted them as *foederati*, autonomous allies, who answered to the authority of their own leaders and remained outside Roman authority. He was forced to confront the usurper Eugenius in 394 CE, defeating him at the Battle of the Frigidus in present-day Slovenia, before he could restore a fragile peace.

Eugenius (*r.* 392–4 CE) was the last imperial claimant who supported polytheism. Theodosius was a zealous Christian, who set out to crush paganism. For centuries, the Roman people had sought the protection of Roman gods, and many people perceived Christianity as owing no specific allegiance to Rome or its people, fearing its introduction would render Rome vulnerable. Theodosius's religious intolerance served to further divide the empire.

On the death of Theodosius, the two halves of the Roman Empire broke apart. This rupture was caused by a range of factors. Both the Eastern and Western Roman Empires had long worked to advance their own interests, rather than looking at the empire as a whole. There was a great deal of political instability which was compounded by government corruption, particularly in the far-flung provinces of the empire, where individual elites were lining their own pockets. The currency was debased, and there was galloping inflation. The Roman army was increasingly dependent on Gothic and Hun mercenaries, who owed no loyalty to Rome, and felt resentful because they were not treated as well as their Roman counterparts. On Theodosius's death, his army rapidly dissolved, and Gothic contingents raided as far as Constantinople. His two sons, Arcadius and Honorius, inherited the Eastern and Western halves respectively, but they were both young and lacked authority.

ROME DIVIDED (4TH CENTURY CE)

312   Constantine wins victory over Maxentius at Milvian Bridge.

313   Edict of Milan: Christianity is encouraged throughout the empire.

325   Constantine executes his rival Eastern emperor in Thessalonika on a charge of attempted rebellion.

330   New Christian city of Constantinople is inaugurated on the site of Byzantium.

337   Death of Constantine; the empire is shared between his three sons.

356–60   Emperor Julian fights the Franks and Alamanni in Gaul.

363   Julian is killed fighting the Persians.

364   Empire is divided between brothers Valentian (west) and Valens (east).

370   Huns, moving from steppes north of the Black Sea, defeat the Ostrogoths and drive the Visigoths westwards, starting a chain reaction.

378   Visigoths inflict a devastating defeat on the Roman army at Adrianople.

379   Theodosius becomes Roman emperor, and revives Constantine's close links between Church and state.

c.380   Roman legions begin to withdraw from Britain, leaving the Celtic population vulnerable.

395   Death of Theodosius; permanent division of the empire.

THE FALL OF ROME

The Germanic peoples who invaded the Roman Empire in the 5th century CE did not set out to destroy it, but to share in its wealth. They were eager to acquire the trappings of Roman civilization, but the refusal of successive Romans emperors to deal with them on equal terms unleashed destructive waves of violence on the faltering empire.

WHEN THEODOSIUS DIED in 395 CE, his young sons Arcadius (*r.* 383–408 CE) and Honorius (*r.* 393–423 CE) succeeded him in the east and west respectively. Honorius, who was aged just ten, ruled under the regency of Flavius Stilicho, a half-Vandal by birth. He was one of the increasing numbers of Germanic soldiers who achieved high rank in the Roman army, becoming the effective ruler of the Western Empire.

At this point, the Goths broke into open rebellion. Under their new leader Alaric (*r.* 395–410 CE), they attacked Constantinople and embarked on an orgy of raiding and pillaging in Greece. They stayed in Epirus, in northern Greece, for four years before attacking Italy in 401 CE. Alaric was making one simple demand: recognition of his people, which would make the Goths legitimate allies of the Roman people and equal partners in the Roman army. The armies of Alaric and Stilicho clashed, but without a decisive outcome, forcing Alaric, whose supply line was stretched to its maximum, to beat a retreat. Meanwhile, Honorius and his court had retreated to the safety of Ravenna in north-eastern Italy.

In 406 CE, the situation deteriorated further. A new wave of Goth invaders swept into Italy, where Stilicho confronted them, defeating them and absorbing them into the ranks of his army. Meanwhile, in the north-east of the empire, a new wave of Germanic invaders, the Vandals, Alans and Suebi, crossed the Rhine in force. They sacked Trier, before crossing the Pyrenees into Spain. In Britain, a new imperial claimant, Constantine III, rose up from the ranks of the army and led his troops into Gaul, where he won the loyalty of the Gallic field army, giving him control of the provinces of Britain, Gaul and Spain.

All these upheavals had a disastrous impact on Rome's economy. Not only was Honorius trying to finance Stilicho's army in Italy, but he had also lost the tax revenues due from Britain, Gaul and Spain, now in Constantine's hands. At this very critical point, Alaric chose to turn the screw, demanding a huge sum of money from the Western Empire in exchange for a military alliance and recognition for the Goths within the empire. The Senate met his demands with incredulity, seeing them as a declaration of war. Stilicho, who advocated meeting Alaric's demands, fell out of favour with Honorius and was executed in 408 CE. Alaric, now despairing of ever reaching an agreement with Honorius, was left with only one option: to invade Italy.

After a protracted and devastating siege of Rome by a huge Goth army numbering some 40,000 men, a military alliance with Honorius was negotiated. However, Honorius had no intention of honouring the agreement, incensing Alaric. After repeated failed negotiations, Alaric finally lost patience and ordered the sack of Rome on 24 August 410 CE. Alaric was a Christian who recognized that the basilicas of St Peter's and St Paul's were sanctuaries, and refrained from stealing from the churches' treasuries. Elsewhere, the Goths efficiently stripped Rome of all its riches, and Romans who resisted were summarily killed. At the end of the three-day sack, certain key buildings were set on fire.

News of this disaster reverberated throughout Europe – a devastating reminder that earthly power was transitory. Nevertheless, Rome had still not been dealt the final death blow.

Against all the odds, the Roman Empire was pieced together again, and much of this was the work of the extraordinarily competent commander-in-chief of Roman forces in the west, Flavius Constantius (370–421 CE). When the Goths who had been occupying Italy moved to Gaul, Constantius turned his attention to the usurper, Constantine III, whom he confronted and defeated. Having reached an accommodation with the Goths, who settled in south-west France, he moved to Spain, defeated the Vandals, Alans and Suebi and brought Spain back under Roman control. A much depleted and considerably impoverished version of the Roman Empire had been revived.

Following the death of Honorius in 423 CE, the long reign of Valentinian III (*r.* 425–55 CE) was beset by further disasters. By the time the Vandals crossed into Africa and captured Carthage in 439 CE, the Western Empire was on the verge of a final breakdown. The Huns were in the ascendancy, with a new leader, Attila (*r.* 434–53 CE), and control of an empire that stretched from the Black Sea to the Baltic and

A consular diptych, commissioned by Anicius Probus in 406 CE to commemorate his consulship, depicting the Emperor Honorius (r. 393–423 CE). While his principal general, Stilicho, who acted as regent for the child emperor, brought some measure of stability until his execution in 408 CE, Honorius's reign was chaotic, bringing the Roman Empire ever closer to collapse.

from Germany to the Asian steppes. Having wreaked havoc in the east, the Huns now turned their attention westwards. In 451 CE, Attila was defeated at the Battle of the Catalaunian Fields by an alliance of Romans, Goths, Burgundians and Celts, but even this famous victory failed to turn back the tide. Attila launched a further successful invasion of Italy, but died on his wedding night when he choked on blood following a nosebleed. The Hunnish threat dissipated with his death, but the Vandals still controlled Africa and the revenues it generated.

By this stage, the divisions between the victorious barbarians and the depleted Italians became increasingly blurred and the Germanic leaders became ever more powerful, as successive emperors ceded power to them, becoming little more than figureheads. The last of all, Romulus Augustus (r. 475–6 CE) abdicated in 476 CE, withdrawing with a comfortable pension to Campania. In a symbolic gesture, Odoacer (r. 476–93 CE), the Ostrogothic king who now ruled in Italy, sent the ceremonial robes of imperial office to the Eastern emperor Zeno (r. 474–5 and 476–91 CE) in Constantinople. Rome's legacy now resided in the east.

RAVENNA:
THE NEW CAPITAL

Ravenna, on the northern Adriatic coast, was a place of safety for the last Western Roman emperors, who created an exquisite Christian capital there, while the barbarians devastated the rest of Roman Italy. Subsequently, Ravenna became the capital of the Ostrogothic kingdom, before it was finally absorbed into the Byzantine Empire in 540 CE.

FROM THE TIME of Augustus, Ravenna had been the headquarters of one of the imperial fleets, and had flourished as a naval base. In 402 CE, it was dragged out of relative obscurity by the barbarian siege of Milan, which prompted the imperial court to retreat to the safety of Ravenna. The site of Ravenna, with its network of marshes and lagoons, threaded through by tributaries of the River Po, made it virtually impregnable, unless – as occasionally happened – a treacherous local guided invaders through the wetlands. The more conventional access to the city was by a means of a raised, and easily defended, causeway.

Ravenna was orientated eastward, with easy maritime access to Constantinople. Honorius was able to weather Alaric's invasions of Italy in Ravenna, and the city became an equally secure refuge for the barbarian kings of Italy. With the imperial court in residence, Ravenna became an important cultural and religious centre, with a lively intellectual life.

Honorius' sister Galla Placidia (*c.*388–450 CE) was forced to make two marriages: the first to Alaric's brother-in-law and successor, Athaulf; the second to Flavius Constantius, the commander of the army and most powerful man in the empire. The latter's six-year-old son, Valentian III, was acclaimed emperor in 425 CE and Placidia ruled as regent until 437 CE. The mausoleum she built for herself and her family, where she was never buried, is a masterpiece of mosaic art, with an arched ceiling that is entirely covered with a dark blue decoration, pierced with gold, which resembles the night sky. The window arches are decorated with a series of masterly rendered mosaic scenes: St Peter and St Paul are depicted as Roman senators; St Laurence with a gridiron, on which he was martyred by burning; and Christ is depicted as the good shepherd.

The Baptistery of Neon was built *c.*460 CE, and again features a magnificent mosaic ceiling with a central roundel showing Jesus baptizing John the Baptist, surrounded by beautifully rendered figures of the Apostles. The exquisite serenity of the scene is in marked contrast to the times in which it was created – the violent descent of the Western Roman Empire into chaos and collapse.

The end of the Western Roman Empire did not bring about the end of Ravenna. When the last emperor, Romulus Augustus (*r.* 475–6 CE), retired to Campania in 476 CE, Ravenna became the capital of the first two kingdoms of Italy, established by the Ostrogothic rulers Odoacer (*r.* 476–93 CE) and Theodoric (*r.* 493–526 CE). These Arian Christian, Latin-speaking kings respected the Roman legacy and adorned their capital with new buildings, palaces and churches. The finest of all is the basilica of Sant'Apollinare Nuovo, with its magnificent mosaics, which include episodes showing the Life of Jesus and his Passion, 36 individual saints holding books and scrolls, and Jesus Christ and the Virgin Mary in majesty, sitting on thrones flanked by winged angels.

Theodoric built a unique mausoleum for himself (520 CE) outside the walls of Ravenna. It is constructed of large white stones from Istria or Dalmatia, and is decagonal in shape, capped by a gigantic circular stone, circled by pierced handles that may have been used for manoeuvring it into place.

The life of Ravenna continued to flourish long after the barbarian kingdoms had fallen. The emperors of the east, based in Constantinople, had remained strong and secure and the Byzantine (Eastern) Emperor Justinian I (*r.* 527–65 CE) actually reconquered a substantial part of the lost Western provinces, although much of this territory was subsequently lost in the 7th century. Ravenna fell in 540 CE and became the flourishing capital of the Byzantine territories in Italy until 751 CE.

THE INHERITORS

The primary motive of the barbarians was not invasion but assimilation: they sought a better life and wanted to be part of the Roman Empire, not its conquerors. The eventual collapse of the empire left the barbarian tribes as its inheritors. The successor barbarian kingdoms varied greatly, and some were much more supportive of the survival of Roman culture and lifestyle than others.

FOR THE MOST PART, the barbarians who invaded the Roman Empire in the 4th and 5th centuries CE converted to Christianity, predominantly Arianism, when they crossed its borders, rejecting paganism in favour of a religion that appeared to be intrinsic to the civilization they were appropriating. Arianism was a belief, taught by Arius in the 4th century CE, that Christ was created by God the Father, and although greater than man, he was inferior to the Father. This was declared a heresy at the First Council of Nicaea in 325 CE, but it took root among many of the people whom Rome called 'barbarians': Visigoths, Goths, Vandals, Suebi and Burgundians.

For many Roman citizens, the end of the empire was by no means disastrous. While the towns and infrastructure were battle-scarred and derelict, relative peace returned to the land, and it was possible to withdraw to estates, villas and farms, and live a prosperous and comfortable life. In many areas, the existing provincial aristocracy retained both land and power, and as long as they accepted they were vassals of the new German elite, they were able to write and worship as before.

The Visigoths, Alans and Burgundians who settled in southern France may well have shared the fruits of civilization with their Roman subjects, and certainly accounts of the Visigothic court at Toulouse in the late 5th century CE paint a picture of an opulent, and in many ways cultured, existence. The Gallo-Roman aristocracy preserved their lifestyle in their villas and country houses. The Church also played a crucial role as the preserver of Roman civilization, providing basic education. Many Gallo-Roman aristocrats became bishops of their native towns, responsible for securing food supplies and protecting their residents against further attacks. In some areas, Romans and barbarians collaborated to create sophisticated law codes, which paved the way for the arrival of the Franks, another Germanic tribe that would take over much of Gaul under the leadership of Clovis (466–511 CE).

The settlement of the Suebi and Vandals in Spain, however, was violent and disruptive, and little of the Roman community survives. The Vandals went on to cross the Straits of Gibraltar to Africa, where they dispossessed many Roman landowners of their estates, appropriating the Roman lifestyle and driving refugees eastwards. The Vandal court at Carthage was nevertheless culturally sophisticated.

In Italy, adjustments were made to the new reality following the Visigothic sack of Rome in 410 CE, and many senators withdrew from Rome to consolidate their country estates, leaving the business of administration to a small number of ruling families. There was a great upsurge in rebuilding following the sack of Rome, and some magnificent new churches, such as St Mary Maggiore and St Sabina, were founded. Rome was refashioning itself as the Christian capital of the West.

From 475 CE, Italy was governed by the Ostrogothic kings, with their court in Ravenna. Odoacer (r. 476–93 CE), who had supplanted the last Roman emperor Romulus Augustus, was himself killed and supplanted by Theodoric (r. 493–526 CE), after a long siege of Ravenna in 493 CE. Both kings were respectful of their legacy, allowing senatorial life in Rome to continue as before, and accepting members of the Roman aristocracy as holders of important offices of state. Odoacer had the Colosseum restored, and encouraged the return of entertainments and hunting displays. Theodoric was renowned as a just and sympathetic ruler. He collaborated with the Roman nobility, encouraged building restoration projects, and effectively managed the Italian economy. He was also respectful of the rights and liberties of Roman citizens.

However, ultimately Theodoric fell out with the Senate when it became more closely allied with the 'orthodox' church of Justin I in Constantinople. This alienated the Arian Theodoric, who began to feel increasingly isolated from his Roman subjects. Following Theodoric's death in 526 CE, there was increasing conflict within his dynasty, culminating in the arrival of the Byzantine general Belisarius (r. 527–65 CE), who reconquered Ravenna (540 CE) and many of Rome's lost territories. The weakened kingdom of the Ostrogoths finally fell in 553 CE. The Byzantine Empire, which survived for several centuries, retained a uniquely Roman identity.

The Mausoleum of Theodoric in Ravenna, Italy. It was under the leadership of Theodoric the Great (r. 493–526 CE) that the Ostrogothic kingdom reached its zenith, preserving many of the traditions and institutions of Imperial Rome. Theodoric spent his childhood in Constantinople as a diplomatic hostage, and he was commissioned by the Byzantine Emperor Zeno in 488 CE to recover Italy from the barbarian king, Odoacer. He set up his capital in Ravenna and built his mausoleum there in 520 CE, six years before his death.

THE CLASSICAL LEGACY

The classical world underpins modern life in innumerable ways. Classicism is prominent in Western architectural conventions, building methods and engineering. Other legacies are pervasive and profound: language and writing; government and justice systems; literature; and the scientific, mathematical and philosophical thought that forms the root of modern intellectual traditions.

FIRST AND FOREMOST, the Greeks invented the political idea of democracy (rule by the people), which is a reality or an aspiration for much of the world today. Cleisthenes' reforms in Athens in 507 BCE effectively handed the power to govern to its male citizens; women, slaves and foreigners were not included. Notions of civic duty were also brought to the fore in Athens: citizens had freedom of speech, could vote for whomever they chose, and had the right to a fair trial. All these precepts are shared by the states of the democratic West today.

Many modern countries' law codes are based on Roman law. Although most contemporary societies would repudiate the harshness of Roman punishments, the basic principles of court proceedings are certainly recognizable. For example, there was a preliminary hearing, much as there is today, when a magistrate decided if there was a case to answer. Witnesses and evidence were brought forward at the trial and cross-examinations and closing arguments took place in just the same way as they do in the modern world.

The Greek alphabet, developed in the 8th century BCE from the Phoenician alphabet, had spread throughout the Greek world by the 7th century BCE, and in turn was the root from which the Latin alphabet emerged. The Latin alphabet is now the most widely used alphabetic writing system in the world, used in western Europe and the Americas, but also in Asia for languages such as Turkish, Malay and Vietnamese, as well as some African and Austronesian languages. Latin, spoken throughout the Roman Empire, became the base for the Romance languages, which include French, Spanish, Italian and Portuguese. English has also incorporated many Latin root words, and Latin is used extensively in the present-day justice system in both Britain and the USA.

At about the same time as the Greek alphabet first appeared, the two great epic poems of the classical world, the *Iliad* and the *Odyssey*, were composed in hexameter verse. Many see these as the foundation works from which all subsequent literature derives; texts such as Shakespeare's *Troilus and Cressida* and James Joyce's *Ulysses* trace a direct line to these great Greek epic poems. Homer undoubtedly inspired the major Roman poets, such as Virgil, Horace and Ovid, who in turn inspired authors such as Chaucer, Shakespeare, Dante and Milton. Shakespeare, in fact, derived many of his plots and references from ancient classical history, notably *Titus Andronicus*, *Coriolanus*, *Antony and Cleopatra* and *Julius Caesar*. Greek theatre, both in its physical space and in the ways in which comedy and tragedy evolved, still underpins all theatre in the modern world.

Greek architecture, with is proportional design, three orders of column design (Doric, Ionic and Corinthian), friezes and pediments, porticoes and colonnades, is highly distinctive. The Greek architectural aesthetic influenced the Romans, who adopted the Greek architectural orders, as well as introducing skilfully engineered features such as domes and arches. All these features were revived in the neoclassical architecture of the late 18th and early 19th centuries, which was extremely popular in both the United States and Europe. The Greek Revival style, which centred on the Doric order, became a US national style in the mid-19th century. Today, the architectural legacy of the classical world can be seen in towns and cities all over the Western world, and many high streets contain banks, town halls, libraries and courthouses in the classical style. The most famous examples include: the Lincoln Memorial and the White House in Washington D.C., the Prado in Madrid, Buckingham Palace in London, Downing College in Cambridge, and the Munich National Theatre in Germany.

Greek mathematicians made an extremely significant contribution to world thought, providing an intellectual basis for a range of subjects, including geometry, astronomy, engineering and design. Greek mathematicians such as Thales of Miletus (*c.*624–c.528 BCE) and Pythagoras (*c.*570–c.495 BCE) laid down many fundamental precepts in the fields of geometry, number theory and irrational numbers. Euclid (325–265 BCE), who lived in Alexandria during the rule of Ptolemy I (*c.*366–282 BCE), wrote *Elements*, which contained 465 geometry propositions and proofs, and is one of the most reproduced text books of all time. Eratosthenes (276–194 BCE) calculated the circumference of the Earth to within 1 per cent of our modern measurements. Aristarchus of Samos (*c.*310–c.230 BCE) proposed that the Earth and the other planets revolved around the Sun.

Greek aesthetics, often passed on via Roman copies, defined standards of beauty that are still recognized today. The innovative naturalism of Greek statues and vase paintings certainly inspired the Romans, but they also introduced their own innovations, not least their ruthlessly realistic style of portraiture.

The Roman invention of concrete was transformative. It enabled them to build very substantial and stable structures, both on land and underwater. The Romans made concrete by mixing volcanic ash from the Bay of Naples with lime and seawater to make a mortar, and then incorporating chunks of volcanic rock into the mortar, the 'aggregate'. Both the Colosseum and Pantheon, two of Rome's most famous surviving buildings, were constructed of concrete. Concrete was also employed widely in the construction of aqueducts, bridges, arches, baths and amphitheatres – all buildings that utilized large-scale arches or curved roofs, characteristic of Roman architecture. Today, concrete is the most widely used man-made substance in the world.

Roman engineering has also had a huge impact on the modern world. The Romans understood the laws of physics and harnessed water flow through their aqueducts, pipes and conduits. They were also able to use water energy to power mines and mills. Their straight roads are legendary and underpin many modern road systems. They also applied their pragmatic good sense to land management, and their techniques of crop rotation, pruning, grafting and fertilization have all been adopted by modern farmers.

Our modern calendar is a Roman invention, although it has changed significantly throughout history. The Julian calendar, launched in 44 BCE, was the first to consist of 365 days, along with a leap year every four years. Our month names derive from the Latin, and everybody recognizes July (Julius Caesar) and August (Emperor Augustus). The Julian calendar forms the basis of the Gregorian calendar, introduced in the 16th century, which we use today. Our everyday life is suffused with the legacy of the classical world...

The Arc de Triomphe in Paris reflects the imperial ambitions of Napoleon Bonaparte, who commissioned it in 1806 after his victory at the Battle of Austerlitz (1805). The arch was finally completed in 1836. It was inspired by the Arch of Titus in the Roman Forum, but deviates from its Roman predecessors by omitting the ornamental columns, which gives it a more massive, top-heavy appearance. In Roman style, decorative high-relief sculptures celebrated the military victories of the Revolution and the First Empire.

FURTHER READING

Baker, Simon, *Ancient Rome*, The Random House Group Ltd, London, 2006

Boardman, John, Griffin, Jasper & Murray Oswyn (eds), *The Oxford History of the Classical World*, Oxford University Press, Oxford, 1986

Cary, Max & Scullard, Howard Hayes, *A History of Rome*, Macmillan Education Ltd, Basingstoke & London, 1935 (reprinted 1991)

Connell, Tim & Mathews, John, *Atlas of the Roman World*, Phaidon Press Ltd, Oxford, 1982

Fox, Robin Lane, *The Classical World*, Allen Lane, London, 2005

Green, Peter, *A Concise History of Ancient Greece*, Thames and Hudson Ltd, London, 1973

Kitto, H.D.F., *The Greeks*, Pelican Books Ltd, London, 1951

Levi, Peter, *Atlas of the Greek World*, Phaidon Press Ltd, Oxford, 1980

Scarre, Chris, *The Penguin Historical Atlas of Ancient Rome*, Penguin Books Ltd, London, 1995

Talbert, Richard J.A. (ed.), *Atlas of Classical History*, Croom Helm Ltd, London, 1985

INDEX

PICTURE CREDITS